THE AFTERGLOW OF INDUSTRY

THE AFTERGLOW OF INDUSTRY

New Zealand Photographs 2012–2022

Chris Corson-Scott

Daylight

Foreword

In writing this foreword I found myself recalling the first time I visited Chris Corson-Scott to learn about his work, probably five years ago. We met at his family home in Mount Eden, a leafy suburb in central Auckland, where he was working in a small spare room. I remember noticing the bookcase in the narrow hall full of well-worn art books, one whole shelf of which was dedicated to the British romantic artists John Constable (1776–1837) and J.M.W. Turner (1775–1851), which Chris told me belonged to his father, the painter Ian Scott (1945–2013). This was unexpected, for neither father nor son showed any obvious debt to these artistic predecessors. Indeed, later, visiting Chris in his studio across town, his own impressive collection of photography books suggested a more obvious set of reference points for the large colour images that distinguish his photographic practice. But now, after thinking about, looking at, and exhibiting Corson-Scott's photographs, I keep coming back to those two British painters as one special clue to understanding what underpins this self-trained artist's practice.

Innovators in their day, Constable and Turner made landscape their subject, turning to nature to capture not just the lay of the land but its elemental forces, seasonal rhythms, intimate details, and awe-inducing scale. Though nature was their subject, their world was always peopled, and encoded in their paintings was a potent sense of the times in which they were living. No longer a backdrop to Christian or classical narratives, their views showed a modern world on the brink of change. Constable sought to memorialise an idyllic rural existence at the very moment small landowners were being forced to leave their holdings to work in the new factories spawned by the industrial revolution; Turner betrayed his fascination for the discombobulating effects of speed and the inevitability of change by dissolving a newfangled steam engine in its own hissing atmospherics and eulogising the last of the 'fighting' sailing ships. And both artists worked at scale, investing extraordinary time and effort into producing their canvases, to grant their scenes the highest order of authority and seriousness.

Working well past the end of the first industrial age, in a far-flung colony annexed in large part to help fuel Britain's economy, Corson-Scott is equally serious (and ambitious) in wanting to document his world, caught at a juncture in its technological and economic history as fraught and consequential as any that has preceded it. He draws on all the formal, visual, and narrative power encoded in his medium to produce large-scale images that capture not the origins but the vestiges of Aotearoa New Zealand's own industrial history and its remnant effects on the landscapes of the country's two major islands. Linked to Britain through his English father, and to Scotland through his mother, he does not shy away from his cultural inheritance, but like his parent before him, he utilises new means to convey his messages.

While his father used acrylic paint to produce hard-edged realist and abstract canvases that bear little trace of his artistic forebears, Corson-Scott likewise counters tradition, making photographs, not paintings. But as Scott senior had a secret respect for the British Romantics, so is his son's work beholden to the visual histories of the West. It is noteworthy that he uses an old-fashioned 8 × 10 inch analogue camera, exploiting this technology's preternatural capacity to capture a maximum amount of detail and for the warmth and responsiveness of its film emulsions. Almost as old as European settlement, photography originally served the needs of New Zealand's colonisers, aiding them in surveying a new land and documenting its people. Cumbersome and mechanical, this apparatus suits Corson-Scott's subjects, which are the old mills, abandoned mines, railway cuttings, gold diggings, shearing sheds, processing facilities, and factories built and used to extract resources from this land in the first waves of settlement in the late nineteenth and early twentieth centuries. Working as both archaeologist and explorer,

Corson-Scott has unearthed old and recent ruins in remote and proximate locations: subalpine escarpments, overgrown gullies, city suburbs, and small-town fringes. His purpose is twofold: to compile an archive of images that document the invasive impact of humans on this landscape, and to recognise and respect the sheer hard work and ingenuity of these efforts, even as he mourns the devastating impact on Aotearoa's ecology and its original inhabitants.

But Corson-Scott is no mere recorder; his ambition is to raise his photographs to the exalted status of high art. Supplementing the indexical veracity of analogue technology, he submits his raw images to a second stage of mediation. After his work in the field and back in his studio, Corson-Scott turns his negatives into digital files, and using his computer (like the painter at his easel), he painstakingly adjusts each image—often over years—to balance tone, colour, and luminosity across each part of the image. He then prints his large and detailed pictures on a professional printer he shares with the artist Mark Adams (b. 1949), thus allowing total control of his output. Finally, framed and hung on the gallery wall at a scale often up to two metres, his photographs rise to their context, allegorising their subjects as both memorials to times past and cautionary reminders of the future hurtling towards us.

Gathered here are some seventy-nine photographs, produced over a decade. They start close to home in Tāmaki Makaurau Auckland, tracing locations that the artist knows intimately and that have helped shape him. They then reach southwards, the result of extended expeditions to ever more difficult-to-access destinations found through assiduous research and via local knowledge. Corson-Scott relishes the book format because it allows him to accompany his images with texts, which he has researched and compiled over a subsequent two-year period, as a means for the reader/viewer to deepen their engagement.

The stories he tells do not explain the pictures, indeed they dip far back in time and extend beyond their titular subjects to embed each image in a history. This accompanying narrative is galvanised by a desire and a duty to attend to the complex realities of human need and effort, to expose the faulty logic of colonial expansion and global economics, and to ponder the impossible balancing act of resource management.

In every sense then, these photographs have the gravitas of history painting. Strikingly dissimilar from the myriad images circulating on the internet, in magazines, history books, and on social media, that serve their range of practical ends—from tourist promotion to pictorial illustration, news photo or snapshot— Corson-Scott's images are to be looked at and read, slowly, with a sense of melancholy, curiosity, and dread, as markers of where we have come from and signs for where we are headed.

Christina Barton
September 2024

In memory of my father, Ian Scott, 1945–2013

THE AFTERGLOW OF INDUSTRY

St Heliers Beach (New Year's Day), Auckland, 2013

Aotearoa New Zealand's largest city, Tāmaki Makaurau Auckland, lies between the Tasman Sea and the South Pacific Ocean, on a volcanic isthmus in the upper North Island. From the downtown port where it was founded, the city sprawls between the estuaries, peninsulas, and beaches of its two harbours: the Waitematā to the north and the Manukau to the south. On the Waitematā, pale sandstone cliffs expose ancient geological layers, below which sandy bays slope to harbours that sparkle in UV-dense light. On the cliffs, the thick twisting branches of pōhutukawa trees, which can live for up to 1,000 years, bloom in summer with seas of red flowers that reach towards the water.

Māori settlement in Tāmaki Makaurau dates back to at least 1350, when the Tainui waka (canoe) arrived from the ancestral homeland of Hawaiki carrying chiefs who settled the isthmus and continued south into the Waikato region. Despite these centuries of settlement, the Waitematā remained breathtaking in its natural beauty up to the point of European colonisation. That point was 1840, and that year Auckland was founded under the leadership of New Zealand's first governor, William Hobson, who sought to control the wider region and open land up for settlers. In colonial style, he named the city after his friend George Eden, the First Earl of Auckland in Surrey, England. Eden never visited this country; however, his career as a politician, First Lord of the Admiralty, and Governor-General of India, speaks to the power of those who would soon lead the colonisation of Aotearoa. By the end of 1841, the British Crown owned almost all of the isthmus.

From the arrival of the Tainui waka, Saint Heliers was known as Te Pane o Horoiwi ('the head of Horoiwi'), after the Tainui chief who first settled on the headland above the beach. In 1841, the Crown bought a 6,000-acre block, which included the Saint Heliers area, for just £100 in cash and £100 in goods (about £22,000 today). This deal deliberately exploited the Māori understanding of land custodianship, rather than ownership; before it was even finalised, the Crown had already turned a percentage profit of thousands by subdividing and reselling the land. One of the purchasers was Auckland's first stud farmer, who, by 1879, owned most of Te Pane o Horoiwi. Making clear his aspirations for the area, he renamed the bay Saint Heliers, after a luxury seaside resort in Jersey, the largest of the Channel Islands. In 1882, he commissioned a 1,500-foot wharf in the middle of the beach, along with the ferry *Tongariro,* as part of a plan to attract weekend tourists and, later, profit from suburban development.

Still reachable only by ferry, Saint Heliers remained mostly farmland until the construction of Tāmaki Drive in 1932. Cut into the sandstone cliffs and built on reclaimed land across rivers, estuaries, and beaches, the road connected the suburb to the central city, and just decades after its construction, nearly every inch of Te Pane o Horoiwi had become suburbia. Today, Saint Heliers is one of Auckland's most affluent suburbs, and some of the most expensive property in the country. The former mangrove estuaries are long gone, and Saint Heliers beach, like others along Tāmaki Drive, is artificially built up. The golden-white sand, for which it is famed, has for decades been dredged from the seabed at Pākiri, a largely Māori community seventy kilometres to the north, despite ongoing protest from locals.

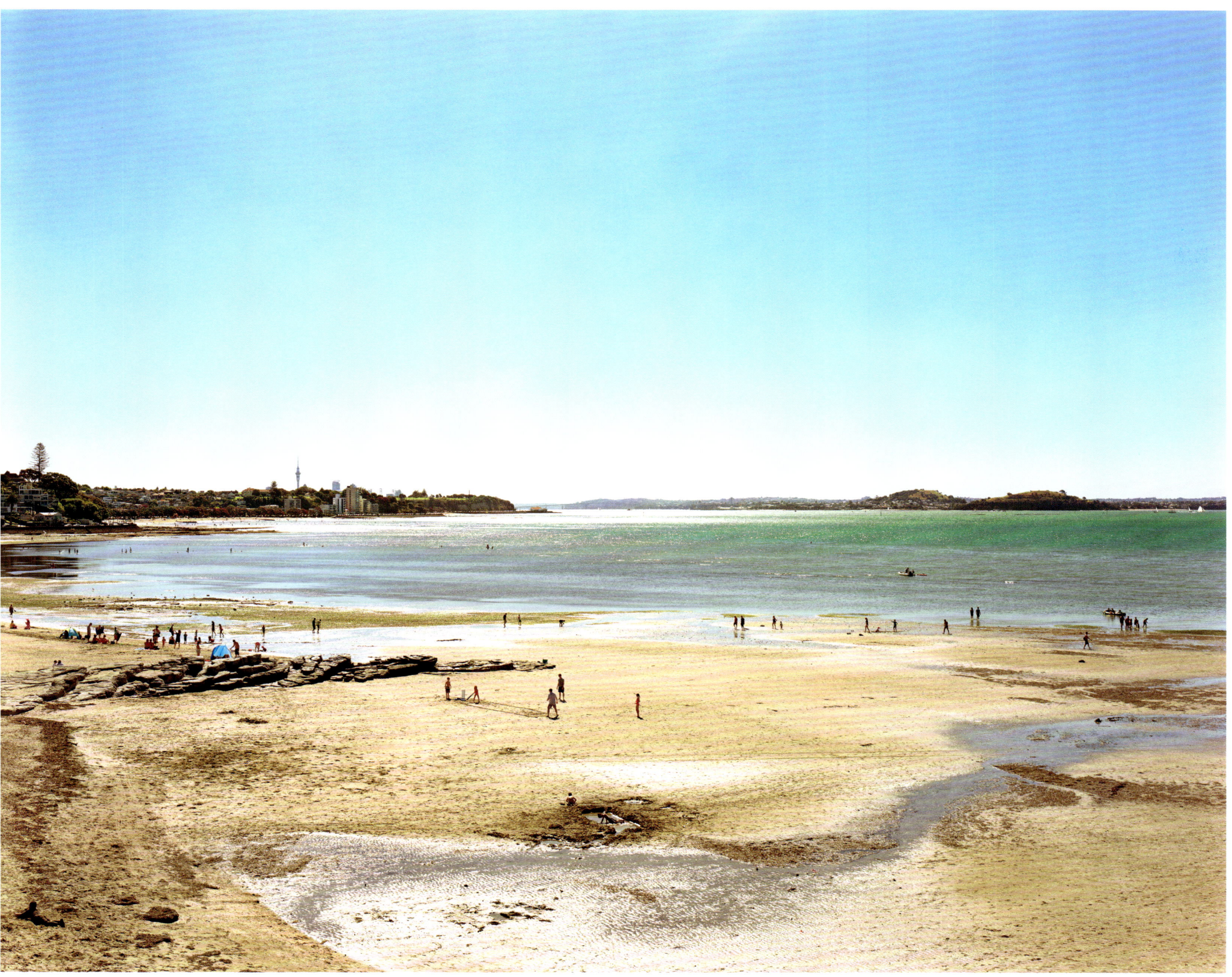

The Neighbour's Garden, Mt Eden, Auckland, 2012

On 20 October 1840, the British Crown was transferred approximately 3,000 acres of land (known as the 1840 Transfer Land) by local Māori, Ngāti Whātua. Spanning Cox's Bay to Hobson Bay on the Waitematā Harbour and running inland to Mount Eden, the parcel included much of central Auckland and many of the suburbs that are now the city's richest, including Herne Bay, Grey Lynn, Ponsonby, Parnell, and Newmarket. The agreement was made between William Hobson, co-author of the Treaty of Waitangi, and Ngāti Whātua rangatira (leader) Āpihai Te Kawau. Both men had very different intentions. Te Kawau sought the deal in a spirit of optimism and generosity, working towards what he hoped would be a new, bicultural society. But almost immediately, the Crown began taking advantage of the situation. For the vast area, it paid only £273 in cash and goods (£31,000 today); less than a year later, forty-four acres had been divided into 'town sections' and sold for more than £24,000 (£2,055,000 today). Hobson also instigated two further, equally exploitative deals for 8,200 acres of land comprising much of the remaining Auckland isthmus.

Before European arrival, the dramatic lava flows of the Maungawhau / Mount Eden area were covered with dense scrub, wetlands, and native pūriri and nīkau forests. Come 1841, migrants from England, Scotland, Ireland, Europe, and Australia were pouring into Auckland. The land was split between farmers and wealthy industrialists, many based 'back home' in Britain. Maungawhau's hills, mountains, and lava flows were quarried, its wetlands drained, and its forests cleared. By the end of the nineteenth century, a town centre with elaborate Victorian buildings sat beneath the mountain Maungawhau, now called Mount Eden, after George Eden, First Earl of Auckland, for whom the city as a whole was also named. As a tramway reached the Mount Eden area from the central city, the farms were subdivided again for profit and turned into suburban plots. By the mid-1920s, villas and bungalows on quarter-acre sections covered the suburb almost entirely.

Inland from the harbour, but a small distance from the city, Mount Eden developed into a predominately middle-class suburb—except for of a handful of streets on ridgelines or hillsides, where views increased land values. Growing up in Mount Eden in the early 1990s, I had as neighbours teachers, musicians, writers, nurses, artists, caregivers, and civil servants. A positive aspect of a suburb composed of similar houses all built at once was that there was a general sense of equality, at least at a superficial level. But it wasn't long before markers of inequality appeared. During my youth, houses started to be renovated, and as their value rapidly increased, many single- and lower-income families I knew began leaving the area.

By the 2000s, whatever egalitarianism New Zealand may have once had was quickly disappearing. The Auckland Housing Crisis set in, and the city soon boasted some of the least affordable housing in the world. Many of Mount Eden's volcanic dry-stone walls (some of which dated back to the first subdivisions) and rambling backyards, where fruit and native trees perched on rocky lava flows, met the fate of bulldozers, chainsaws, and concrete. Since this time, houses have grown larger, while sections have been halved and quartered, the pyramid of speculation ensuring that those able to buy early, and hold on at critical moments, continue to accumulate wealth.

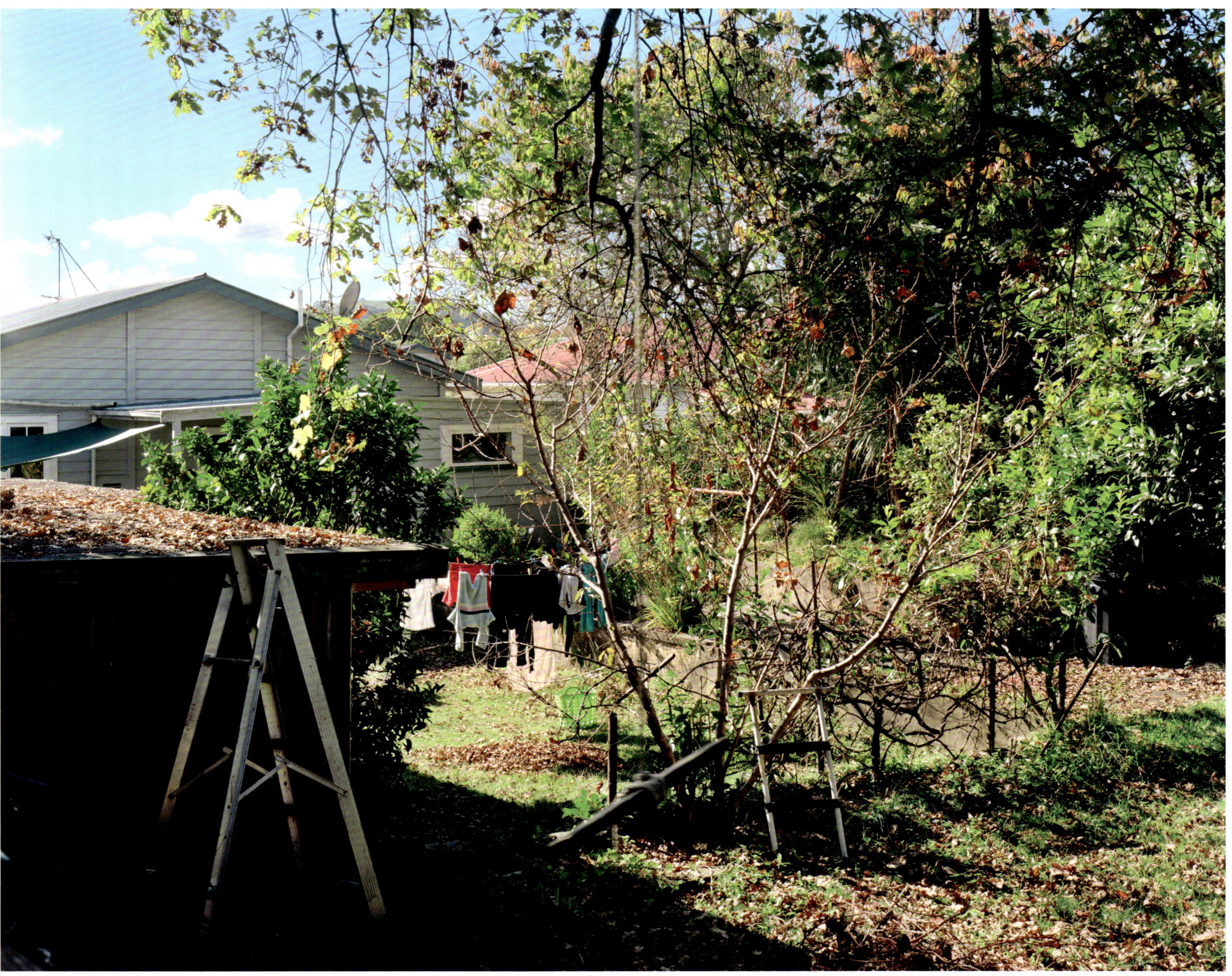

Remains of the Controlled Mine Base, Rangitoto Island, 2013

Tāmaki Makaurau Auckland sits on a field of more than fifty-three volcanoes covering almost 500 square kilometres, from the Waitematā Harbour to the rolling hills that become Waikato, beyond South Auckland. Erupting just 600 years ago, Rangitoto Island is the youngest of these volcanoes and the only one dormant rather than extinct. Lying at the mouth of the harbour, barely ten kilometres from the central city, and rising 260 metres from the ocean in a near-symmetrical cone, Rangitoto is so prominent that it is difficult to imagine Tāmaki Makaurau without it.

In 1854, the British Crown purchased Rangitoto from Ngāti Pāoa for just £15 (£1,400 today), yet still felt it had overpaid for an island that was 'all rock'. In 1898, the Auckland Council opened a scoria quarry near Islington Bay on the east side of the island. Over more than thirty years, thousands of tons of scoria would be blasted and cut from the lava flows. Most of it travelled just a short distance across the harbour, where it was used in vast land reclamations that expanded Auckland's central business district and port and created Tāmaki Drive. From 1925 to 1936, the justice department stationed prisoners on Rangitoto, which they described as 'the Dominion's third-class waste land', for 'reformative' hard labour. The prisoners took over the backbreaking work at the quarry and were tasked with building the island's kilometres of gravel roads. Their labour was especially gruelling, as the mostly treeless island offered little shelter from the sun, which intensified as it reflected off the water and was absorbed by the black lava flows.

During the Second World War, the Japanese invasion of Pearl Harbour in 1941 caused panic that Auckland, New Zealand's largest port, could be a future target. The Government began planning a defence system for the Waitematā Harbour, and in 1943 work was completed on the Controlled Mine Base, which sat on the water's edge beneath the sheer cliffs of Rangitoto's former scoria quarry. Built to maintain and control a giant field of underwater mines to defend the harbour entrance, the base was also made large enough to house part of the United States Navy in case the war moved further into the Pacific. However, this never eventuated, and the buildings were demolished in the 1970s.

Today, Rangitoto and its summit walk have been a tourist attraction for many decades, with ferries leaving from central Auckland several times a day. Despite being located on one of the island's most beautiful coastal tracks, the mine base remained contaminated, its surface strewn with shattered asbestos roofing and walls, broken timber, concrete, and tangled rebar. In 2014, it was added to the Government's Contaminated Sites Remediation Fund priority list, a top ten of toxic locales, including early gold mines, defunct factories, and polluted rivers. In 2019, the Department of Conservation, which manages the island, finally received funding to remediate the area. Following the removal of hundreds of bags of contaminated material, it was reopened to the public in 2020. Meanwhile, in 2011, after a four-year eradication programme that built on decades of work, Rangitoto and neighbouring Motutapu were declared pest-free. Rangitoto is now home to the world's largest population of pōhutukawa trees and is visited by over 100,000 people a year.

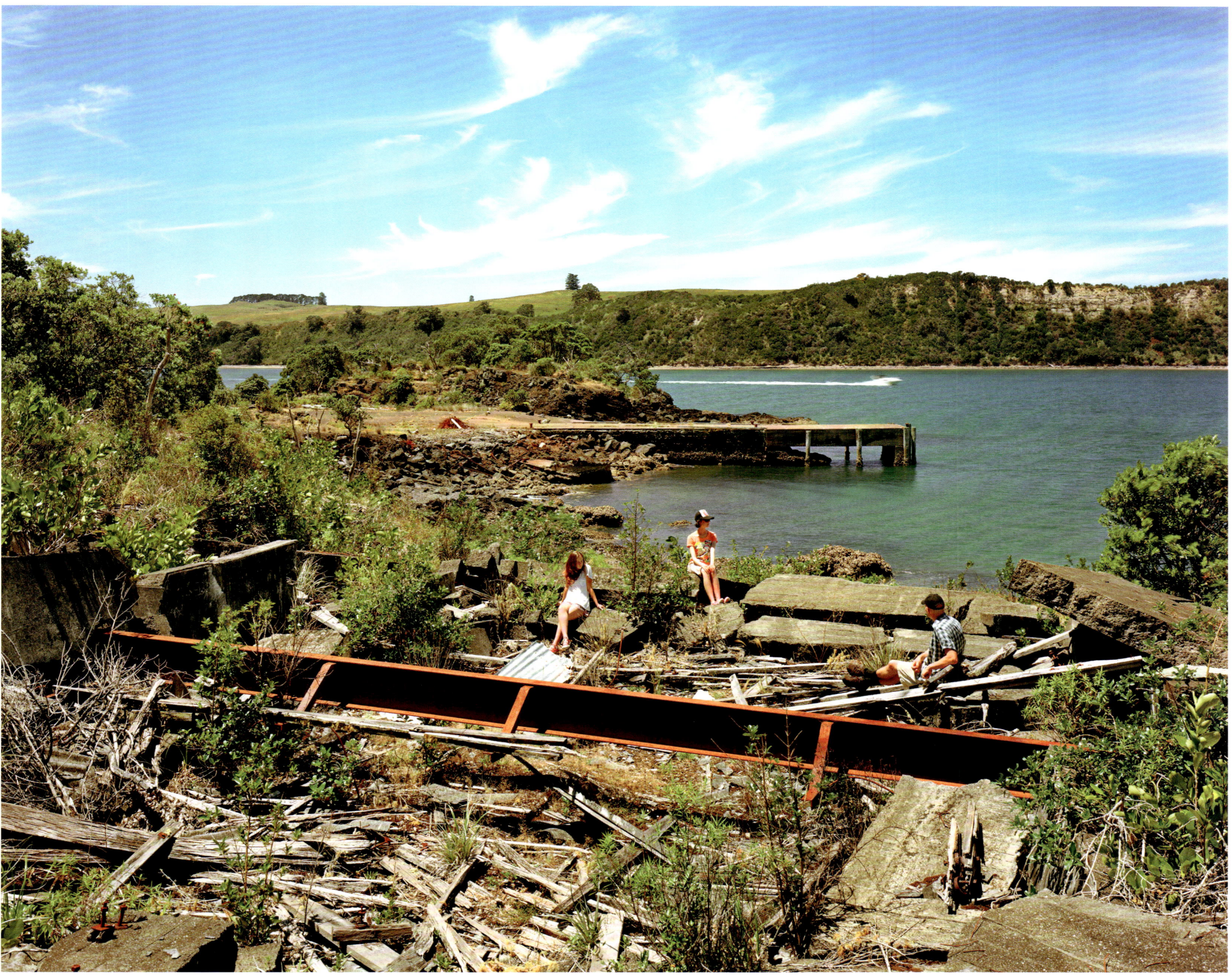

Fuel Pump in a Clearing, Rangitoto Island, Auckland, 2013

Six years before the Rangitoto quarry opened in 1898, the *Auckland Star* newspaper wrote, 'It is probable that before very long Rangitoto Island, whose scrub-clad lava slopes have not hitherto presented any particular attraction to Aucklanders, will become the scene of a new and important local industry … a small syndicate [forming] for the purpose of establishing a salt refinery and manufacturing works.' Initially, the enterprise thrived, but a year after its opening, the *Star* reported, 'During Thursday night's south-easterly gale some damage was caused at the newly opened salt refining works. … The windmill used to pump up salt water was blown clean away and could nowhere be found, [and] a sixteen-foot open boat lying at the small wharf at the salt works was also smashed up.' The storm spelled the end of the salt works, and from the early 1900s, Rangitoto embraced a different type of industry.

In 1912, the *Herald* wrote, 'The attractiveness of Rangitoto Island as a holiday resort has been enhanced by the discovery of three large caves.' Another piece from 1919 noted, 'On Easter Monday it was with pleasure, with hundreds more, to spend a day among the rocks and caves [on Rangitoto]. I was bewildered with its beauty. It is still almost in its natural state, and the question is how to improve it.' The first 'improvements' were licensed campsites, and numerous private baches (small holiday homes). From 1925, prisoners were stationed on the island and put to work cutting a road to the summit. The *Auckland Star* noted, 'The idea at the back of the scheme is to develop Rangitoto as a scenic asset. At the present time its full beauty is not realised owing to the inaccessibility of so much of it.' By 1932, the *Herald* would boast of the island's 'swimming pool, diving platform and a sports ground, while a motor road traverses nine miles of Pohutukawa groves, taking in the summit in its sweep of the island'. However, no mention was made of the unpaid prison labour used in construction.

Tourism soon had an adverse effect. A letter to the *Herald* from 1933 lamented, 'Rangitoto is a wonderfully unique island, botanically and geologically, and is visited by scientists from all parts of the globe … [but] last August I observed bulbs, apparently daffodils, sprouting beside the track near the summit, not to mention many other imported plants near the houses.' In addition to this, Australian wallabies had become acclimated to the island, and deerstalkers had to be commissioned to control the population, which was 'seriously damaging the native trees'. In response, in 1933, the New Zealand Institute of Horticulture held a meeting urging the Rangitoto Island Domain Board that exotic plants should be eradicated and no further holiday shacks should be allowed. Four years later, the board notified the 137 bach owners that their structures 'must be cleared off the island within the next twenty years'.

By 1957, around forty of the baches had been removed. The remaining structures were given a stay of thirty-three years, on the condition that they couldn't be sold, rented, or altered, and would be demolished upon the owner's death. In 1990, the Department of Conservation, which manages the island, placed a moratorium on further demolition, and a few years later, the last thirty-five baches were listed with the New Zealand Historic Places Trust. They are now under the care of a charitable trust which houses an island museum in one, and offers three for public bookings year-round, with plans in place for restoration of others.

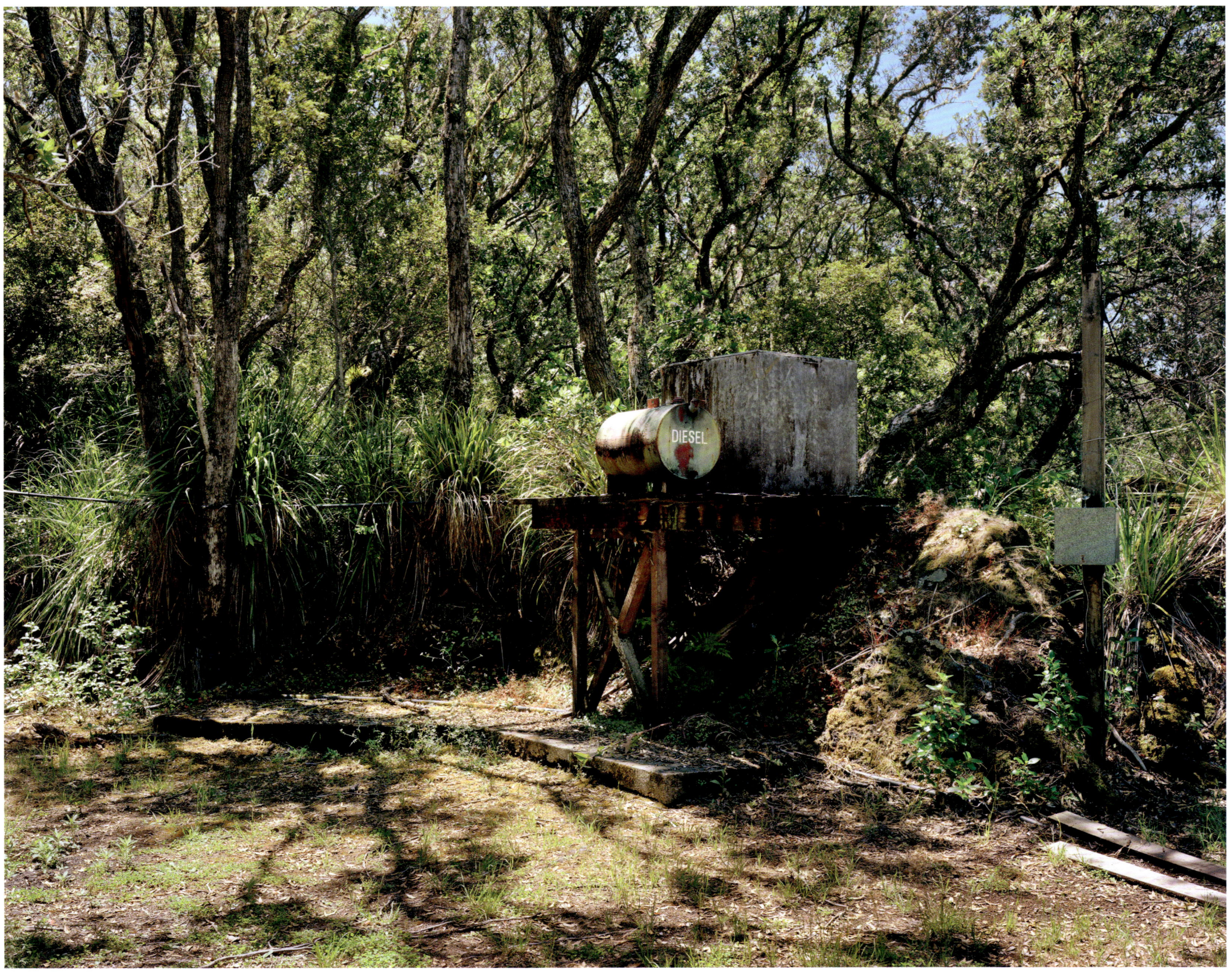

Reservoir Pipeline at Dusk, Big King / Te Tātua-a-Riukiuta, Auckland, 2013

In the centuries before the founding of Auckland, most of the mountains in the region's vast volcanic field were at some point occupied by Māori. These tūpuna maunga (ancestral mountains) supported vast pā (settlements), which could be fortified with palisades, trenches, and deliberately steepened slopes. Terraces were created, providing space for housing, the storage of kai (food), and gardens where crops like kūmara (sweet potato) were cultivated.

As Europeans began arriving in Auckland in the 1840s, extensive quarrying and clearing of the maunga began. Summits, cones, smaller peaks, and foothills were swiftly cut away. At Maungarei (Mount Wellington) and Maungawhau (Mount Eden), entire mountainsides became sheer quarry walls and pits. Other maunga were quarried away completely. In 1967, a stadium was built in the land depression where Rarotonga (Mount Smart) had once risen 100 metres above the surrounding land. From 1888, beginning with Maungawhau, concrete reservoirs, both above and below ground, were installed at almost all of the remaining maunga. In just decades, most of the tūpuna maunga and their Māori history had been blasted and crushed into material for the construction of Auckland's roads and railways or buried beneath concrete.

Perhaps the most telling story is that of Te Tātua-a-Riukiuta (Big King). The area was once home to three prominent peaks called by the British the Three Kings, a large volcanic crater, two further mountains, and more than a dozen hills spanning kilometres. Before quarrying, it was described as the most historically and geologically complex site within the Auckland volcanic field. In the seventeenth and eighteenth centuries, it was extensively occupied by Māori, who developed complex terraces and kūmara pits. But in 1845, one of Auckland's first major quarries opened at Three Kings, and by the 1920s nearly all the mountains and hills were gone. The 133-metre-high Big King was the sole survivor.

In 2008, quarrying finally ceased at Big King, and its thirty-metre-deep pit began being filled with earth from rural land flattened for subdivisions. New Zealand's largest building company, Fletcher Challenge (the quarry's owners since 1988), which was partly Government owned, went public with plans to construct a subdivision of 1,500 apartments, seventeen metres below street level in the former quarry pit. Public opposition was immediate, and in 2016 a resident group took the issue to the Environmental Court, which ultimately ruled in their favour. Fletchers was forced to spend further years refilling the quarry to nine metres below ground level, and the number of apartments was decreased to better respect the features of the landscape.

Finally, in 2014, as part of a Tiriti o Waitangi (Treaty of Waitangi) settlement, Te Tātua-a-Riukiuta was one of fourteen tūpuna maunga returned to mana whenua (people with authority in the land). The mountains are cared for by the Tūpuna Maunga Authority, which comprises mana whenua, Auckland Council, and a non-voting Crown representative. Since the redress, many maunga have been replanted with native trees and shrubs, and boardwalks have been constructed to protect what remains of their fragile archaeology.

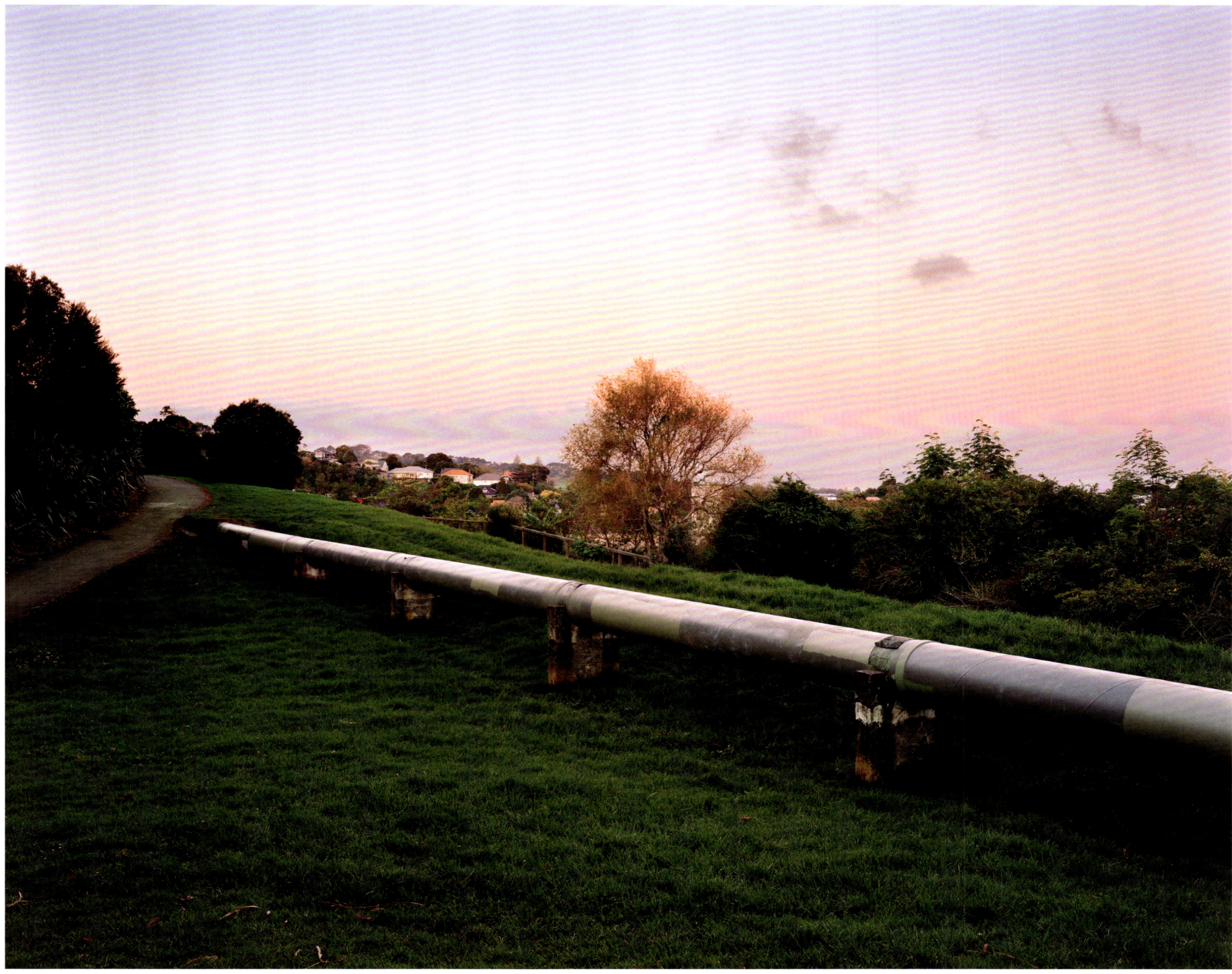

Gorse in a Development, Pinehill, Auckland, 2012

Despite housing affordability rapidly decreasing in the city from the early 1990s, the idea of an Auckland housing crisis was not seriously reported on until at least 2007. By that time, the average house price had almost doubled in less than a decade, and at the peak of the crisis in 2021, the increase over twenty years was a staggering 450%. Amid this, the wealthy, and those with access to low-interest finance, had realised that buying houses in Auckland was more profitable than working. So bad was the speculative bubble at certain points, that more than once, articles reported houses being resold as little as a week after purchase for profits of over 20%.

Auckland's growth, and high building costs due to New Zealand's geographic isolation, were factors in the crisis, but its main driver was a cultural shift in which housing became an asset class. A key element was New Zealand's lack of a capital gains tax. Of the thirty-eight similar nations that comprise the OECD, only New Zealand has no such tax. From 2007, the centre-right Government under which the housing crisis bloomed vigorously denied the problem, claiming that unaffordability was a good thing and showed that New Zealand was a place people wanted to live. The market was healthy and functioning and would—as the capitalist parlance goes— regulate itself. In hindsight, though, it is hard not to link their position to the disproportionately large number of investment properties owned by party members. With regulation, tax, and even acknowledgement of the issue off the table, more housing became the only answer.

In a few short years, vast areas of the most fertile pasture and fruit-growing land on Auckland's fringes were carved up into low-density and car-centric suburban developments. One such development, emblematic of the housing crisis, is Pinehill, which rapidly buried what once lay beneath it. While carrying out research at the Auckland Council archives, I found an aerial photograph of Pinehill taken in 1963. At its centre is a block of native forest, around which tree ferns regenerate along creeks that criss-cross the sloping hills. To one side, above the creeks, native shrub grows beneath radiata pine self-seeded from the forest of the neighbouring sawmill. A clay farm track follows the ridgeline through the bush, where today the major Greville Road motorway off-ramp cuts through the middle of Pinehill. Beyond the road, river valleys, orchards, and farmland appear in the distance.

Sometime before 2010, work began on a large suburban development at Pinehill, which was then still farmland. In 2012, bankruptcy filings temporarily halted the development, allowing gorse (*Ulex europaeus*) to recolonise the land. The plant was introduced to New Zealand in the nineteenth century by British settlers who were accustomed to using it for farm hedging, capitalising on its sharp spikes. Here, however, gorse spread rapidly. Long considered this country's most prevalent weed, it has spurred decades of eradication programmes. Recently though, it has been found that gorse acts as a nursery plant, allowing native bush to regenerate naturally over time. As work resumed on the Pinehill subdivision, the gorse was removed and with it the chance for forest regeneration. The area's once-gentle slopes, valleys, and creeks have been flattened into sites for identical suburban homes, and the name 'Pinehill' has acquired an ironic edge, given that barely a tree remains.

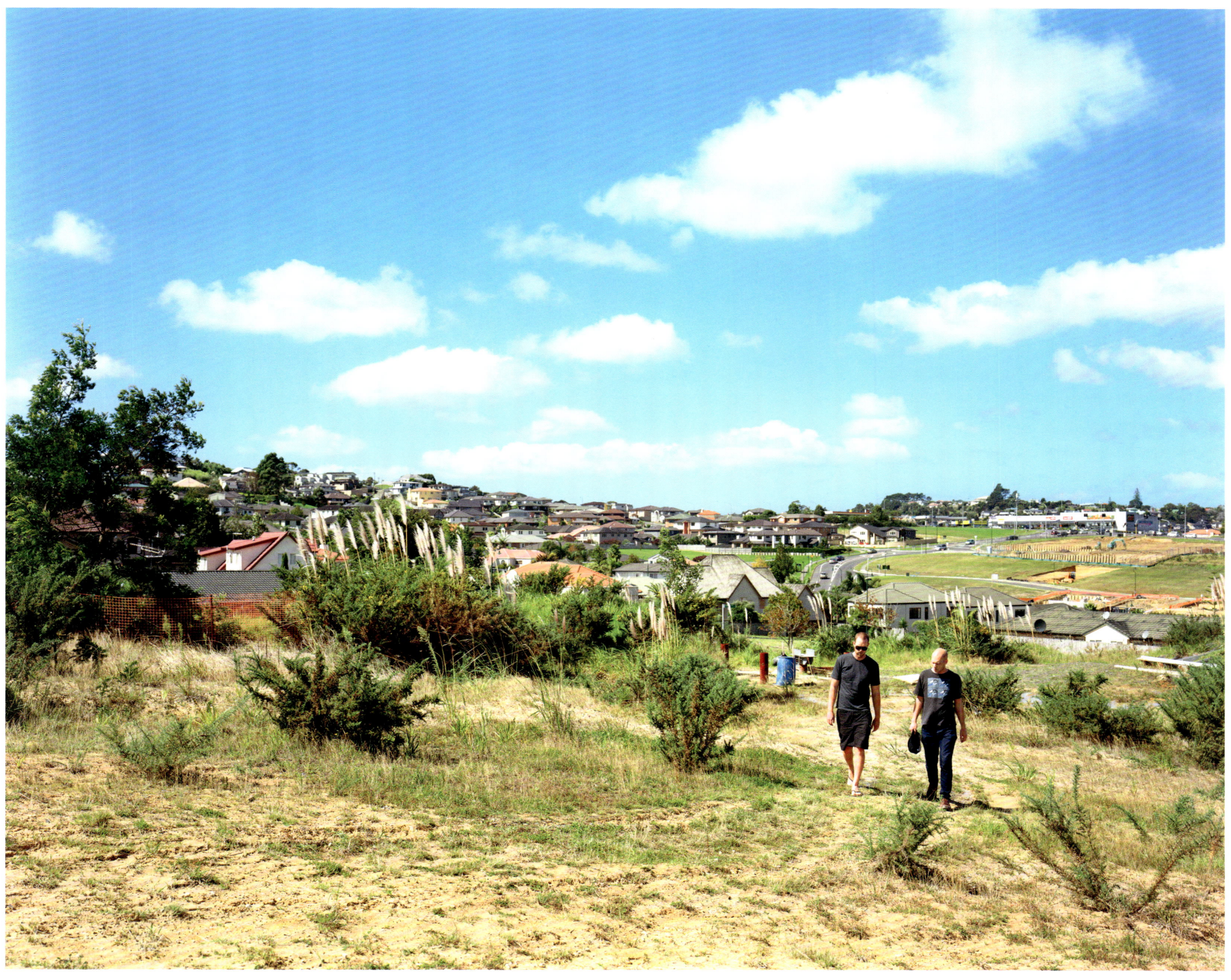

A Pōhutukawa Saved from Development, Rosebank Road, Auckland, 2013

As central Auckland grew in the 1840s, European settlers were also venturing into west Auckland. Although lying barely ten kilometres west of the central city, the Rosebank Peninsula was at the time said to be a no man's land of wetlands and bogs, left after kauri forests were cleared by Māori centuries before. Following abandoned Māori trails around the area in 1842, missionary and explorer William Colenso wrote in his journal, 'We travelled on, over open and barren heaths. … Observed nothing new in these dreary and sterile wilds.' His account was echoed in 1859 by the German geologist Ferdinand von Hochstetter, who described witnessing 'nothing, but waste, dreary, sunburnt heaths of notorious sterility … upon which nothing but dwarfish manuka shrubs, and scanty ferns can grow'.

How 'sterile' these 'wilds' actually were remains open for debate, but over the next five decades generations of farmers gradually improved the soil until they could plant grasses, orchards, and trees, and raise cattle. By the early 1900s, nearly all the forty families who owned land in the still rural area listed their profession as nurserymen, fruit growers, or orchardists, and for decades to follow Rosebank Peninsula remained agricultural. By the 1960s, though, the area was under increasing pressure from an ever-expanding Auckland. Within barely a decade, most of the market gardens and orchards that had taken nearly a century to cultivate had been cleared and paved for suburban, commercial, and industrial development.

In 2007, the last 'undeveloped lot' was sold by Bob O'Connell, whose family members were among the first market gardeners in Auckland. Nearly seventy years earlier, as a young boy, Bob planted a pōhutukawa and an oak tree behind the homestead on his family's twenty-two-acre property. Adjacent to Rosebank Road, which was now a busy arterial route, over time the two trees had become a prominent landmark. But, in 2009, without warning, or public consultation, Auckland Council approved a resource consent to fell the trees as part of an industrial development. A professional valuation estimated that with the trees standing, the site would lose $600,000 of potential value, no doubt factoring into the council decision. Then, later that year, despite public opposition, the Avondale Community Board endorsed naming the new street through the former O'Connell property and beside the trees Jomac Place after the development company, discarding other suggestions, including 'O'Connell Place' and Māori names.

The trees became emblematic in a battle for urban tree protection, and for the next three years, the decision to allow the felling was fought by local residents and a nonprofit organisation, the Tree Council. Numerous legal proceedings saw the dispute reach both the high and environmental courts, until in May 2011, Auckland Council granted both trees protection on the Schedule of Notable Trees. With the possibility of another office or warehouse extinguished, in 2014, the developers sold the site to a progressive childcare centre, which integrated the trees into their landscaping, building a boardwalk playground around them.

In 2015, under a National Government, the Resource Management Act was permanently altered to remove automatic protection that existed for native and significant trees over a certain height on private property. The law change, which remains in place today, permanently clears the way for similar trees to be felled, without public consultation or council consent.

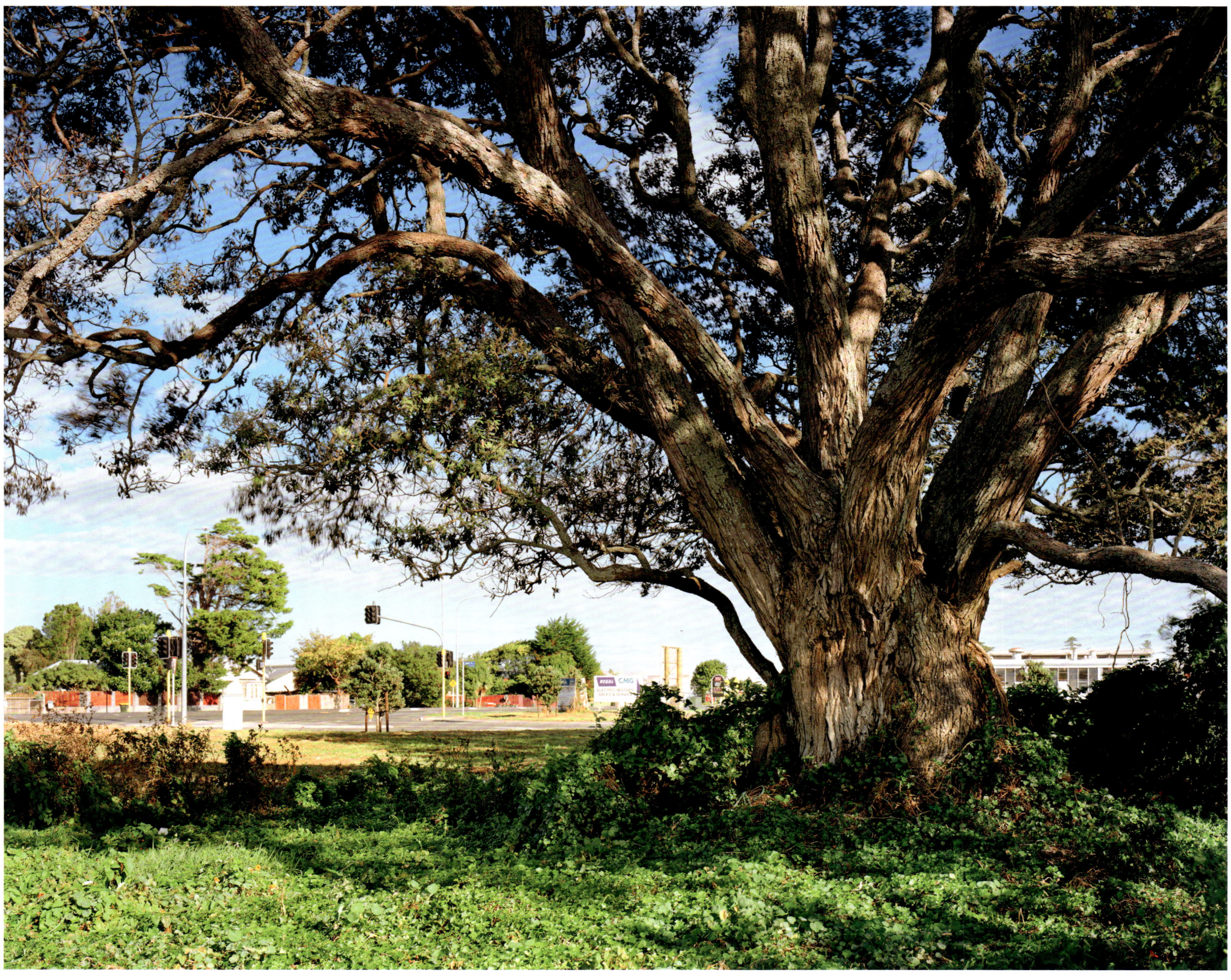

A Boathouse Among Pōhutukawa (After Winkelmann), Hobson Bay, Auckland, 2015

In 1879, the artist Alfred Sharpe painted a watercolour of Newmarket Gully and the creek which runs through it into Hobson Bay. In the picture, sparkling water flows between punga ferns and ancient pūriri trees above a waterfall, the distant gully vanishing into a romantic wash of colour. A photograph by Henry Winkelmann, taken in the same area over twenty years later, looks towards Hobson Bay, across what became Auckland's most expensive suburb, Remuera. A solitary farmhouse stands on pasture-clad hills that gently roll towards a mangrove estuary. The tide is out, and creeks weave through mudflats towards the harbour. On the distant shore, pōhutukawa trees cling to sandstone cliffs above boathouses. On the headland beyond, Parnell's first villas bite at what was then Auckland's fringe.

By the turn of the century, however, Newmarket Creek had become the open sewer of the growing suburbs, and Hobson Bay had become polluted. Not long before, the bay had hosted a children's regatta, and photographs show children swimming in clean water beside the boathouses. A letter to the *Herald* newspaper from 1900 reads, 'As a resident of Remuera I often ride along the Beach Road, and the odious smell arising from the gully which empties itself into the bay is something to be remembered, considering the possibility of the bubonic plague paying us a visit. A few days ago, I was riding a horse unaccustomed to town atmosphere, and I could not get the animal along the road on account of the frightful smell, the water in the above gully being as black as you could make it.'

In response to the outcry, an underground sewer was constructed in 1903, its route following the creek before crossing mudflats and 'discharging in a tidal creek'. As Remuera continued to grow, the scheme was expanded between 1910 and 1913. A new sewer inside a concrete box rose three and a half metres above the high-water line, and ran nearly four kilometres across Hobson Bay, Wilson's Beach, and Ōkahu Bay, before emptying into underground holding tanks (which are now Kelly Tarlton's aquarium). Suspiciously, the location selected for the outlet—from which sewage was discharged into the Waitematā Harbour with the outgoing tide—was just beneath the headland of Ōrākei pā, the main Māori settlement in the area.

Running just metres off Wilson's Beach, the elevated sewer also ended the boating and swimming at Hobson Bay. Later, between 1927 and 1932, the bay was twice more cleaved by causeways—first for the eastern branch of the main trunk railway line, and second by the coastal ring road Tāmaki Drive. On top of this, even with the new pipeline, heavy rainfall still regularly caused sewage to overflow, and now blocked by sluice gates beneath the railway, Hobson Bay was soon polluted again. The causeways led to deep mud build-up in the bay, and native flora was swamped by a mat of algae and seaweed, which allowed invasive Asian date mussels, giant Pacific oysters, and barnacles to take hold. In 2004, the Auckland Council supported plans for a new multilane eastern motorway across the bay, but after strong public protest, the plans were eventually abandoned.

In 2010, the elevated concrete sewer was finally removed. Overflows into Newmarket Creek caused by stormwater continue to make Hobson Bay unsafe for swimming or food gathering.

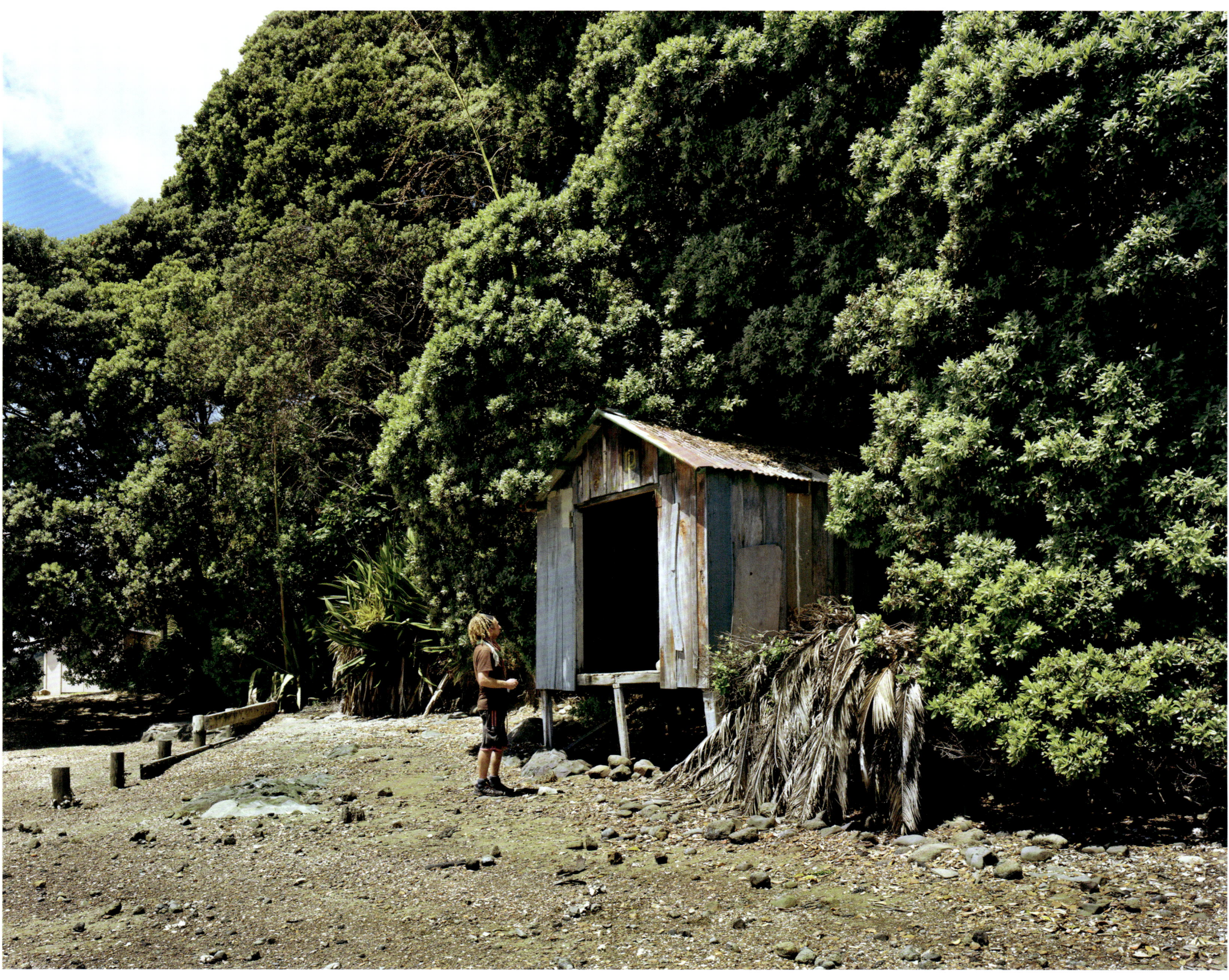

Kotanui Island and Rangitoto (After Kinder), Whangaparāoa, 2013

In the middle of the nineteenth century, as the medium of photography was growing in popularity, thirty-six-year-old John Kinder set sail from London to Auckland to take up a position as headmaster at the recently established Church of England Grammar School in Mount Eden. Kinder's childhood had been one of privilege. His father's success as a London high-street merchant had provided his family a large home with ornate furnishings, and daily life had included chauffeured carriages and private tutors. But by Kinder's teenage years, problems with his father's investments saw the family fortune crumble. His father departed indefinitely for South America to try and salvage his investments and reputation, leaving Kinder, his mother, and his sisters 'consigned to the hands of God'.

Although Kinder had graduated from the University of Cambridge, the sudden responsibility to provide for his mother and younger sister saw his academic dreams dashed. John pivoted into school teaching, and this became the profession he was known for in New Zealand. After arriving here, however, he also began a parallel, and almost secret, career as an artist. From the 1860s, and mostly within a decade, he produced over 400 glass plate negatives, and later, hundreds of watercolours—often working from earlier photographs. Incredibly, except to an intimate circle of his friends, the works remained unknown in his lifetime, and for several decades after his death in 1903. Not until 1937, when his adopted son Harry gifted a substantial portion of work to several national museums, did awareness of his achievement begin.

Among the best known of Kinder's photographs is a suite made around Matakatia Bay at Whangaparāoa in 1868, during a brief stay with his friend Monsieur Direy, who was one of the first European settlers on the then-remote and bush-clad peninsula north of Auckland. During this trip, Kinder produced images of Matakatia Bay, a pontoon on the beach, sandstone cliffs seen from the headland, and several views of Kotanui Island, many of which have since become iconic. The formal rigour of Kinder's images, though, is almost incongruous with the fact that he only showed his work twice publicly in his lifetime, and seemingly had little interest in being known as an artist. Even today, more than a century after his death, the ideology and motivations behind his work remain enigmatic. Compared with the images of other early colonial photographers, his pictures—showing subjects like deforestation in the Waitākere Ranges, scorched hillsides cleared for gold mining at Coromandel, and railway cuttings through banks—seem uniquely contemporary, almost prescient of the American New Topographic photography movement of well over a century later.

A lack of commentary by Kinder himself leaves us only to speculate about meaning. Are images that seem to question the virtue of colonial expansion into Aotearoa's natural landscape really that, or are they simply expressive of the prevailing viewpoint that such destruction was a manifestation of order and progress, a rightful 'taming of the wilderness'? Beyond his images, Kinder leaves one clue in an unpublished memoir. Following a visit to Rotorua, he wrote, 'after European settlement the landscape and place … was now shorn of its most attractive features'.

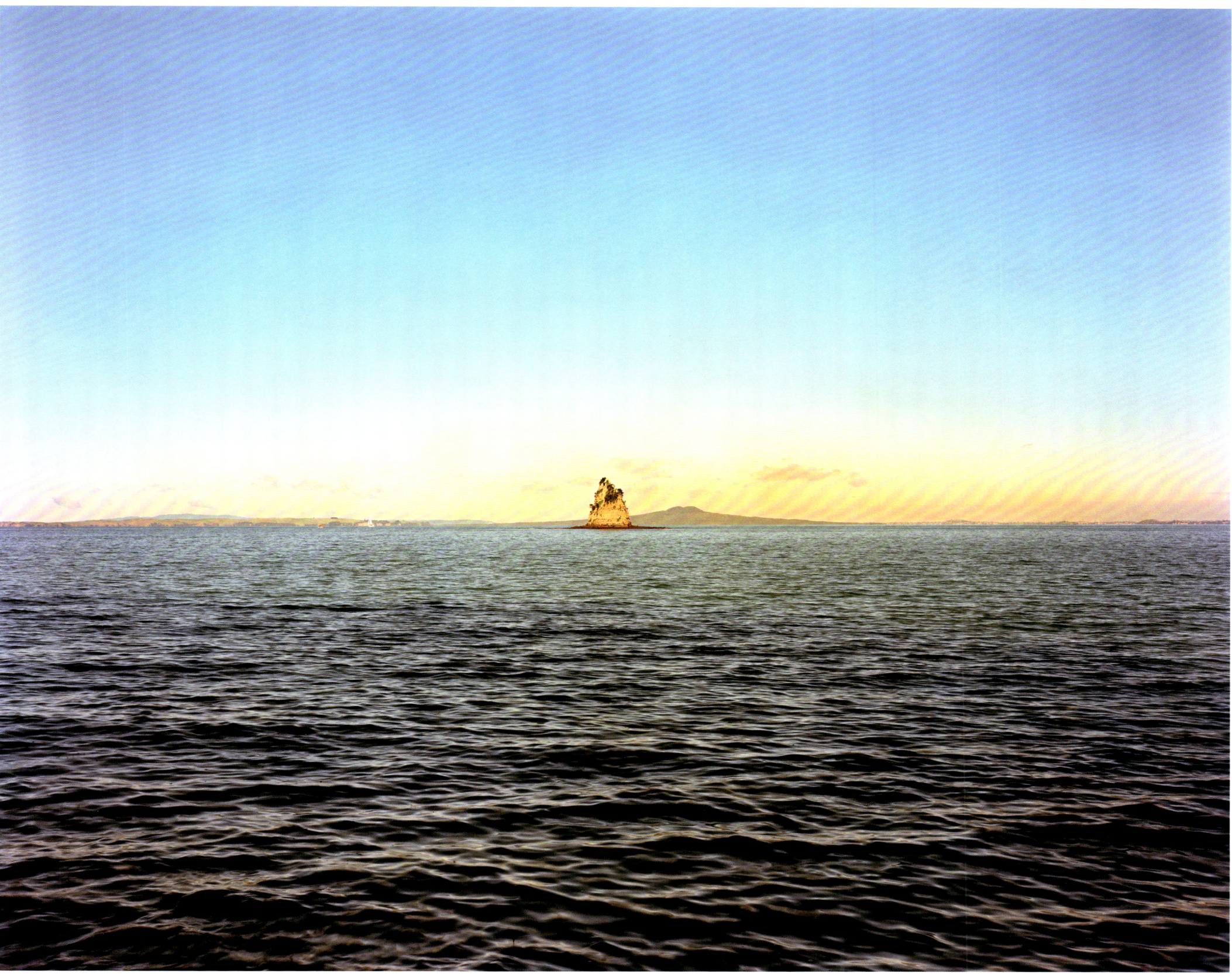

My Father (Ian Scott) Painting Beneath a Pōhutukawa, Okoromai Bay, Whangaparāoa, 2013

My father, Ian Scott, was born in April 1945 in the West Yorkshire village of Baildon. Human habitation in this part of England reaches back almost 3,000 years to the Iron Age, with even the town of Baildon being 1,000 years old. For most of these centuries, Baildon was a small farming community, but during the industrial revolution it became a hub of the woollen industry. Opening in 1823, its Providence Woollen Mill occupied the centre of the village like a medieval church. Its importance to the community was made clear during the Second World War, when tanks and searchlights were stationed on the surrounding moors to protect it. At that time, my grandfather (who was a cinema projectionist) was enlisted to screen films for the troops, but as the war ended, Britain fell into an economic depression. Industrial towns like Baildon were hit particularly hard, and seeing little opportunity in post-war Britain, my father's parents immigrated to New Zealand in 1952. Less than a decade later, in 1964, the Providence Mill closed its doors for good.

Arriving after a two-month journey at sea abord the *Captain Cook*, my father's family settled in Sunnyvale, a new Government subdivision at the foothills of the Waitākere Ranges. My grandfather took one of the only jobs going as a local butcher, and my grandmother became a typist. In England, my father's early interest in art had been nurtured by his grandfather, an amateur artist who taught him watercolour painting on the Yorkshire moors. Now, living by the comparatively wild Waitākeres, landscape painting became his obsession. With the encouragement of his teachers, his skill quickly developed, and by the age of fifteen he was regularly selling his paintings.

By his late teens, modern art had overtaken his interest in landscape painting. He attended classes with renowned modernist Colin McCahon in 1963, then enrolled at the University of Auckland's Elam School of Fine Arts the following year. While there, he painted large post-pop figurative landscapes that soon gained attention. Meanwhile, his parents moved to Whangaparāoa, and after art school he rented the unit beneath their house, where in a small space with a low ceiling, he produced the early examples of his best-known series, the *Lattices*. Weaving interlocking diagonal grids of colour, the works referenced suburban environments as well as traditions of craft and geometric abstraction. In 1978, a work from the series won the country's national art award, judged by the director of the National Gallery of Australia, James Mollison, who had famously acquired Jackson Pollock's *Blue Poles* a few years earlier.

Although he is today best known as an abstract artist, my father continued to paint landscapes privately throughout his life. During my childhood, the closest thing we had to holidays were trips to the Coromandel and Whangaparāoa Peninsulas, where I followed him on endless walks over hills and around the coast while he painted. By the time this photograph was taken, he had been fighting cancer for several years. On a day at the end of summer in 2013, we visited a distant spot on the Whangaparāoa coastline where my father had painted in his twenties and where I hoped to find the location of a photograph of coastal cliffs by John Kinder. I helped my father descend a steep, trackless bank he would have run down just a few years before. As he sat on a boulder looking out to sea, after spending a few hours making watercolours, his painful tiredness was evident. It was one of the last trips we took together. He died three months later, in June, on the night of my twenty-eighth birthday.

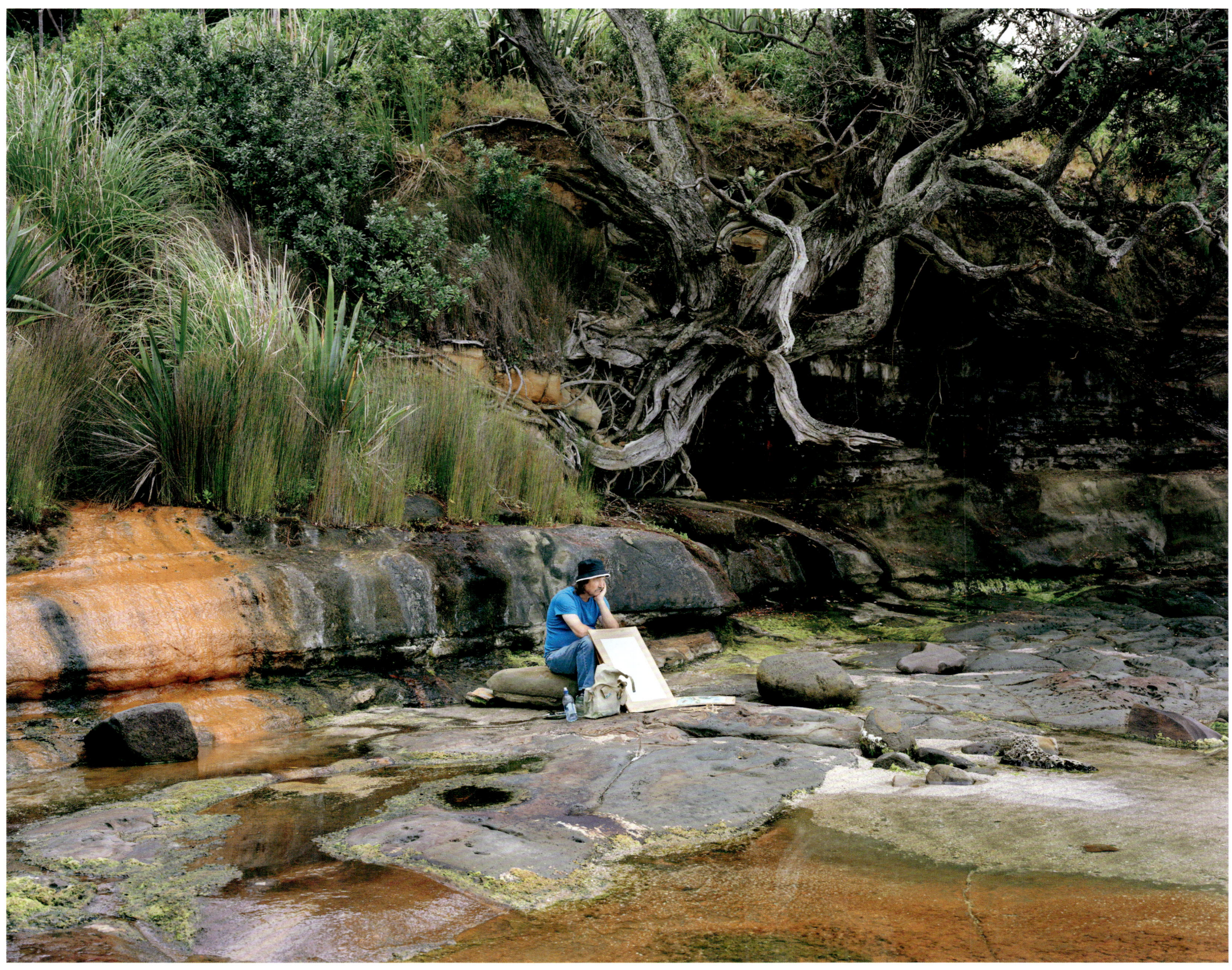

Land Development Beside Waikumete Cemetery, Glen Eden, Auckland, 2014

Two years after Auckland's founding in 1840, its first cemetery opened at Symonds Street, at the far end of the Karangahape Road ridgeline two kilometres from the downtown port. At this time, the town's population was still just 2,000 people. On the cemetery's eastern bank, bracken fern traced the slopes of Grafton Gully above native forest remnants that grew along the Waipārūrū Stream. For decades, the area remained semi-rural; in 1850, Partington's Flour Mill and its famous windmill opened near the cemetery's edge. By the 1880s, though, most of the land around the cemetery had been sold, and as the population increased, a new location was sought.

In 1880, Auckland's western rail line reached Glen Eden, then on the edge of the Waitākere rainforest. Industry in the area centred on logging, and burning trees to clear pasture, and so dominant was this line of work that the neighbouring suburb Henderson, was even named after the most prominent Waitākere sawmiller, Thomas Henderson. The surplus of former forest land, combined with the optimism that West Auckland would be a new city centre, saw a site just above the Glen Eden railway station selected for the new cemetery. Opened in 1886, and covering 267 acres, Waikumete became the largest cemetery in Australasia. A regular Sunday train service was established to increase access to the still-remote location, and this included a separate funeral carriage for the deceased and accompanying mourners that arrived at its own platform.

As the forest was pushed back, Glen Eden became farms and pasture, and nurseries and orchards were also developed. Gradually, the area also became synonymous with winemaking. Although there were local attempts at viticulture from the 1850s, it wasn't until Dalmatian immigrants with winemaking knowledge and experience arrived in West Auckland in the early 1900s that the craft succeeded here. Their legacy was such that the 1960 *Encyclopedia of New Zealand* noted, 'Henderson and Oratia made up 80% of Auckland's vineyards and orchards.'

Immigrating to New Zealand from England in 1952, my father entered this bucolic environment, where orchards and vineyards lay beneath the regenerating forest of the Waitākere Ranges. His family bought a new house in a Government-built subdivision on Awaroa Road, which runs from the northern end of Waikumete Cemetery to the Sunnyvale town centre. Coming from a dying industrial town in northern England, to my father the area was like paradise. In his youth, he and his brothers and friends often spent their free time in the rambling cemetery, and he later worked at local orchards.

When he died in 2013, after a long fight with cancer, my mother and I made the decision to bury him at Waikumete. His plot, beneath old pine trees, looks south-west to the Waitākeres and east to the city centre. It is also near the site of this photograph. Here, as a child, and when the land was still overgrown, my father walked each day, through the cemetery between school and home.

Today, Waikumete is the resting place of over 70,000 people.

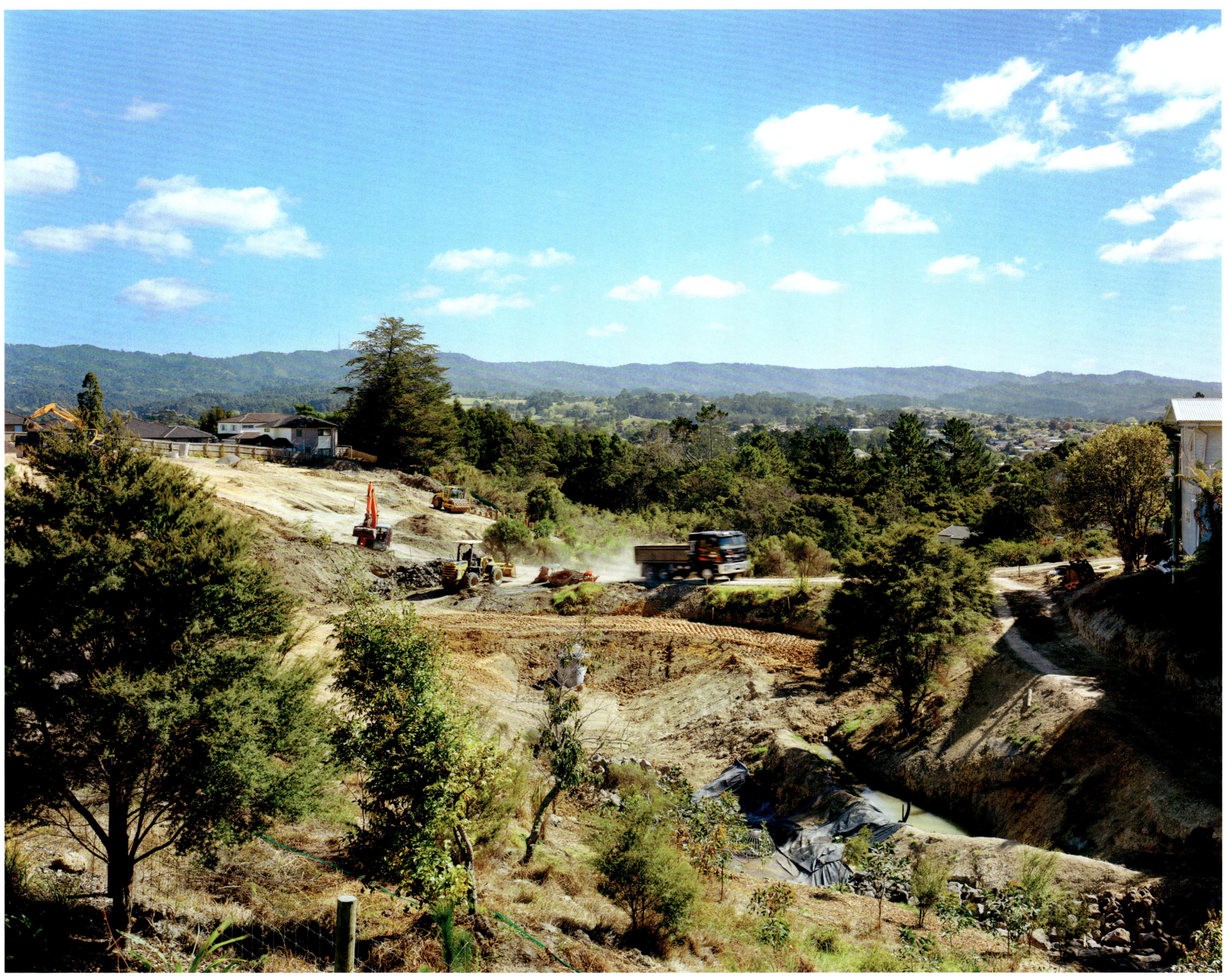

Nihotupu Auxiliary Reservoir, Waitākere Ranges, Auckland, 2014

When Europeans first sailed into the Manukau Harbour and saw the cliffs of the Waitākere Ranges, ancient kauri trees stretched over the hills and valleys as far as the eye could see. The visitors reacted with awe, describing a cathedral-like forest, in which pale grey trunks metres wide rose a hundred metres into a dense canopy. Yet within just decades, only isolated patches of the forest remained. Trees were felled for timber or burnt to clear land for settlement and pasture. Over time, though, an awareness of the loss grew. A public outcry, led by Algernon Thomas, professor of biology at the University of Auckland, and several other prominent Aucklanders, saw the creation of the Waitākere Ranges Regional Park in 1894 and the protection of a small area of forest from logging.

At about the same time, Auckland was suffering from increasingly severe water shortages. As the population swelled, the city's main source of water, Western Springs, began to run dry, a problem exacerbated by summer droughts. In 1898, the worst drought to date took place, said to be so severe that another week without rain could have led to deaths. That year, the *Observer* newspaper wrote, 'For nearly twenty years past the inadequacy of the Auckland water supply has been admitted. For nearly twenty years past the Auckland City Council have been paltering with the question of procuring a supply that shall be permanent and inexhaustible.' After a lengthy, and widely lambasted, period of indecision, the council selected the Waitākere Ranges as the site for a new reservoir scheme. There may have been no good alternative, but the decision condemned some of the area's most pristine rivers, waterfalls, and valleys to permanent flooding.

The project began with the construction of a twenty-kilometre pipeline that traversed sheer terrain by bridge and tunnel to reach the struggling pumping station at Western Springs, and in 1902, the first dams opened on Nihotupu Creek and Quinns Creek. Despite the scale of the project, though, it still proved inadequate. In 1910, a much larger concrete reservoir, Waitākere Dam, opened, flooding an area of 62 acres, and in 1915, construction began on a second concrete dam to replace the earlier one at Nihotupu Creek. The project was almost immediately marred by problems. The First World War caused material and labour shortages, and a blasting accident saw a rock fly 100 metres into the site office, killing the head contractor. In addition, high rainfall and flooding made roads impassable and working conditions more dangerous.

After four years of delays, construction began on an auxiliary reservoir above the main dam at Nihotupu as a stopgap. But this project, too, was beset by bad weather and inaccessibility through muddy clay roads, and by the time the reservoir opened in 1921, the winter period of water collection had been missed. The auxiliary reservoir operated for just a single season before, after eight gruelling years of construction, the Upper Nihotupu Reservoir opened in 1923. Rarely used thereafter, the Nihotupu Auxiliary Reservoir was decommissioned in 1985, with holes cut through the front and back faces of the dam to reopen the creek.

Today the area of the Auxiliary Reservoir is home to regenerating bush. It is part of the Waitākere Ranges Regional Park, which includes more than 39,500 acres of protected native forest and coastline.

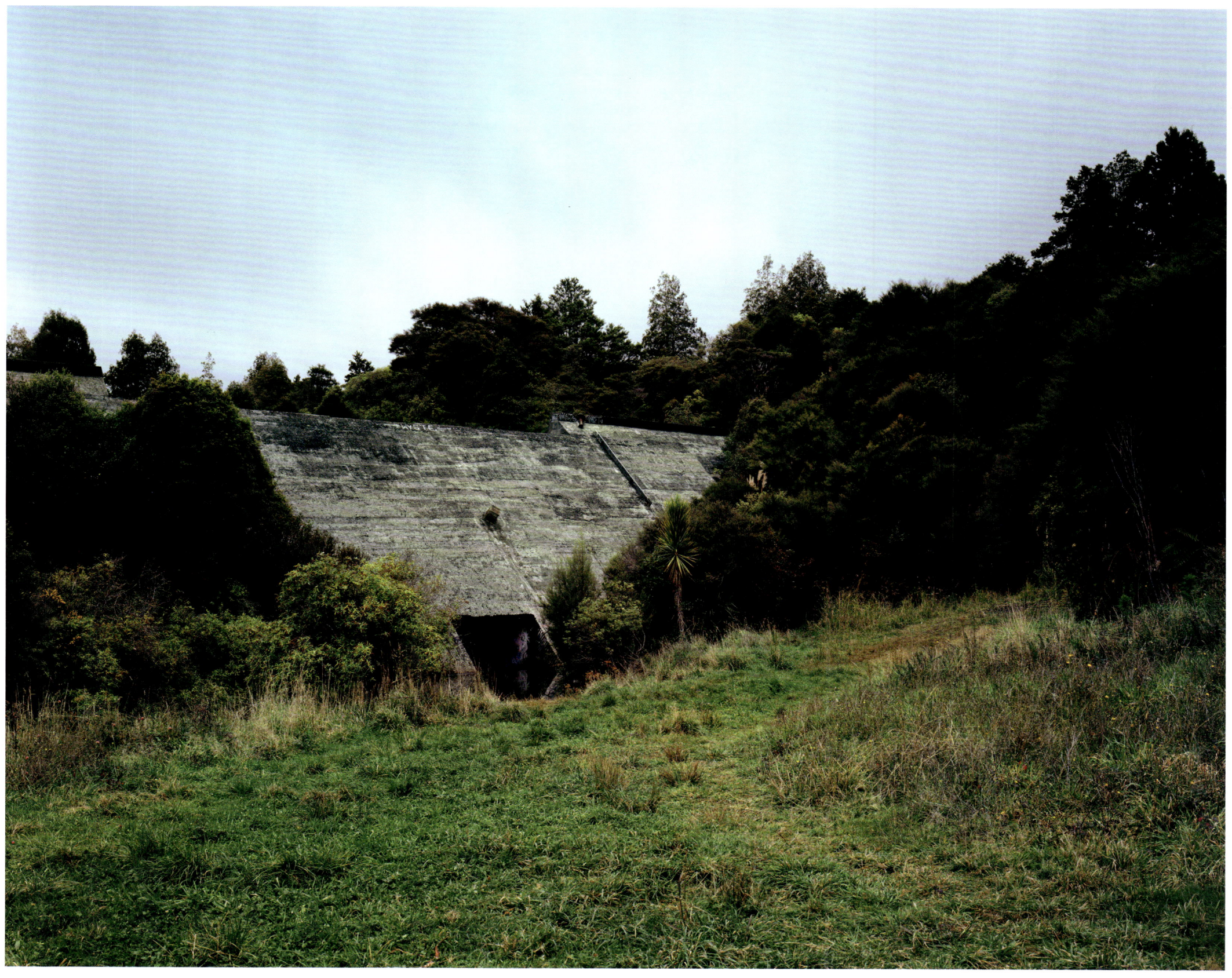

Remains of Black Rock Kauri Dam, Piha Gorge, Auckland, 2014

At the age of twenty-one, Dr Frederick Rayner, a dentist and graduate of the University of Toronto, married Ethel McLeod, a wealthy Canadian meat-empire heiress. During their subsequent global travels, which included a visit to New Zealand, the couple decided to make the country their home. Soon after arriving, Rayner bought land at Lake Rotoiti, and in 1898, he built Moose Lodge, a 6,000-square-foot house that later hosted Queen Elizabeth II. Based in Auckland, he lived conspicuously, proudly owning one of the first cars in the city, running the automobile association, and establishing the American Dental Parlour on Queen Street, from which five dentists worked eleven hours a day, six days a week. In advertisements, the firm claimed to see 1,000 patients a month and fit 1,000 dentures a year.

In 1907, Rayner acquired the Waitākere forest surrounding Karekare, Piha, Anawhata, and Whatipū beaches for next to nothing after the Government liquidation of a forestry contractor. Lacking road access for logging at Karekare, he built steep rail inclines and a tramway, which traversed sand dunes and the rugged coastline to reach a wharf at Whatipū for export. In 1910, the sawmill moved across the hill to Piha, and within three years nearly all of its ancient rainforest was removed, the kauri turned into items like butchers' chopping blocks and planks for train carriage chassis, or exported to Australia. In 1913, Rayner sold the mill (but not the land) to the Railways Department, which logged neighbouring Anawhata after discovering that Piha had no forest left. A decade later, an inquiry by a new Government found that the department had lost tens of thousands on the operation, while Rayner had made a profit of £104,488 (£5.5 million today). That Rayner was able to get away with this trickery was linked by many to his close relationships with politicians.

From the spoils of his deals and the destruction of these forests, Rayner built a second Moose Lodge (today known as Rannoch) in Mount Eden in 1914. He saved a block of ancient pūriri forest around it as a curio, while also having poison injected into his neighbour's trees to clear a view of the harbour. In 1922, he and Ethel opened Auckland's first jazz cabaret, the Dixieland Dance Hall, which soon burned down in what was widely said to be insurance fraud. He later became known for his extravagant gambling, alongside other early Auckland capitalists like J. J. Craig, a brickmaker whose inherited transport company owned seventy ships. Rayner's final act before he died in 1931 was to set in motion the subdivision of Piha's remaining wilderness into suburban sections.

A 1923 article in the *New Zealand Herald* wrote of Rayner's effect on Piha, 'Much of the original beauty of the western hills has been lost, even within the last few years. … Hillsides of magnificent bush have been ruthlessly devastated, while in recent years the destruction of the peerless seaside forests of Piha has left Auckland immeasurably the poorer. The old-time beauty of the Piha gorge, of the noble tracts of bush that swept up from the ocean to the crest of the ranges, was something that should have been handed on from generation to generation; today, the hillsides and valleys are scarred and rent and torn, and only the merest vestige of former beauty remains to sadden the heart of those who witness the desecration that has been wrought.'

In 1938, the family of Sir Algernon Thomas gifted 100 acres around the Piha Stream to the council, which became part of the Waitākere Regional Park. The small waterfalls and deep pools of Piha Gorge, in which kauri logs are still stuck a century later, are a popular spot for canyoning enthusiasts.

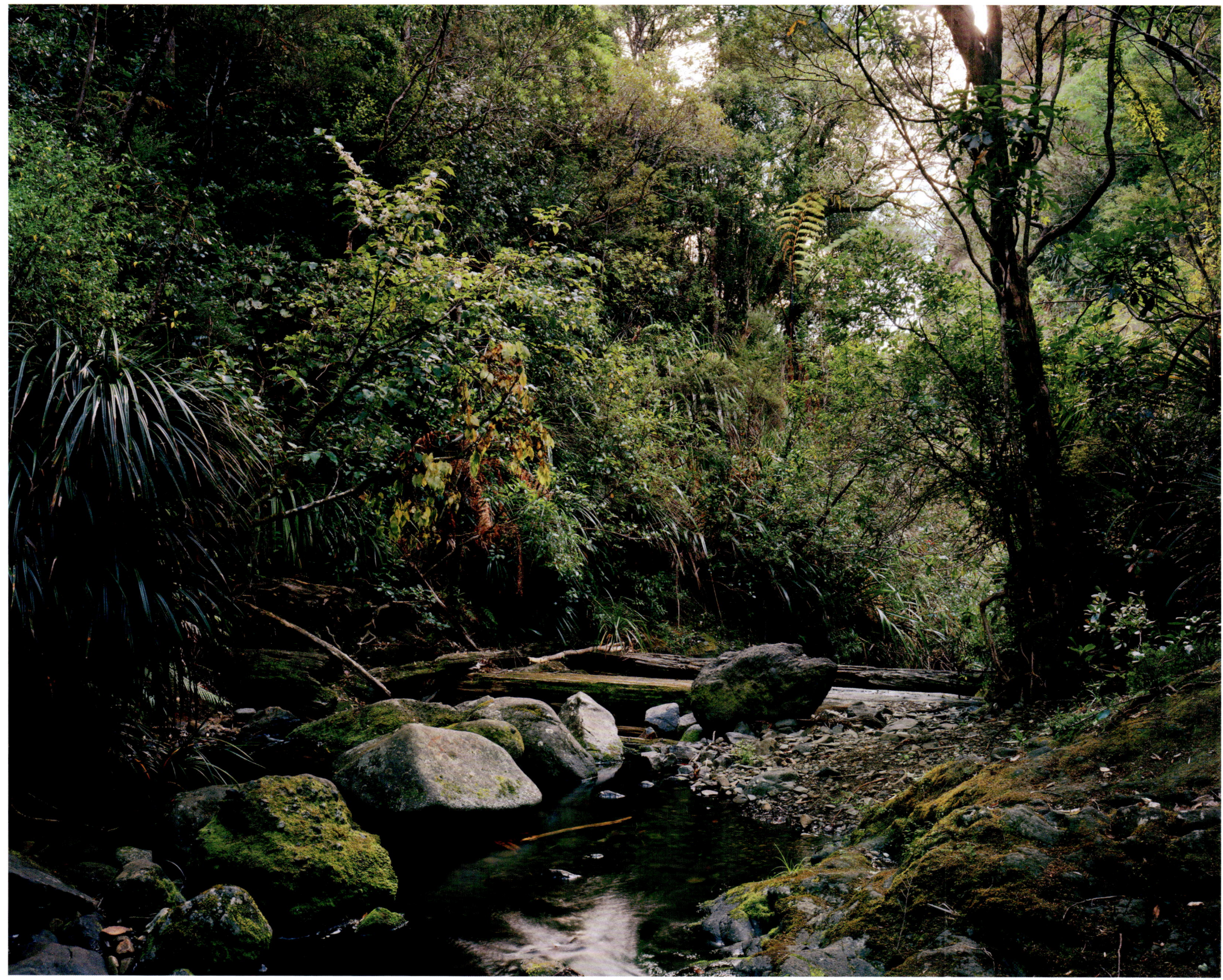

Rain over a Development, Whangaparāoa Peninsula, 2014

The noise, pollution, and crime that went hand in hand with the industrial revolution saw large areas of many cities become places where few lived by choice. Often confined to crowded slums, factory workers experienced living conditions vastly different to those of their managers, who could return each evening to estates beyond the urban smog. Towards the turn of the nineteenth century, though, labour movements had won battles for increased wages and shorter working hours, and these gains coincided with the development of social programmes and public transit networks. Concurrently, urban planning theories such as the 'garden city' grew in popularity, together with the desire for clean air and space. As the twentieth century advanced, these factors made the aspiration of suburban living a possibility not only for the upper classes but also for working people.

In a 2007 essay on a Stephen Shore photograph, artist Joel Sternfeld summarises the ideology of American suburban expansion: 'When the town/country duality is made, town is portrayed as the dark urban merchant, evil in comparison to the bright virtues of nature and rural living. Nothing trumps Nature—it is pure, it is good. Its mythic credentials run deeper than those of any old 'tun' (town).' The ideology Sternfeld here describes also explains a key motivation for European colonisation of the wilderness of Aotearoa in the early nineteenth century: a desire to escape the evil of the cities. It is a persistent irony that this same impulse is a direct cause of the consumption of nature by city suburbs.

As cars became widely available and were enthusiastically adopted in the 1930s, suburban expansion increased in ferocity. At the time, these seemed like natural developments. However, it became clear that they were spurred on by American car and oil companies, which worked to encourage dependency on their products by dismantling urban tram systems, while also funding and advocating motorway networks to encourage suburban development. In 1947, the archetypal subdivision of the 'automotive city' was constructed in Levittown, New York—a model of urban planning that would come to dominate New Zealand and much of the rest of the world. Eventually consisting of over 17,000 almost identical single-family homes (with up to twelve new houses being finished every day), Levittown redefined the suburb in terms of its dependence on cars and disengagement from former city life.

From the post-war years to the present, the majority of New Zealand's housing has followed almost exactly the Levittown model of suburban development. This is especially true in Auckland, where new subdivisions have been dramatically expanding the city since its inception. In the 1970s, the wave of development reached Whangaparāoa, a narrow peninsula stretching fifteen kilometres off the east coast, north of Auckland. For decades, it had been a modest beach and retirement community, but by 1998 New Zealand's first luxury marina-subdivision 'Gulf Harbour' was taking shape across one of the peninsula's most untouched estuaries and hillsides, its style inspired, seemingly without irony, by Seaside, Florida, the failed planned community that later became the set of *The Truman Show* (1998).

Since the establishment of Gulf Harbour, Whangaparāoa's estuaries and farms have continued to be filled with low-density housing, including treeless developments like the depicted Woodridge Villas and a nearby retirement community, the Botanic, which promises a place for 'people who desire a life full of purpose, nature, wellbeing and joy'.

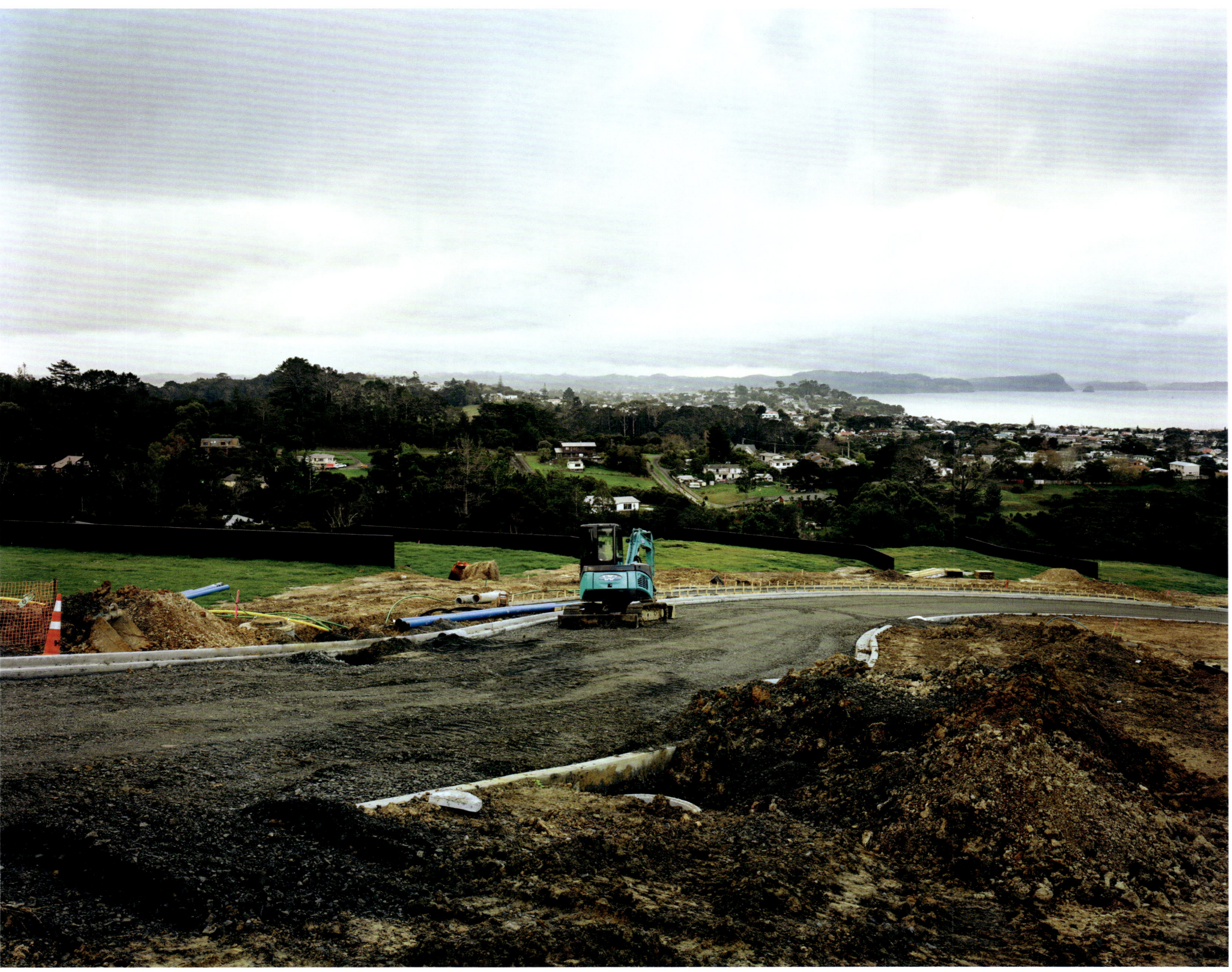

Mark Adams Retouching Photographs at Studio La Gonda, Karangahape Road, Auckland, 2013

For over 600 years, Te Ara o Karangahape was a trail used by Māori to travel between the Waitematā and Manukau Harbours. Following an elevated ridgeline behind what is now the central business district, it encompassed nearly panoramic views of the lush isthmus landscape. As Auckland grew, from its establishment in 1840, the arterial Queen Street sprawled uphill from the port, and by 1882, it had reached the trail, which it absorbed into the city grid as Karangahape Road. Largely due to the prevailing wind, which made it smell better than the manure-lined open sewer of Queen Street, Karangahape Road became Auckland's most affluent shopping district. It housed ornate Victorian buildings and arcades, and, by 1902, electric trams ran at all hours of the day on streets paved with wooden tiles.

With the mass adoption of cars in the 1930s and 1940s, New Zealand rapidly changed. By 1955, road usage had increased such that the Government purchased a swathe of residential property in Newton Gully, just south of Karangahape Road, for a new motorway. The resulting interchange, Auckland's first and largest, came to be known as 'Spaghetti Junction'. As with urban motorway projects by Robert Moses in New York, it constituted an act of social engineering, displacing more than 50,000 lower-income residents, many of whom were artists and other creatives. The motorway also disconnected Karangahape Road from its surrounding neighbourhoods, leaving its department stores and small businesses to atrophy while suburban shopping malls grew. By the 1970s, the once boutique shopping area had become the city's red-light district. Eventually, though, Karangahape Road began to flourish again, as spaces became available to artists and specialist businesses at affordable rents, spurring new creative life.

In the 1990s, photographic artists Mark Adams, Haruhiko Sameshima, and later John Miller (Ngāpuhi) formed a partnership and shared workspace, Studio La Gonda. The name was borrowed from the former owner of the art deco building where the studio is located, La Gonda Fashions, which was among New Zealand's leading makers and designers of modern clothing before the 1960s. By sharing costs, and carrying out professional photography of art and objects when necessary, they have been able to sustain three of Aotearoa's most important art practices for decades, while remaining almost entirely outside the commercial art world. Studio La Gonda has also become a meeting place for the photography community in New Zealand.

As with other cultural centres around the world, the creative revitalisation of Karangahape Road has left it vulnerable to gentrification. Its red-light district mostly banished, despite some resistant grit, the area is now home to high-end apartment conversions, design firms, expensive stores, and, briefly, a Tesla dealership. For more than a decade, as rents have risen, the existence of Studio La Gonda has been under increasing pressure, a problem exacerbated by New Zealand's lack of regulations like rent control to support continuous tenancy. For now, though, Studio La Gonda holds on. Its dimly lit staircase, with varnished wood panelling and worn patterned carpet, is a remnant of another time, like the film view-cameras, processing chemicals, and analogue darkroom within.

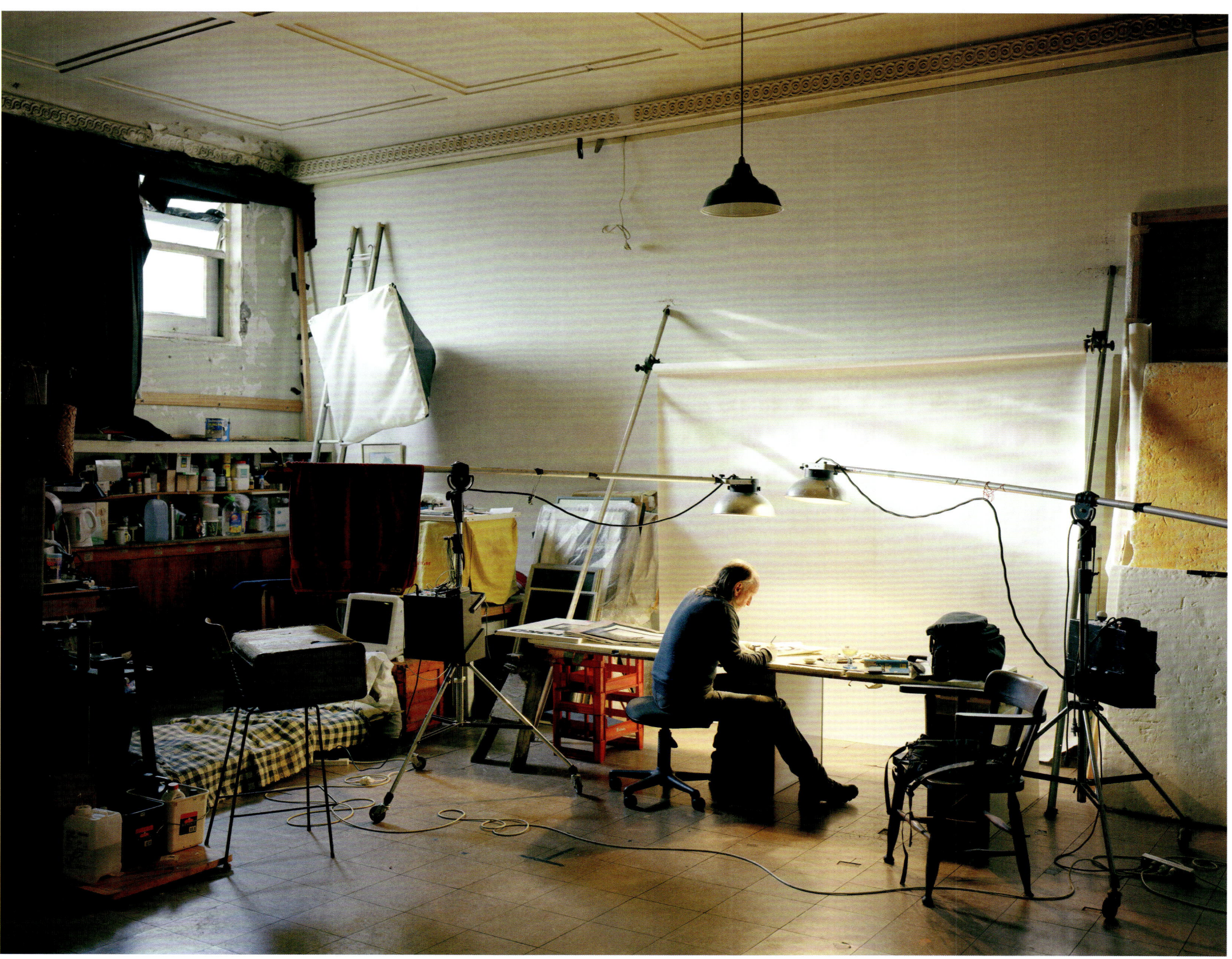

My Father's Studio, Three Months After His Death from Cancer, Mt Eden, 2013

Standing atop Maungawhau (Mount Eden) in 1913, looking south-west towards the Manukau Harbour and Āwhitu Peninsula, artist Henry Winkelmann created a three-frame panorama with his plate camera. In the foreground of the image, the few hundred villas that made up the suburb cluster around a town centre. Just beyond them, horses graze above valleys of rocky lava flows, on which ancient forests had stood just years before. In the middle distance, Mount Eden stops abruptly at Balmoral Road, now the suburb's centre. Its dry-stone walls, made of volcanic rock, and pine windbreaks mark the change to rural land that then ran all the way to what is now South Auckland. Finally, in the middle of the image are the towering peaks of Three Kings, the terracing of abandoned pā (Māori settlements) visible, but soon to be quarried away, along with the mountains.

When Winkelmann made the panorama, it's likely he knew that this rural boundary would soon disappear. The open land in his pictures would in just a few years be filled with Californian bungalows, copy-pasted in quick succession. In 1981, my parents bought one of these bungalows, halfway between Balmoral Road and Three Kings. For the three-bedroom house on a quarter-acre section, they paid just $52,000 ($240,000 today). The relative affordability of housing in Mount Eden, and its location on the city fringe, saw the suburb become a creative centre; during the twentieth century, countless painters, photographers, writers, journalists, and potters would call it home.

At the back of my parents' section were metres-high lava flows, upon which the sole large tree on the section grew: an oak at least fifty years old. Almost immediately after buying the house, my father assembled a kitset double garage on a concrete foundation beneath the tree. For the next thirty years, it was his studio. Almost every day, he would walk from the back door across a path of colonial bricks beside kawakawa, hydrangeas, and pink geraniums to the 'shed' to paint.

By the 2010s, the Auckland housing crisis was changing Mount Eden. Within just two decades, the cost of a house on my parents' street had jumped from $200,000 to $1 million, and then to $2 million. As prices drastically increased, so did council rates and the cost of living, and it wasn't long before much of the creative community that had enhanced Mount Eden for over a century was driven out. In their place came people who cared more about money than about art or ecology. They replaced low hedges with tall stone walls, and garden paths with electric gates and intercoms. Old fruit trees and native trees, like pūriri, pōhutukawa, and kōwhai, met their fate beneath chainsaws, making way for invasive palms, concrete, and ever larger houses.

In the wake of my father's death in 2013, my mother and I were left to contend with his lifetime of art making, which now filled the shed and rooms in her house. Alongside the important works were decades of experiments and studies, stretchers, rolls of canvas, and materials bought for paintings that would never come to be. For a long time after his passing, the studio sat silent, with everything as it had been. On one side sat Ian's last *Lattice* painting, the masking tape of its making yet to be removed. Beside the red garden chair he sat in while looking at paintings, his glasses lay on his workbook—still open in anticipation of the next day's work.

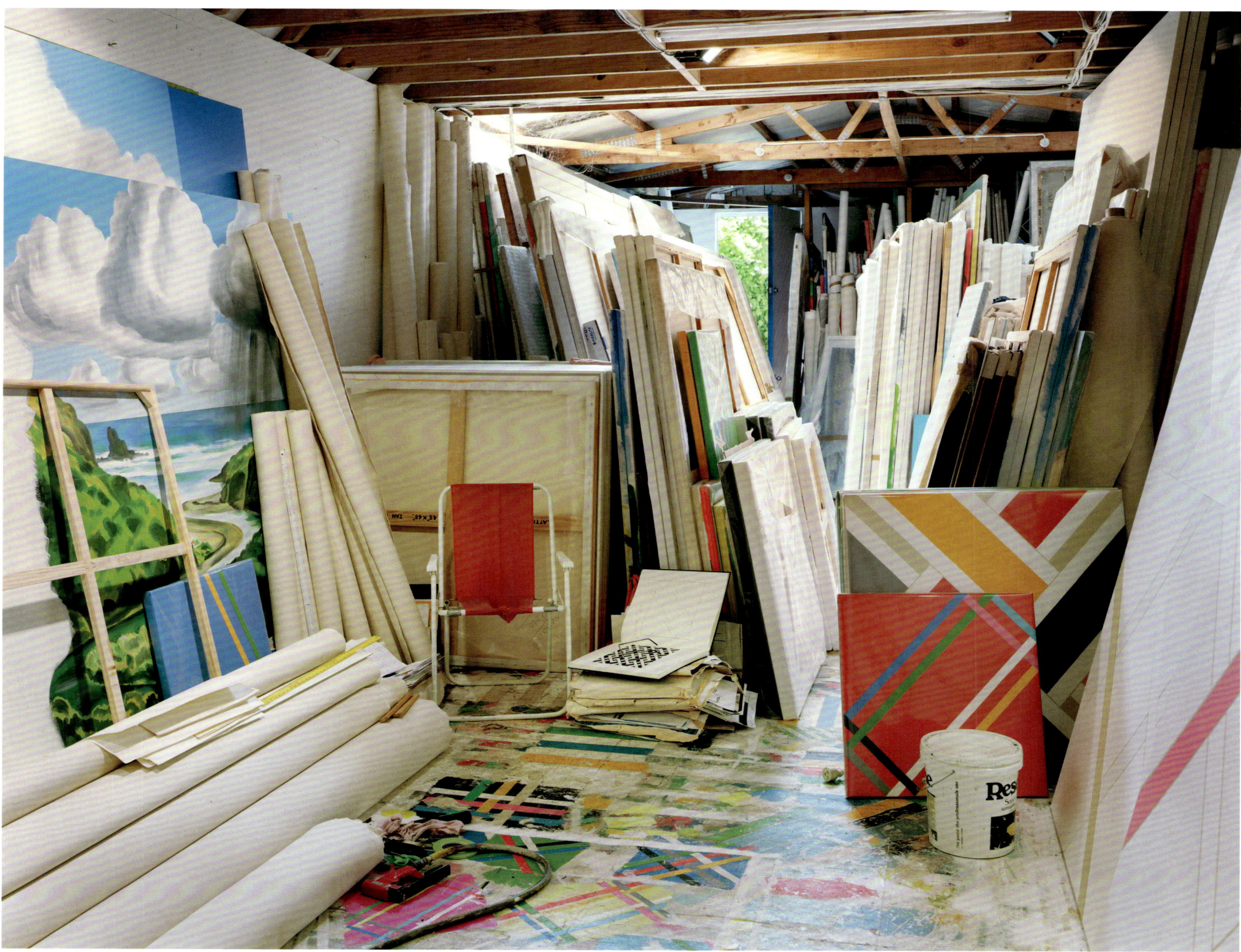

Bulldozed Farmland in Albany, North Shore, Auckland, 2014

Before the Auckland Harbour Bridge opened in 1959, the main access to the city's North Shore was by boat or ferry. Inaccessibility from the city meant that the area remained largely unpopulated, save for pockets of European settlement along rivers and the harbour's edge. Even before European arrival, much of the North Shore remained clad in a dense and ancient kauri forest. Among the few Māori settlements inland was a small pā above Lucas Creek, in what is now Albany. By as early as 1840, however, just a few years after European settlement commenced, most of the North Shore's forests had been cleared and milled; all that remained were scattered clusters of old-growth trees retained as curios.

The main industry on the Shore became the digging of kauri gum, which fell from cracks in the bark or was produced in larger blocks when trees were deliberately bled. Following the discovery that gum could be used for making varnish, an industry and market developed for its export to Britain and America, and by the 1890s, nearly 70% of all oil varnishes made in England were produced with kauri gum from New Zealand. Mostly Māori or Dalmatian, the kauri-gum diggers would laboriously pick over the scrub and swamp forest remains, digging as far down as twelve metres in their search. To make the work easier, wetlands were drained and scrub burnt away, the fires sometimes spreading to whatever bush remained. Draining the wetlands went hand in hand with flax milling, since native harakeke (Phormium tenax) grows in these environments. This systematic movement of industry through wetlands, creeks, and estuaries ultimately left little of the area's native flora intact.

By the middle of the 1860s, most of the North Shore had been dug over and cleared. Now the land was divided into large farming blocks, with creeks and estuaries often forming boundary lines. Farmers soon found that what was left of the soils was best suited to fruit growing, and by 1890, the area at the Shore's northern fringe that would become Albany was almost entirely orchards. Named after a well-known and similar horticultural region in Western Australia, well into the 1950s, even as the rest of the North Shore became residential, Albany remained productive land. Not until 2005, when the North Shore City Council accepted a development proposal marketed as a 'happy mix of businesses, hotels, shops, apartments, and entertainment' was the fate of its last green space finally sealed.

The 2008 global financial crisis stalled plans, but by 2013 the development went ahead. Albany was rezoned as a Special Housing Area by the New Zealand Government, a policy intended to address the growing Auckland housing crisis by opening large tracts of agricultural land on the city fringe for fast-tracked development. In the following decade, over 150 Special Housing Areas would be zoned and constructed across Auckland until the project ended in 2019. The review that ended it concluded, too late, that 'Special Housing Areas benefits did not outweigh their costs, and that in some cases the subsidised houses were 5% more expensive than those outside them'.

The original Māori name for Albany is Ōkahukura, which means 'the place of Kahukura' or 'the place of butterflies'.

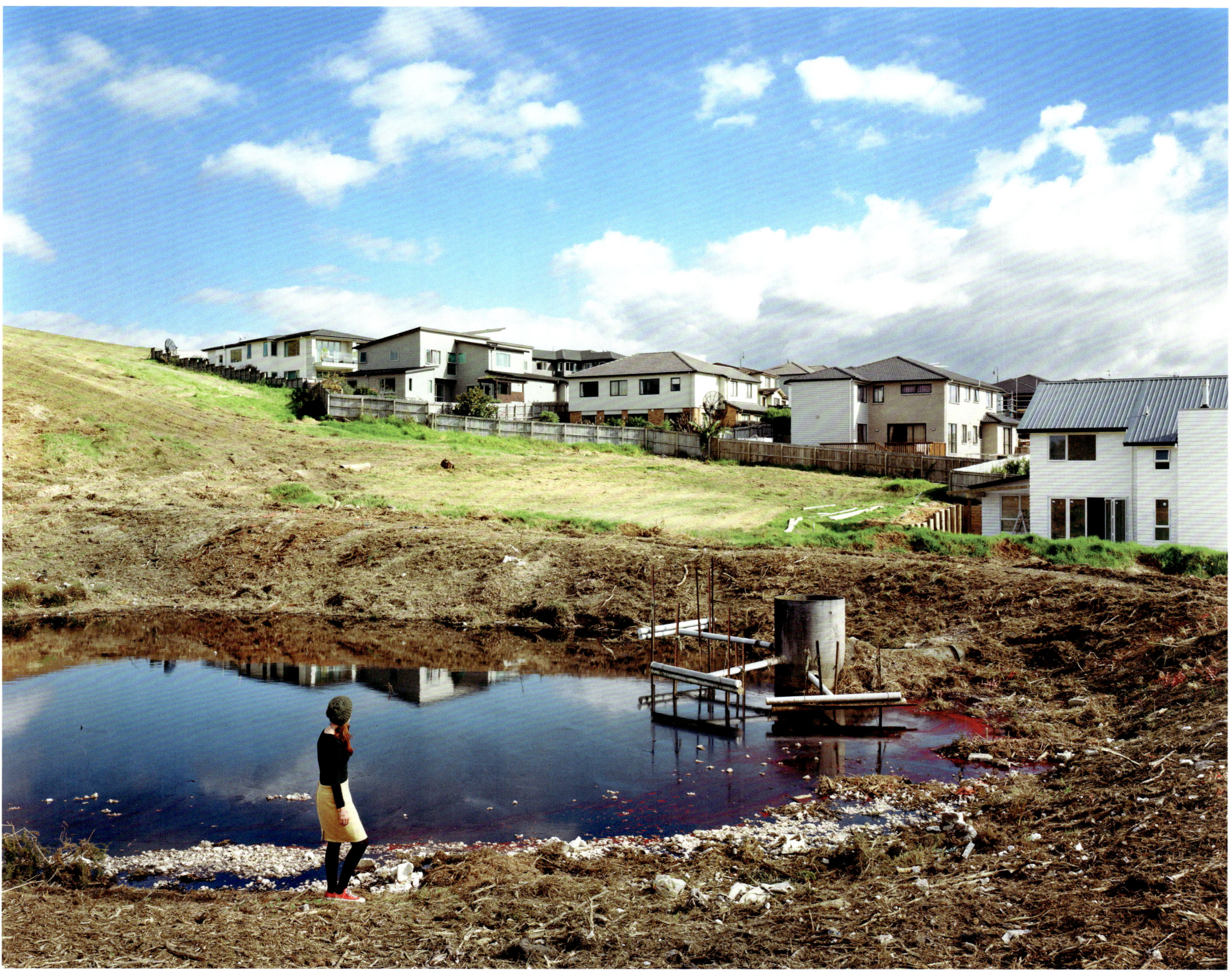

George's Tunnel, Waitākere Dam Tramline, Auckland, 2015

In January 1898, the *Observer* newspaper wrote, 'At occasional intervals, the imminence of a water famine stares [the Auckland City Council] in the face, and a great cackling arises among the City Fathers. They decide that something really must be done to allay the public alarm, and that something usually takes the form of a series of pleasant picnics to all the creeks and waterfalls within a radius of thirty miles. They gaze upon the beauties of nature and discuss the gastronomic charms of succulent ham sandwiches washed down with libations of sparkling champagne, as they lie a-basking in the sun after their exertions in climbing to the falls.' Such was the sentiment in Auckland that year, when the city faced another of its increasingly serious summer droughts.

In the early 1900s, the Waitākere Ranges was selected for a new reservoir scheme, and a site above Waitākere Falls was chosen for the first reservoir, Waitākere Dam. At ninety-five metres, the falls were the highest of many in the Waitākere Ranges, and, surrounded by regenerating forest, they had been a popular attraction among hikers and picnickers since the arrival of Europeans in Auckland. To the colonial day-tripper, the remoteness of the falls was part of their charm, but with access to the gorge limited to a walking track, a tramline had to be constructed before work could begin on the reservoir. Three years of arduous manual labour in challenging conditions ensued to finish the tramline. By the time water finally flowed down the pipeline from Waitākere Dam to Auckland, over six years had elapsed since the whole project began.

Two decades later, the northern half of the tramline was removed, and what remained between George's Tunnel and the reservoir was scaled down to a 'narrow gauge'. Retained by public water company Watercare for pipeline maintenance, over time the tracks became a popular walking spot. In 1976, volunteers established the Waitākere Tramline Society, which offered tours along the line on miniaturised trains. Carrying twenty passengers in narrow, open carriages that faced outwards towards the gorge, the tours provided broader access to the unique ecology of the Waitākere Ranges, taking passengers deep into the rainforest via narrow tunnels, cuttings, and bridges, before reaching Waitākere Dam. Twenty years later, in 1998, another tour, the Rainforest Express, was established nearby on the Nihotupu tramline, which was built in 1912 for the construction of the Nihotupu Dam.

In 2011, rockfalls along both tramlines caused leaks in the pipeline that triggered slips. Watercare suspended public access to the lines and commissioned a land stability and risk assessment report. This suggested that an incident occurring during public use had odds of 'possible to once in 100 to 1,000 years', with the risk of a death being 'not credible to once in more than 10,000 years'. But despite the minimal risk, and a flawless safety record over four decades on both lines, the cost of a remediation that 'could not completely account for potentially undetected or future risks' was estimated at $11 million. In response, Watercare indefinitely suspended the leases of the Waitākere Tramline Society and the Rainforest Express in 2014, ignoring public petitions and campaigns by the volunteer societies.

The remediation was never undertaken, and although both lines are still used for maintenance by Watercare, they have remained closed to the public. As of 2024, negotiations to reopen the Rainforest Express at Nihotupu are ongoing.

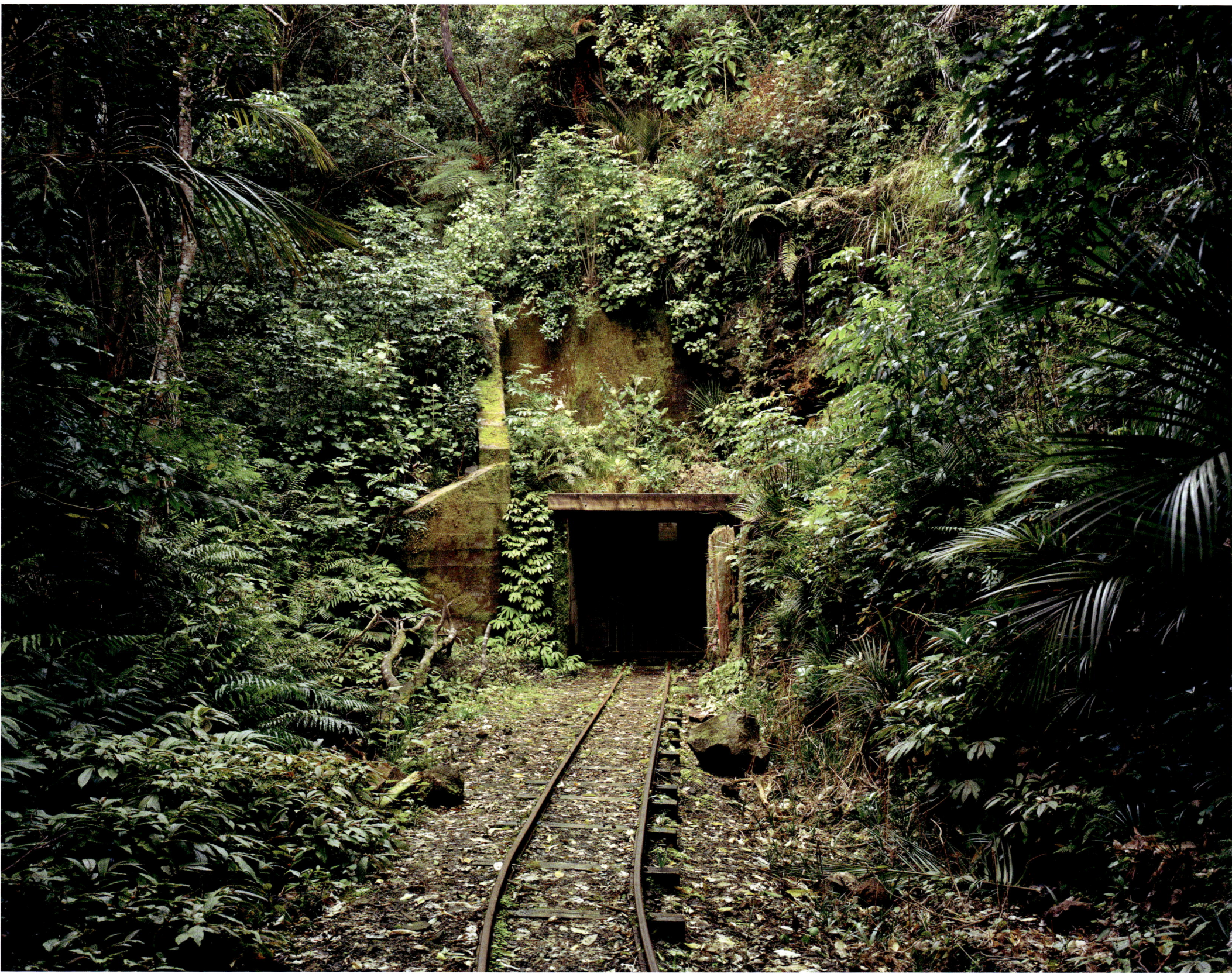

Evening, The Frank Sargeson House, Esmonde Road, Auckland, 2015

Frank Sargeson was New Zealand's first full-time writer, known for his meticulously crafted short stories. In 1927, at the age of twenty-four, he boarded a ship from Auckland to Europe to experience 'the music I couldn't hear, the theatre I couldn't see'. However, five months spent reading at the library of the British Museum left him feeling 'the intolerable weight of so much civilisation'. He concluded, 'I knew that I was only indirectly a part of it all … for better or worse, and for life, I belonged to the new world.' After sixteen months away, he returned to New Zealand, never to leave again.

In 1929, following a consensual homosexual encounter, Sargeson was convicted of 'indecent assault', for which he served a suspended two-year sentence of labour on his uncle's farm. Afterwards, he moved into a modest fibrolite bach (small holiday home) his family owned at Esmonde Road on Auckland's North Shore. He described it as 'a small one-roomed hut in a quiet street ending in a land of mangrove mudflats that belonged to the inner harbour … decayed, with weatherboards falling off'. The Harbour Bridge connecting the central city to the Shore was yet to be built, and Sargeson's location across the Waitematā Harbour on a no-exit street was about as secluded as then possible in Auckland. Beyond this, the location provided a cheap place to live and room to grow vegetables, but Sargeson faced harassment from neighbours. After various complaints of his residence being messy, it was condemned and demolished by the local council in 1946.

The present structure was constructed in 1948. The original design by modernist architect Vernon Brown, a friend of Sargeson's, was altered and built by George Haydn to make construction more affordable, though signature elements by Brown, such as the sloping flat roof and ceiling, remained. With a modest place to write and live, and a large vegetable garden in the backyard to sustain himself and others, Sargeson had found a home. Here he helped to cultivate a New Zealand intellectual and literary community. Writers and artists congregated at the house, drinking 'Lemora'—a cheap and notorious grapefruit and lemon wine made by a local Russian immigrant—into the night. Of Sargeson's many guests and protégées, Janet Frame is the best known. From 1955 to 1956, following her release from a mental institution, she lived in an old army hut in his garden, where she wrote her first novel, *Owls Do Cry*. In 1990, her memoirs were turned into the feature film *An Angel at My Table*, directed by Jane Campion.

At Esmonde Road, Sargeson also found love. He lived there with his partner, Harry Doyle, for decades, although publicly they could only be referred to as 'roommates'. Even in 1968, they felt it necessary to add a second bedroom to the home to quieten local accusations, as until the passing of the Homosexual Law Reform Act in 1986, male homosexual relationships remained illegal in New Zealand. Before the law had passed, though, Sargeson died, on 1 March 1982. His ashes were spread under a loquat tree in front of the house. Later that year, his property was subdivided to establish and fund a charitable trust that maintains the house as a private museum. Unfortunately, the garden and the hut Frame and others worked in was lost in the process.

Esmonde Road became a State Highway off-ramp after the completion of the Harbour Bridge in 1959. In 2008, the road was widened to four lanes and consumed more than a metre of the front yard, including the loquat tree.

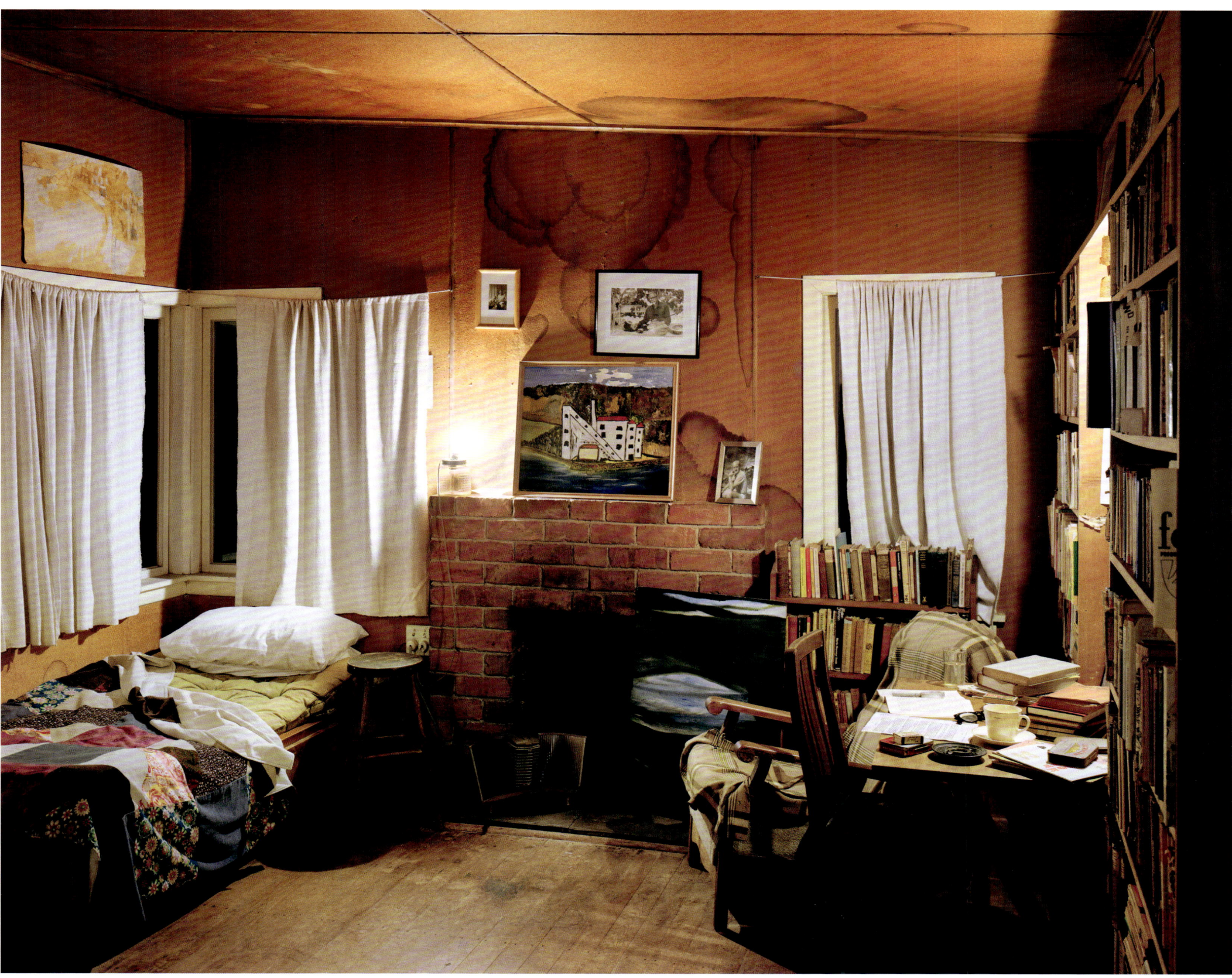

John Perry in His Workshop, Former Regent Cinema, Helensville, 2015

Beyond Auckland's fringe, State Highway 16 winds north through fifty kilometres of sheep and cattle pasture before reaching Helensville, south of the immense Kaipara Harbour. Where the town now stands was once the Māori settlement of Te Awaroa, which sat within a great kauri forest that stretched hundreds of kilometres. From the modest docks by the bridge across the Kaipara River into town, the forest was shipped away in the nineteenth century as planks, some travelling as far as San Francisco and London. Near the river, the decaying Kaipara Dairy Factory marks the next chapter in the town's story. A farmer's cooperative dairy industry filled the void after settlers ran out of trees to fell, but it was ultimately unable to compete with larger conglomerates.

At the other end of town, just before the highway winds back over the river, stands one of Helensville's largest and most prominent buildings, the Regent Theatre. Built in 1939, it replaced one of the country's first cinemas, the Lyric, which was constructed in 1915 and later destroyed by fire. Once part of a bustling town centre, the disused Regent today has a melancholy air. Faded blue paint peels from its façade, while green lichen drips from its once-golden trim. The former grandeur of the building is a monument to cinema's golden age as much as the regional prosperity of the early twentieth century, when similar theatres were proudly built in nearly every small town in New Zealand.

Around the start of the new millennium, after the Regent had shown its last picture, the theatre began a new life as the home of John Perry and his Global Village Antiques. John was at various times an artist, curator, writer, teacher, and art and object expert. During his tenancy, the Regent was less an antique store than a kind of informal museum. Behind a small shop in the former lobby, the body of the theatre contained Perry's lifelong collection of art, craft, and 'Kiwiana'—the objects filling every inch of the space, including the stage and the projection area, which was converted into an apartment. Over the decades, Perry continued to be driven by a desire to expand the scope of what constitutes art in Aotearoa. In the 1970s, as director and curator of the Rotorua Museum of Art and History, he built a unique and diverse collection, where prescient among museum professionals, he sought to value and understand as art a broad range of media, including Māori weaving, photography, and ceramics.

Perry's personal collection, housed in the Regent Theatre, expanded upon these ideas, taking in historical, folk, and industrial relics too. In later life, he planned to open the collection and theatre to the public as a gallery and museum, but council fire and earthquake regulations prevented him from doing so. A few years ago, he decided to sell a portion of his collection, to lighten his burden and to fund plans to travel the world. In 2021, though, Perry died after a sudden illness at the age of 76. The following year, what remained of his collection began to be dispersed through a series of auctions.

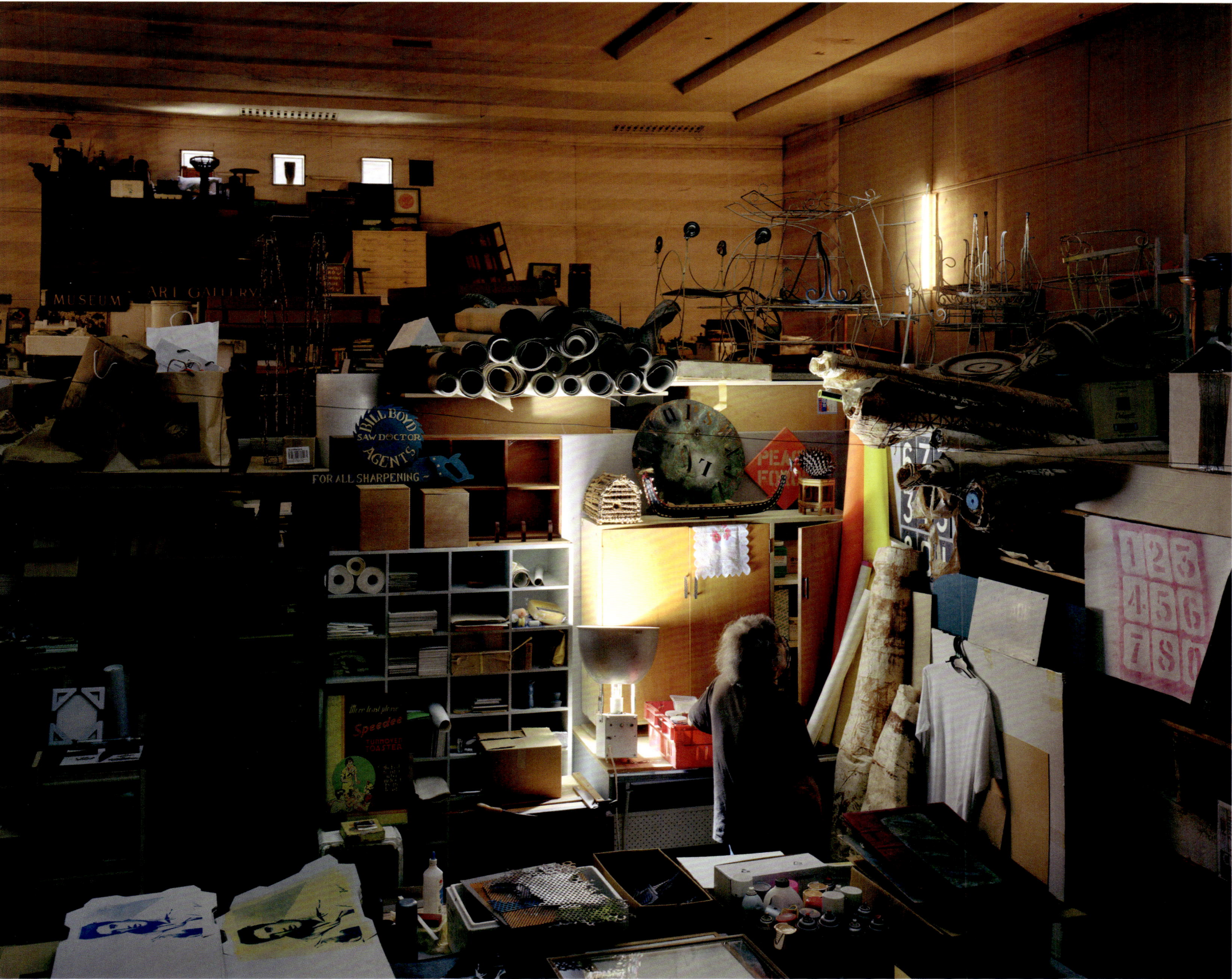

Mark Adams at a Former Garden and Settlement Site, Āwhitu Peninsula, 2015

Long before the human settlement of Aotearoa, 135,000 years ago, Taranaki and other volcanoes of the Central North Island Volcanic Plateau began erupting. In the wake of this activity, iron sand, white quartz, and pumice convulsed together, flowing down the Waikato River south of Āwhitu, towards the Tasman Sea. Here strong ocean currents pulled the fragments up the coast, gradually depositing them along sand dunes which had started forming the Manukau Harbour two million years ago. Over this vast timescale, these currents slowly compressed the rock fragments and dunes until they rose as the forty-kilometre-long Āwhitu Peninsula.

It was only 7,000 years ago, though, that the Manukau Harbour on Āwhitu's eastern shore became filled with seawater. Before this, it was a densely vegetated valley of kauri forest, undulating over a web of creeks and hills and joining the Waitākere Ranges to the north. Over the past two million years, the process of transformation from seabed to land and back again in the Manukau Harbour is now known to have occurred as many as thirty times. In 90% of these periods, in which sea levels fell significantly before rising again, the cause was a dramatic cooling of the earth.

Āwhitu Peninsula and the shores of the Manukau are also thought to be among the earliest sites of Māori habitation in Aotearoa. Centuries later, when Europeans arrived on ships from Europe in 1836, they stationed missionaries on the Manukau at Āwhitu's Ōrua Bay, and from here began a destruction of people, culture, and ecology at a rate foreign to both Māori and geology. Before this time, more than half of Āwhitu still retained its original forest, mighty pūriri standing to the south and kauri to the north. Only a few decades after European arrival, though, less than 7% of the forest remained. The rest, then thousands of years old, had been logged for timber or thoughtlessly burned to clear the way for pasture.

Around 1900, Pātara Te Tuhi, a leader in the Māori King movement, recalled his grandfather's memory of geographical change at Āwhitu before the arrival of Europeans. In his grandfather's youth, a plain known as Paorae reached kilometres into the sea off Āwhitu's west coast:

> A flat land, and mostly sand, a famous place for the cultivation of the kūmara and the taro … with freshwater lagoons abounding in eels and wild duck. … Large canoes were drawn up on the sand, and in the summer months were launched day after day. … Each year, the sea would eat a piece of the Paorae; the waves would roar right up to the plantations, and the growers of the kūmara would be edged back and back. The great waves of the Tai-Hauauru (West Coast) dashed against that land of sand and washed portions of it away, and so in time the ocean rolled over it all. … There was no great or sudden catastrophe. The land did not disappear by earthquake or hurricane. It vanished over generations.

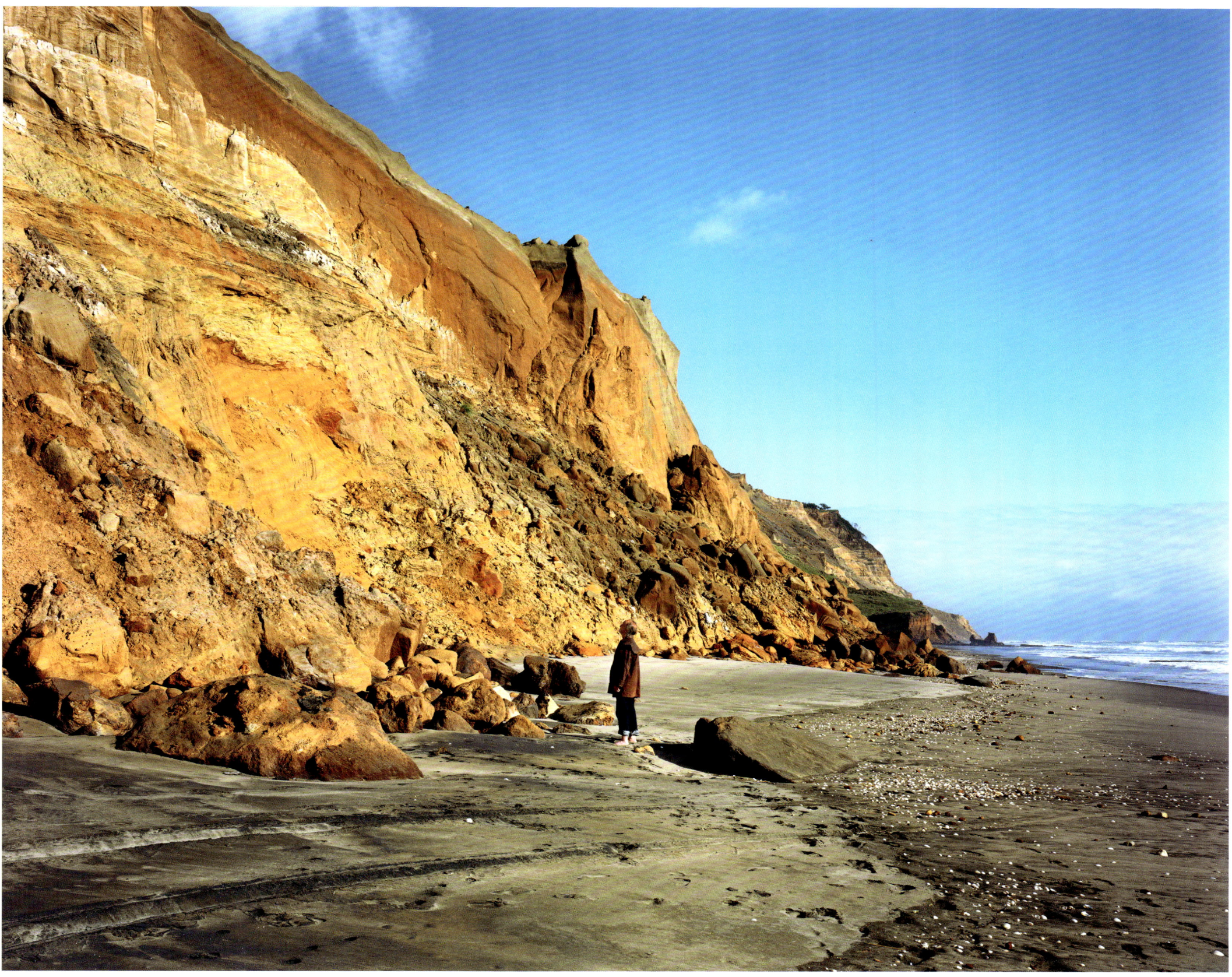

Kauri Dam Remains, Coromandel Ranges, Near Tairua, 2015

In the early nineteenth century, the challenge of logging old-growth forests in mountainous regions of North America and Germany led to the invention of timber driving dams. Built across creeks beneath slopes where trees were felled, the dams slowly filled with water while logs accumulated. Once the dam was full, a gate was 'tripped', releasing the logs on a torrent of water and sending them crashing through the creek to sawmills below. In the 1840s, this idea made its way to New Zealand, most likely with goldminers from California, and by the end of the century, more than 1,000 dams had been constructed across the upper North Island. The structures were known here as 'kauri dams', after the trees they logged almost exclusively, and from which they were typically constructed. Despite the proliferation of the dams, though, no original and intact example remains today. Often, the only traces are foundation logs preserved from decay beneath shallow water, or indentations left by bolts in rocky gorges.

Besides its alpine plateaus and basins, most of New Zealand was covered by forests before human habitation, and, of these, the kauri forest was the most vast and ancient. The antecedents of the kauri reach back as far as any forest on earth, the still primordial-looking tree a direct descendent of species that developed during the Jurassic period over 140 million years ago. Through those millennia, kauri forests covered most of Aotearoa's upper North Island, an area of nearly three million acres. In Northland's Waipoua Forest, the best-known kauri, Tāne Mahuta (also the name of the Māori god of the forest), stands over fifty metres tall with a girth of nearly fourteen metres. Tāne is estimated to be more than 2,000 years old, though prior to logging, it is believed there were trees even larger, and as many as 3,000 years old.

Kauri was seldom felled by Māori, as tōtara was the preferred timber for waka—though kauri was sometimes used for larger vessels—while lighter woods like kānuka and tree ferns were used in the construction of pā (settlements). Consequently, even after centuries of Māori life in Aotearoa, the North Island's kauri forests largely remained as they had been for millennia. From the time Europeans first encountered Aotearoa, however, they desired the kauri for its long straight trunk, which, unweakened by side branches, was perfect for ship spars. Well before the first influx of settlement, it was being used for repairs by navigators and whalers, as well as British naval supply vessels working off the northern coasts of New Zealand. It is even said to have been used by the fleet of Vice-Admiral Horatio Nelson at the Battle of Trafalgar (1805).

As colonisation began in earnest in the 1840s, kauri timber quickly became a major export. It was sent in vast quantities to Australia, California, and Great Britain, and notably used extensively in the rebuilding of San Francisco after the 1906 earthquake and fire. In New Zealand, it built much of the North Island's first houses and cities, though shockingly, near equal amounts were simply burned to clear space for grazing land or industry like gold mining. Within barely fifty years of European settlement, the vast kauri forests of Northland, Auckland, Coromandel, and the Waikato were almost entirely gone. Today's estimates are that less than 2% of Aotearoa's original kauri forests remain.

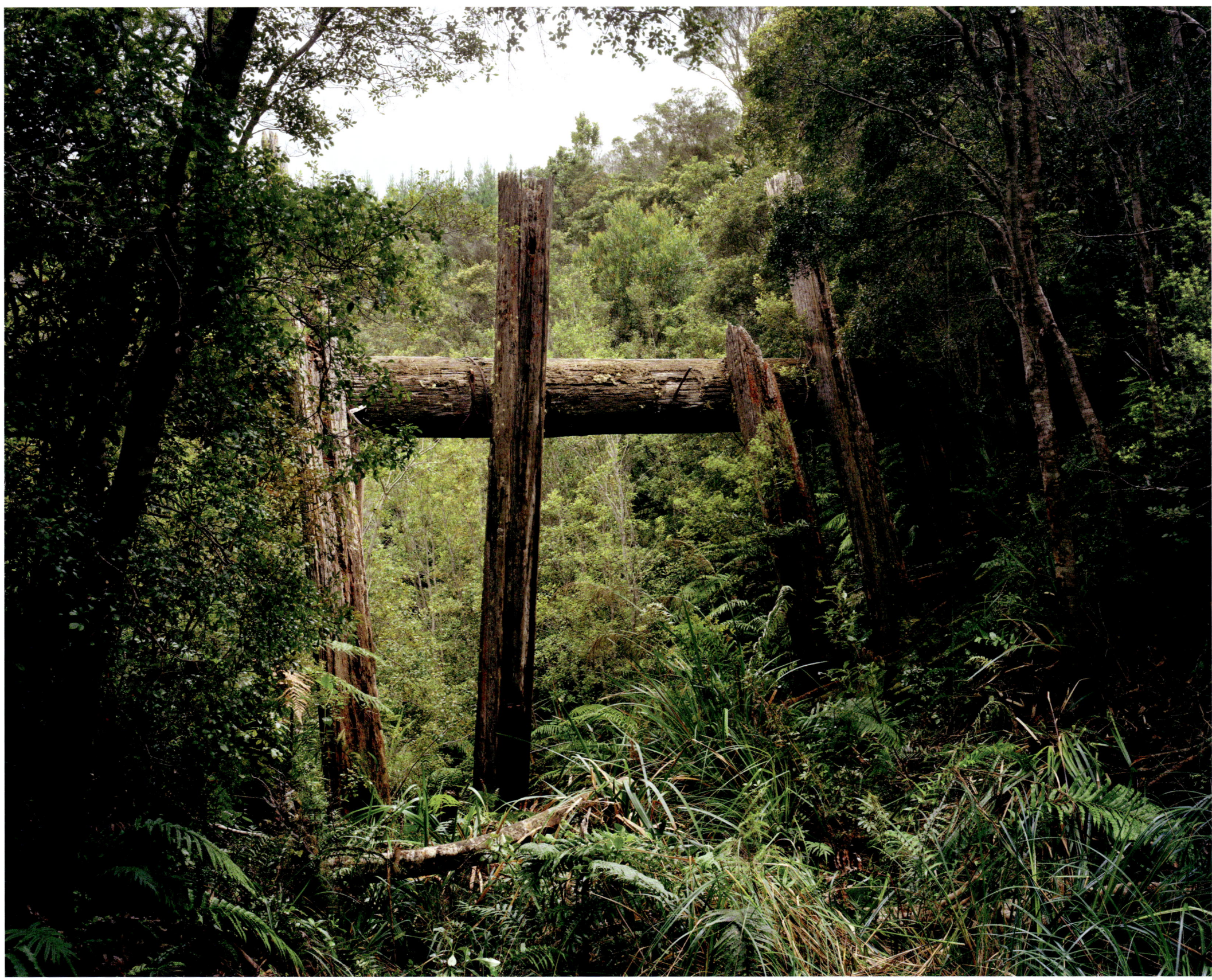

Pūriri Tree in Waterfall Gully, Shakespear Regional Park, Whangaparāoa Peninsula, 2022

North of Auckland, the Whangaparāoa Peninsula juts fifteen kilometres off the east coast into the Hauraki Gulf. Archaeological evidence suggests that human habitation began around 850 years ago, when the first waka (ocean-going canoes) landed on these shores, with the land occupied by a number of groups afterwards. At Whangaparāoa, oral tradition traces the emergence of Ngāti Kahu, the mana whenua (people with authority in the land), to before the middle of the 1600s; however, through intermarriage, the iwi's ancestry reaches back to the first settlement of the area. Later on, connections to the people of the Mahurangi Peninsula to the north and the Waitematā Harbour to the south enabled Ngāti Kahu to live in peace at Whangaparāoa for over a century.

Near the end of the peninsula is one of the Auckland region's few forest remnants, dating to before the human settlement of Aotearoa. For Ngāti Kahu, the forest was an essential part of their existence, providing sustainable building materials, medicine, birds to hunt, and berries from trees like kahikatea, pūriri, taraire, and titoki. Whangaparāoa was also home to a vast shark-fishing ground, and the location of the peninsula, halfway between Mahurangi and the Waitematā, made its natural harbour desirable. Tragically, though, these assets saw Ngāti Kahu driven from the peninsula. In 1821, a Ngāpuhi war party arrived from Northland armed with European muskets, and they overwhelmed Ngāti Kahu's pā on the Weiti River in a lopsided attack.

Although decimated by Ngāpuhi, Ngāti Kahu returned to Whangaparāoa in the late 1830s. However, in 1841, the British Crown purchased eighty kilometres of eastern coastline, including the peninsula. After the battles of the late eighteenth century, Hauraki tribes also claimed authority in the area. Without involvement from Ngāti Kahu, a sale was finalised in January 1853, and its people were left landless. One of the largest subsequent purchasers from the Crown was Sir Robert Hamilton, Baronet of Stratford on Avon (later Sheriff of Warwickshire), who had served nearly fifty years with the East India Company. By 1883, despite never visiting Aotearoa, Hamilton had acquired most of the eastern part of the peninsula, as well as Ōkura Bush, at the mouth of the Weiti River. After his death in 1887, the entire property was passed to his grandson, Robert Henry Anson Shakespear, and his wife, Blanche, beginning the area's long association with the Shakespear family.

Now in control of Ngāti Kahu's garden and settlement sites, the family began the task of converting the scrub and bracken-covered hills into pasture. Their farm was successful, and besides wool and dairy, they cultivated pumpkins (developing the Whangaparāoa Crown variety) and watermelons, which were sailed to market in Auckland, up to 600 melons at a time. In 1967, the Shakespear farm was acquired by Auckland Regional Council, becoming the city's second regional park. Named after the family, it is today one of Auckland's most popular outdoor recreational spaces, and large projects have been undertaken to restore its natural environment; gullies have been fenced off to allow bush to regenerate, the Okoromai Bay wetland has been restored, and an on-site nursery raises seedlings at a target rate of 10,000 annually.

In 2010, a wildlife sanctuary was established with the construction of a pest-proof fence across the peninsula, and all predator species have since been removed. Each year, planting days are held and members of the public assist in reforesting.

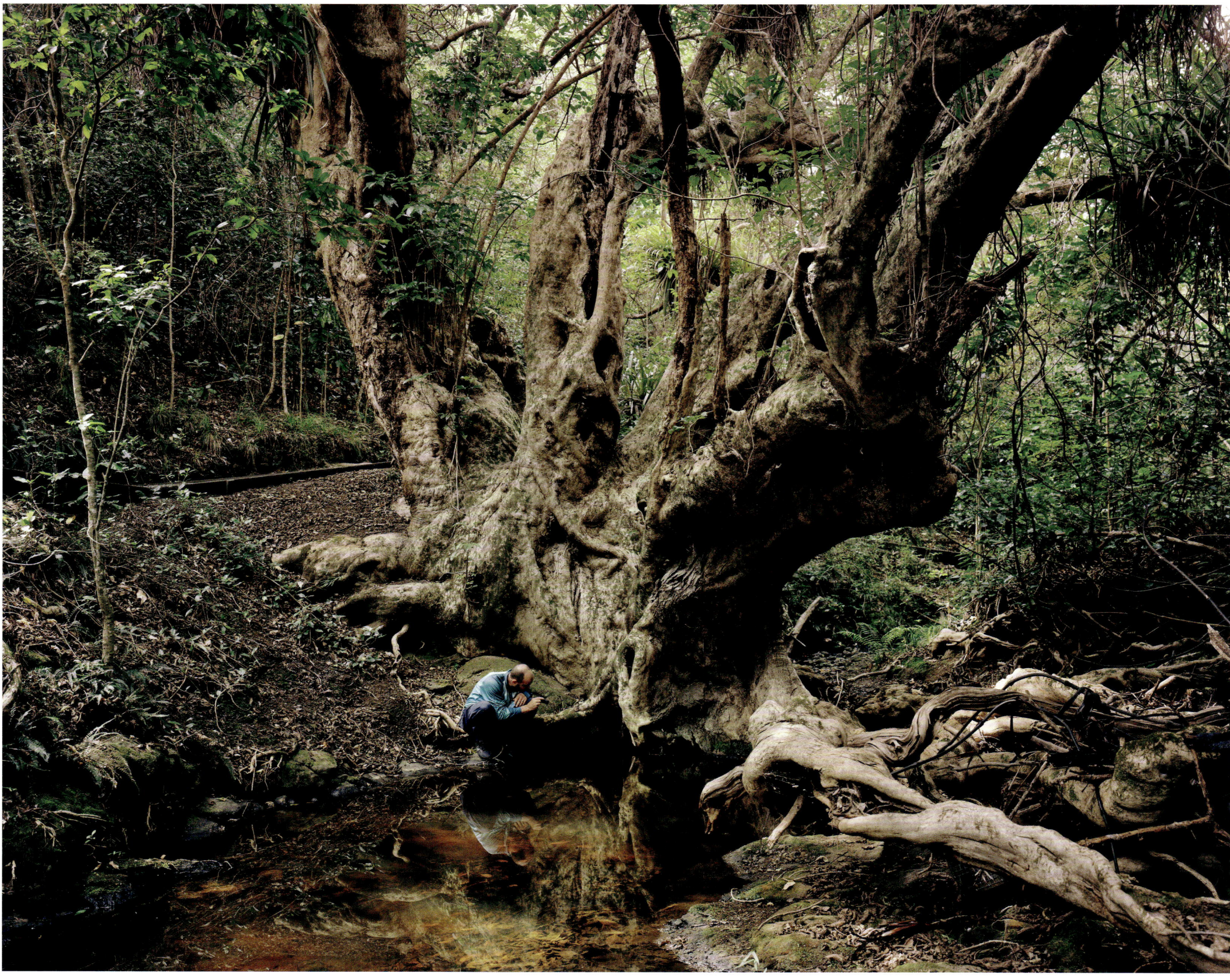

Undersea Cables, Former Degaussing Station, Pink Beach, Whangaparāoa, 2015

During the Second World War, Germany made use of new underwater explosives, known as 'magnetic mines'. The devices were dropped by plane into shipping channels, where they would detonate when triggered by the magnetism of a vessel passing above. Just months into the war, numerous British steamships, and over 200,000 tons of cargo, had already been destroyed by the mines, which were undetectable by radar. And, despite developing similar technology towards the end of the First World War, the British were yet to engineer an effective defence, beyond physical minesweeping.

In November 1939, a German plane tasked to drop a magnetic mine in the Thames River near Shoeburyness came under heavy anti-aircraft fire. As the pilots rushed to flee, the mine they dropped missed the channel, landing instead on the river's sprawling mudflats. A malfunction in the mine's fail-safe saw it survive, allowing the British Army to recover and reverse-engineer it. Within five weeks, several new methods had been developed to counter magnetic mines. The best was 'degaussing', a process invented by Charles Goodeve and named after Carl Friedrich Gauss, a German scientist specialising in magnetism. It involved internally 'encircling the ship with a cable through which an electric current was kept flowing to neutralise the field'. Before a vessel left for hostile waters, it would pass over the underwater cables of a degaussing station, which checked and helped to reconfigure a ship's magnetism until it was safely neutralised.

In New Zealand, the most direct threat during the Second World War was a potential invasion by Japanese forces. In Auckland, observation posts and gun emplacements were built around the Waitematā Harbour. At Whangaparāoa, the New Zealand Army purchased 321 acres of land from the Shakespear family for a military base on the peninsula's north-western tip. They installed a 130-ton gun emplacement (which could fire a 380-pound shell over twenty miles), large ammunition stores at Te Haruhi and Okoromai Bays, observation posts, pillboxes, and over a kilometre of tunnels and bunkers. In 1940, a degaussing range was built in the shipping channel between the peninsula and Tiritiri Matangi Island, with a base to control the operation at Okoromai Bay. When the station opened, the *Gisborne Herald* noted, 'As the ship steered various courses over the range, readings of the neutralising effect of the ship's gear were recorded ashore, and corrections were made. In cases where a ship's degaussing gear was not working satisfactorily, she was sent back to port for adjustments.'

Following the war, the degaussing station was decommissioned. In 2000, the historic buildings of the Whangaparāoa military base were condemned, and a decade later they were removed and replaced. In 2018, the Marutūahu Collective of Hauraki iwi initialled a redress deed, and a number of historic and public reserves around the Waitematā Harbour, including Whangaparāoa and its military base, were subsequently returned. For the time being, the New Zealand Army has retained its installation, now in a lease agreement with Marutūahu.

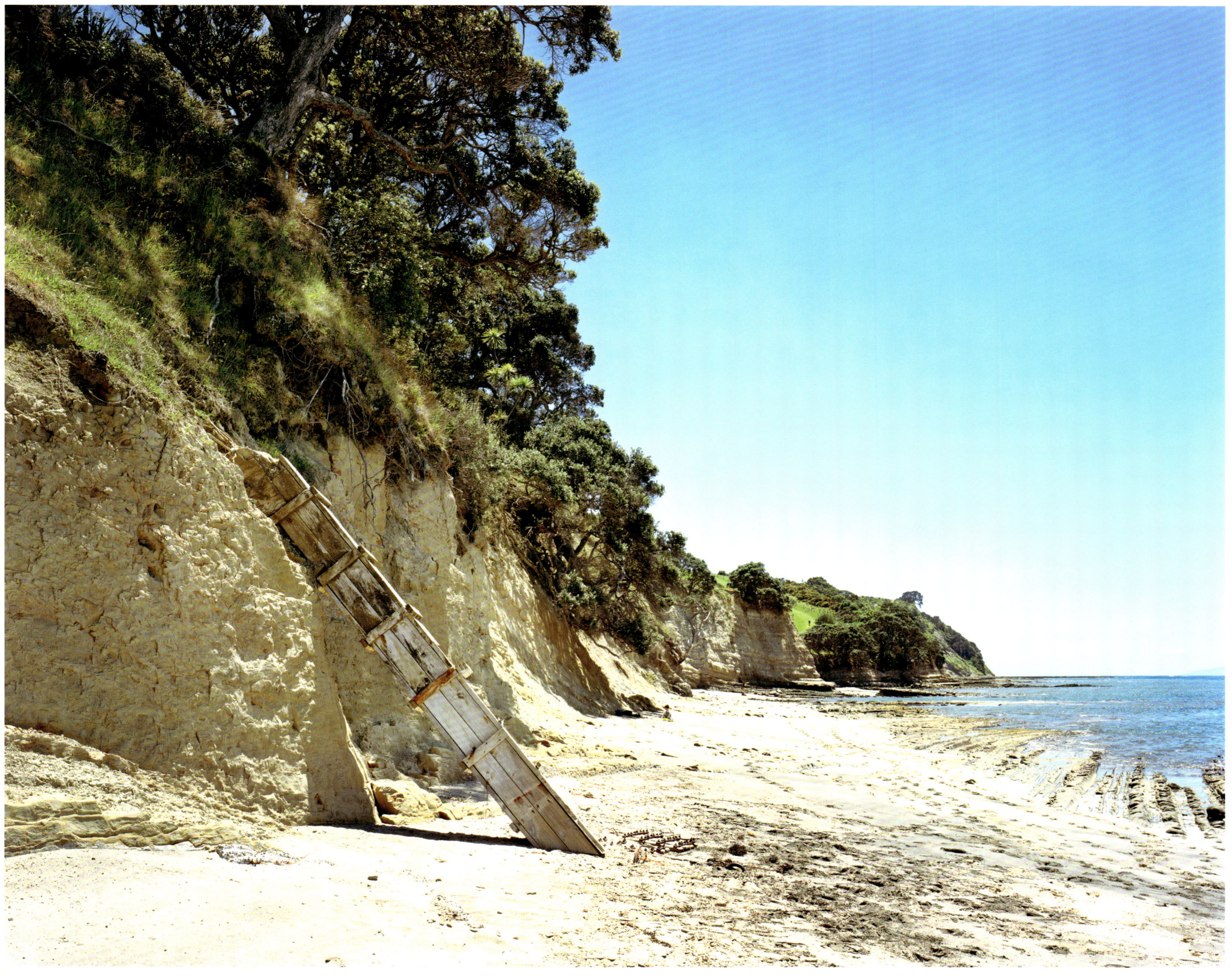

Poutu Dam and River Diversion, Rangipo, Tongariro, 2015

As the Māori tohunga (priest) Ngātoro-i-rangi traversed the Central North Island, his footfalls are said to have created the hot springs of Rotorua, Tongariro, Taupō, and Tokaanu. Reaching the Poutu Stream, which flows from Lake Rotoaira to the Tongariro River, he leapt across at a narrow point, leaving a footprint in the sandstone still visible today. Finally, at the summit of Ngāuruhoe, he claimed the land as far as he could see for his descendants, Ngāti Tūwharetoa. In the centuries that followed, a settlement arose at Tokaanu, its sacred springs used for bathing, cooking, and heating cultivations. Attractive to Europeans, too, by 1874, a hotel stood beside the springs, and a steam ferry connected the settlement to Taupō.

Fearing further encroachment of settlers upon their land, in 1887 the chiefs of Ngāti Tūwharetoa protected the sacred summits of Tongariro, Ngāuruhoe, and Ruapehu by surveying them as reserves in the land courts. Following this, in 1894, the Government passed the Tongariro National Park Act, creating the world's fourth national park and this country's first, but also decreasing Māori control of the reserve. A year later, in 1895, the Government then instituted the Native Townships Act, and with its new power, they seized most of the remaining Tongariro and Tokaanu area. In 1898, California rainbow trout were released into the region's rivers and lakes, almost wiping out the native kōaro (climbing galaxias) in just a few years. Finally, in 1929, the Chateau Tongariro opened, and huts and a ski field were placed on Ruapehu, the area becoming the site of tourism that it remains today.

By 1964, an energy crisis was looming, and the Government announced plans for the Tongariro Hydro Electric Scheme, one of the largest industrial projects in the country's history. The headwaters of the Whanganui, Whakapapa, and Tongariro Rivers would be dammed and partially redirected through over fifty kilometres of tunnels, tailraces, and canals around Tongariro into Lake Rotoaira to feed three new power stations. Extra water flowing into the Waikato River from Rotoaira via Taupō would also dramatically boost the production of nine existing stations. The scheme—which would require huge resources and drastically alter the landscape—was protested by Ngāti Tūwharetoa, environmentalists, tour operators, fishermen, local councils, and residents. Despite this, the Government insisted there was no alternative, and construction began, albeit with over $1 million dollars ($5.2 million today) of screens and nets added to protect the now important rainbow trout industry.

In 2011, the right-wing National Government was elected to a second term, and they soon began the process of partially privatising four state-owned power companies. One was Genesis Energy, which owned the Tongariro Scheme. Left-wing opposition was immediate, and in 2013 a referendum was held in which 67.3% of voters rejected privatisation. Prime Minister John Key indicated that the Government had always intended to ignore the result, since the election had given them a mandate, and by 2014, the asset sale had taken place.

A concurrent Waitangi Tribunal report stated that local iwi had never relinquished ownership and control of their waterways and, 'In operation, the scheme's impact on lakes and rivers has resulted in a loss of water quality, habitat, and food and fish resources, particularly at Lake Rotoaira.' In 2008, a Treaty settlement saw the Central North Island Iwi Collective, of which Ngāti Tūwharetoa is part, returned a portion of land worth $196 million and rental revenue of $223 million. Another settlement was reached in 2015, with thirty-two Crown-owned sites returned to Ngāti Tūwharetoa. An agreed historical account was issued, the Crown made a formal apology, and the iwi received compensation of $25 million. As of 2024, the claim around Tongariro National Park remains in progress.

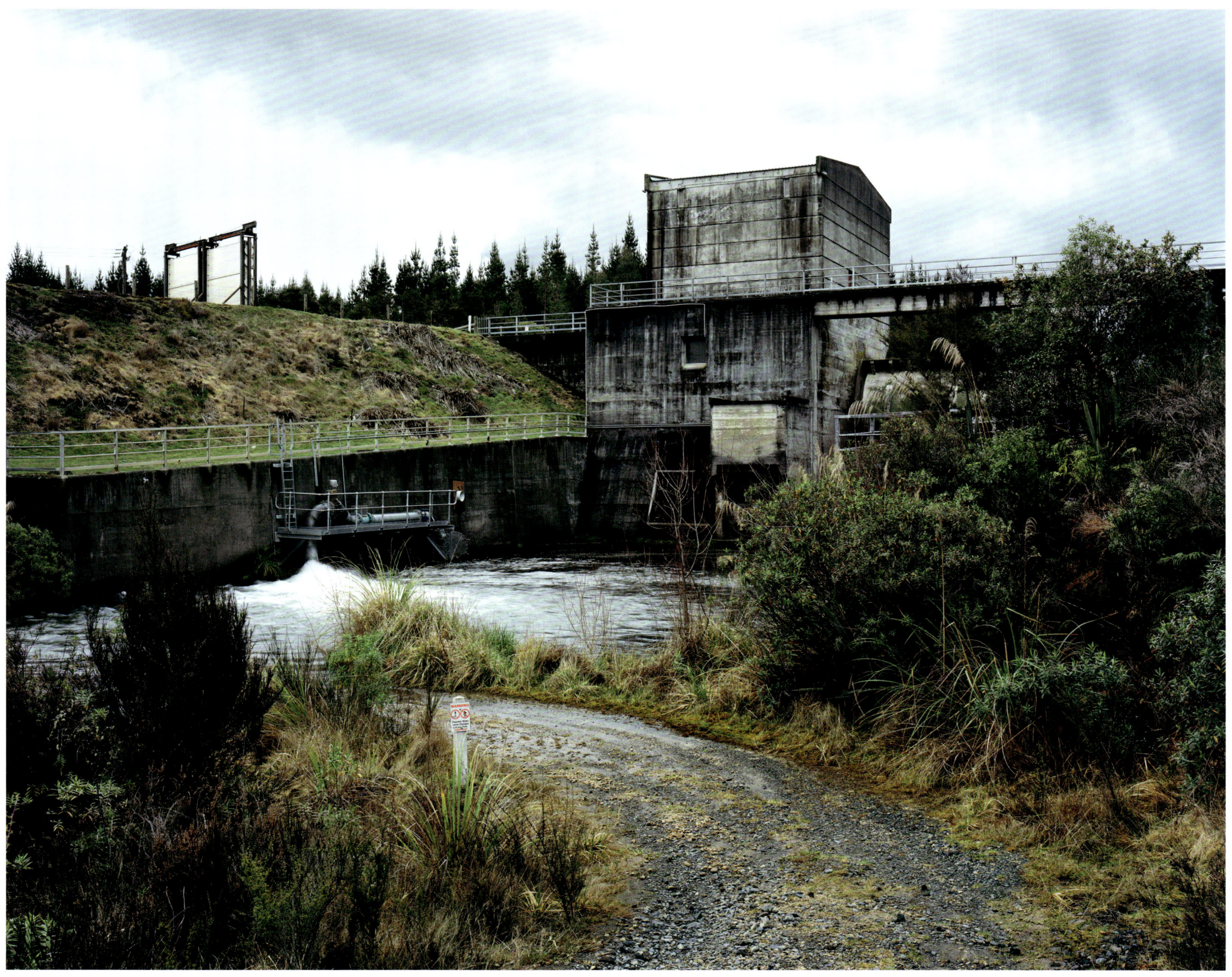

Former New Zealand Shipping Company Offices and Wool Store, Tokomaru Bay, 2016

Although the use of spices in medicine and cooking in Asia dates almost to the beginning of recorded history, their popularity in Europe began only during the Middle Ages. Almost overnight, spices became hugely valuable, and networks for their trade developed. Central to this was the Byzantine Empire and its capital, Constantinople, where routes converged and goods were sold. However, in 1453, the city fell to the Ottoman Empire, trade was barred, and longer and more dangerous routes were required to circumvent the now hostile territory. Partly in response, the Portuguese monarchy commissioned the navigator Vasco da Gama to find an ocean route from Europe to India in 1497, a voyage that would become synonymous with the so-called 'Age of Discovery'.

After months at sea charting winds and currents south through the Atlantic Ocean, da Gama mapped the southern extent of Africa. Finding that permanent westerlies lay below it, he followed the winds north off Africa's eastern coast until he reached India. Halving the time of overland travel, the sea route greatly increased Portugal's colonial power. Building on da Gama's discovery, in 1611, the Dutch navigator Hendrik Brouwer set out to establish trade routes to the Dutch East Indies (now Indonesia) and found that the westerlies at 50° and 60° southern latitude also made for the fastest circumnavigation of the globe. From Brouwer's path, the 'Clipper Route' developed. Named after the fast ships of the time, it passed south of Australia and New Zealand (or through its Cook Strait), before rounding Argentina and crossing the Atlantic Ocean to Europe.

Placing New Zealand and Australia on the line of global trade, the Clipper Route greatly aided the colonisation of both countries in the nineteenth century, in practical and financial terms. Departing from England then, a typical voyage to New Zealand took just over three months, but if vessels ran into bad weather, or needed to stop at remote islands for repairs, the journey could take as much as a year longer. For example, in 1871, two ships from the English line of Shaw, Savill, and Company arrived in New Zealand within months of each other, one six months late, the other delayed and with its cargo ruined by seawater. After decades of British control of shipping into New Zealand, this was the final straw. Two new lines emerged: the New Zealand Freight Company and the New Zealand Shipping Company, founded in 1872 and 1873 respectively, both with the proviso that shares would be held only locally.

By the early twentieth century, the New Zealand Shipping Company was responsible for much of the transport to and from the country. In 1912, following the opening of a cooperative freezing works the year before, they opened a regional office and a wool store at Waimā, a cove at the northernmost end of Tokomaru Bay on the East Cape. Their move to the region followed the construction of a new cooperative freezing works the year before. Beyond providing work and storage space, the building hosted functions, including a dance and supper in aid of the English Church fund, a sermon by the Bishop of Waiapu, and a meeting of the Reform Party. By 1927, though, the freezing works had gone bust. The local Harbour Board took over the Shipping Company's premises, using the building to store various commodities, and later installing a maize-drying facility. Eventually, the building fell derelict, and, in 1992, it went into private ownership. Although it now holds a Category 2 historic place listing, which prevents external modification, this also makes remedial work prohibitively costly and complex.

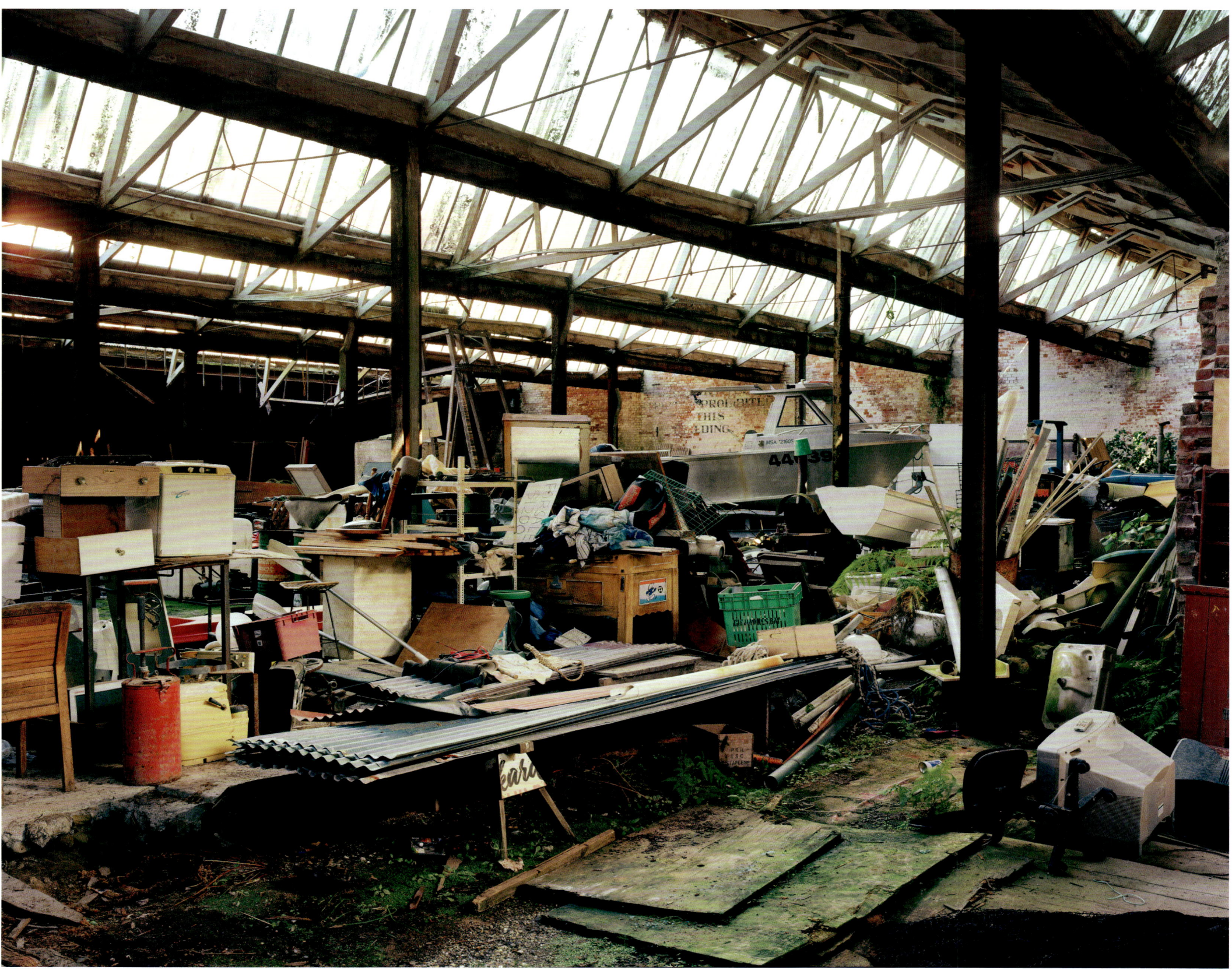

Last Light, Tokomaru Bay Wharf, Waimā, East Cape, 2016

East of Rotorua and Taupō, the East Cape reaches nearly 100 kilometres into the South Pacific Ocean, its coastline of sheltered bays and stony braided river mouths spanning over 350 kilometres. Above its coastline, the steep Raukūmara Ranges, which occupy most of the Cape, rise to a peak of 1,725 metres at Hikurangi. In the south-west, they meet the Huiarau Ranges, which separate the East Coast from the Central North Island. Between the two ranges, the winding State Highway 35 connects Ōpōtiki and Gisborne, the only vehicle access to the small settlements around the Cape, a single and vulnerable coastal road.

For hundreds of years before European arrival, the settlements of the Cape—many dating back to the first arrival of Māori in Aotearoa—could only be reached by sea. Just over halfway around is Tokomaru Bay and, at its northern end, Tokomaru Bay Wharf, in the sheltered cove of Waimā. Europeans began visiting the area around the early 1830s, and the sale of dressed flax to them became a source of income for local Māori. By the end of the decade, however, Europeans were landing permanently, and they established a large whaling station at Māwhai Point at the Bay's southern end. Around this time, the English missionary William Colenso and others also travelled to the Bay and began converting Māori to Christianity—a mission they continued with fervour, and much success, around the entirety of the Cape.

In 1874, a settler began sheep farming in the area, and, just a decade later, the first shipment of sheep left Tokomaru Bay for the freezing works at Gisborne. With a mostly Māori staff, it was the first freezing works to be established in an area that would become famous for this industry. The distance to Gisborne, however, proved impractical. In 1909, a collective of farmers raised the capital to construct a freezing works at Waimā, partnering with Māori who exchanged land for shares in the new company. The bay rapidly became a hub of production, and in 1911, a new timber wharf was constructed to allow larger vessels to dock. At 365 metres, it was the longest wharf in the country, necessitating the addition of a tramway a year later. Soon, Tokomaru Bay's exports through the New Zealand Shipping Company were regularly arriving at the Tooley Street Docks on the River Thames in England. In 1940, economic success enabled the wharf to be upgraded again at great expense, its aging wooden supports replaced with state-of-the-art concrete pillars.

In the years after the Second World War, the local freezing industry hit hard times as demand dried up in the post-war recession both locally and overseas. As the coastal road around the East Cape was upgraded, ocean freight from small local operations like Tokomaru Bay ceased to be viable, and, in 1952, the freezing works closed for good. Once a lifeline, from which women cried as men went to war, and half the goods the cape produced left for London, Tokomaru Bay Wharf was left to decay. Over time, however, it became an icon of the coast, like its counterparts at nearby Hicks and Tolaga Bays. Recently, after decades of fundraising, Tolaga Bay Wharf was restored and reopened, and has since become a successful tourist attraction. Tokomaru Bay Wharf, half collapsed into the ocean and fenced at multiple points to prevent entry, now awaits the same revival.

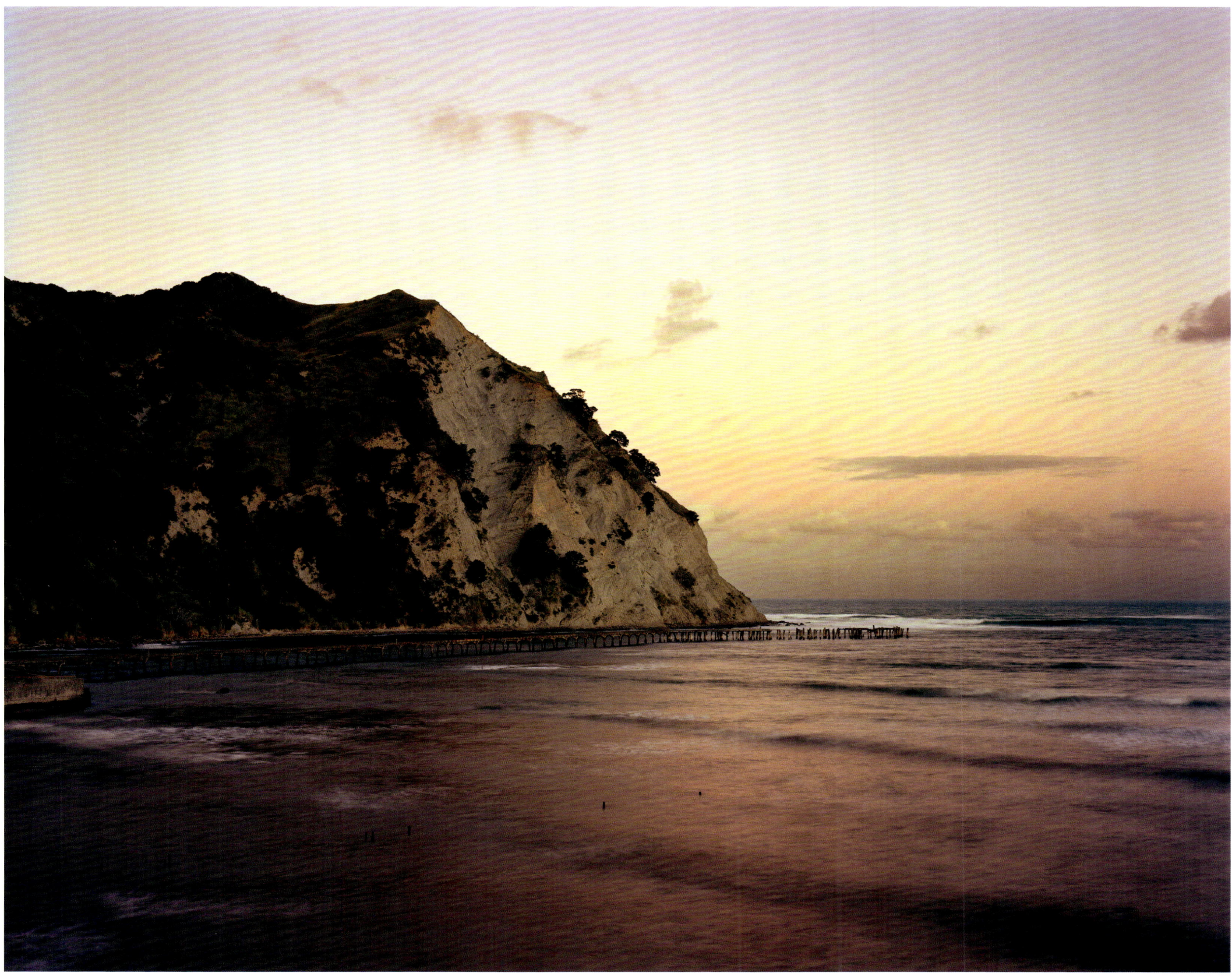

Collapsing Roof, Gisborne Sheep Shearers Wool Store, Tokomaru Bay, 2016

Leaving Whakatāne, the East Coast's narrow, two-lane road follows the contours of mountains, between coastal cliffs and the South Pacific Ocean. It climbs towering hills, passes through valleys, and crosses long, flat bridges spanning wide stone-filled rivers as it wraps round the coast. On the hills behind the settlements are vast farms and radiata pine forests, many owned and operated by Māori. An uncommon level of local ownership exists here; in many other parts of Aotearoa, overseas companies control much of the farming and especially forestry, since that industry's denationalisation in the 1980s.

Continuing around the coast, vestiges of European incursions are seen in passing: wooden Anglican churches built in the late nineteenth century, the ghostly remnants of regional dairy factories, freezing works, and ports. But beyond these colonial markers, other connections between the Cape and wider world come to mind, too: novels and films set or produced there. At Waihau Bay, the film *Boy* (2010) by Taika Waititi, in Whāngārā, Witi Ihimaera's book *Whale Rider* (1987) and Niki Caro's 2002 film adaptation, and at Hicks Bay, David Ballantyne's *Sydney Bridge Upside Down* (1968).

It's late afternoon when we arrive in Tokomaru Bay. In the middle of winter, far outside any tourist season, payment at the campground operates on an honesty system. As we pull in, heavy clouds hang above the wild sea, which breaks along the rocky coast, and someone offers to sell us weed. On the main street, the buildings are modest, a century old, and one or two-storeys high: a general store, a New South Wales Bank, a Bank of New Zealand. Nearly all are boarded up, their balconies sagging, and paint sandblasted to a patina by salt spray, their occupants and contents concealed behind layers of curtains and cardboard taped to the windows. Past the street, following the coast north, are old beachside cottages, some collapsing. Beyond them the dilapidated concrete of the defunct freezing works looms on the road's edge and the Tokomaru Bay Wharf comes into view, half disintegrated into the ocean beneath eroding cliffs.

It was 1952 when work stopped at this place and the wharf and the buildings of the once-bustling freezing works were left to crumble. Now, the concrete façade of the old wool store is overgrown with vines, which pry at gaps and rub away the faded yellow signwriting that reads 'Gisborne Sheep Shearers Wool Store'. At street level, multi-coloured tagging sits on a background of thick blue paint that hides previous graffiti. Above the building's raw concrete walls, which are everywhere boarded up to prevent entry, a grey sky weighs down on the buildings, their roofs ready to fall in the next storm, if they haven't already.

Although the complex was made a Category 2 historic place in 1984, protecting at least its exteriors from alteration, there has never been a budget to preserve or restore the buildings. Instead, rain, wind, and weeds slowly work their way through the structures. The roof and floor of the wool store, still somewhat intact in this photograph from 2016, are now fully collapsed.

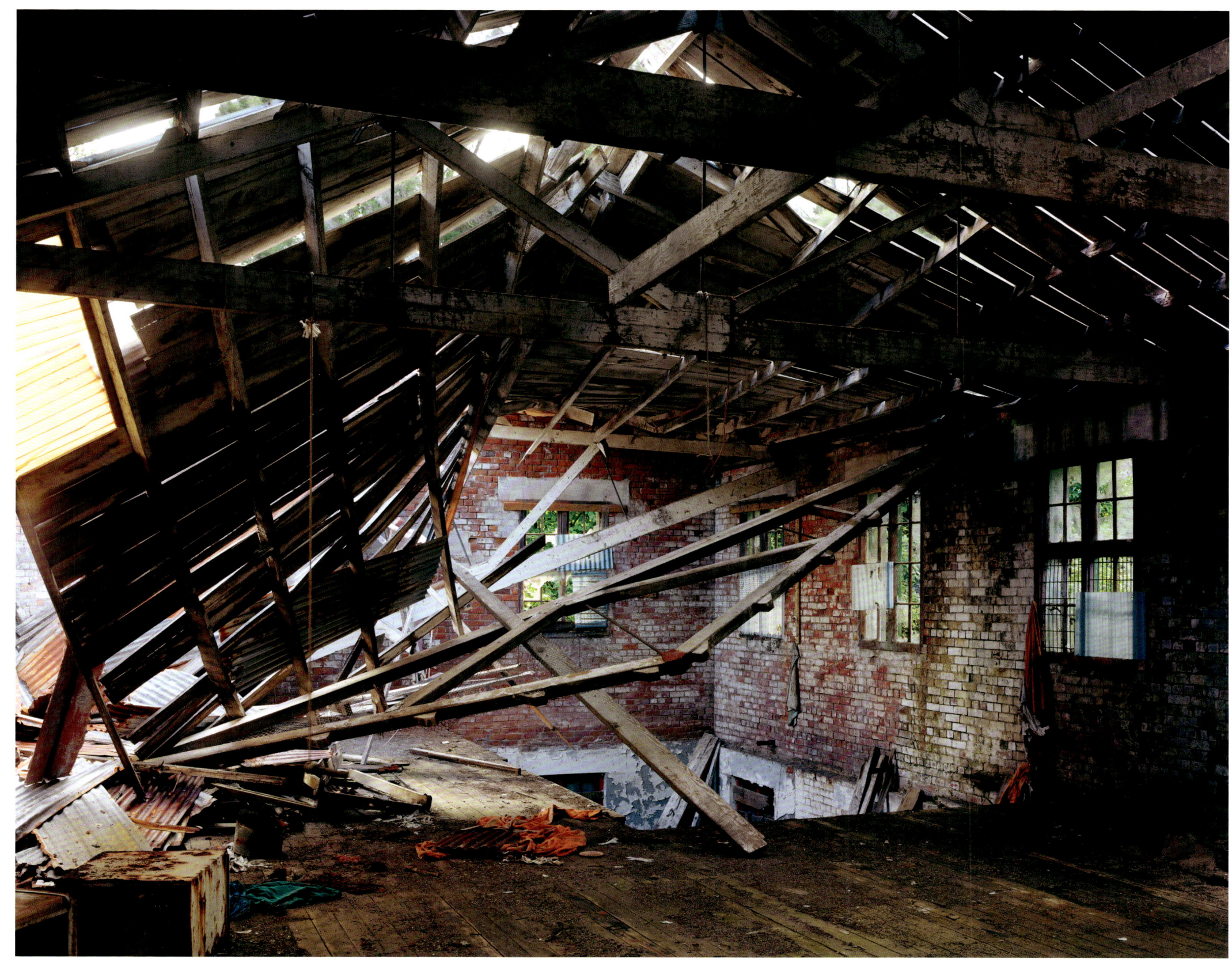

Waikaretāheke River Diversion (After Lusk), Lake Waikaremoana, 2016

Hydroelectricity was used for the first time in 1880, when a theatre and store frontage in Grand Rapids, Michigan, was illuminated with power from a dynamo connected to a turbine. Brought to New Zealand by American gold miners, the technology was first used in this country six years later at the remote mining camp of Bullendale, Otago. Despite the camp's location some ten kilometres beyond the still-notorious Skipper's Road, a huge twenty-stamp battery was assembled on site. Three kilometres of No. 8 wire then connected a turbine in one valley across a hill to power the stamping battery in another. Forty years later, the power-generating potential of hydroelectricity had exponentially increased, and plans were laid for the North Island's first major hydroelectric scheme at Lake Waikaremoana.

100 kilometres south of Rotorua, within the mountainous region of Te Urewera, Lake Waikaremoana formed over 2,200 years ago when a landslide dammed the Waikaretāheke River. The water that pooled behind the earth formed the North Island's deepest lake and the world's second largest landslide dam, 582 metres above sea level. Clad in dense forest, Te Urewera is the rohe (traditional home) of Ngāi Tūhoe, who have long fought to resist colonisation. Following attacks on the area in 1913 and 1914, the Crown began to assert its control over Lake Waikaremoana, in the interests of tourism and recreational fishing. Ngāi Tūhoe, Ngāti Ruapani, and Ngāti Kahungunu petitioned the Native Land Court in 1913 to investigate the ownership of the Waikaremoana lakebed. Hearings were held over four years, and the Court ruled that the lakebed was Māori customary land. Nonetheless, the Crown lodged an appeal in 1918 and—in the words of the 2001 Lake Waikaremoana and District Scoping Report from the Waitangi Tribunal—'continued to act as if it was the owner of the lake'.

In addition to taking control of the lake for tourism, the New Zealand Government began constructing a hydroelectric scheme, opening the Tuai, Piripaua, and Kaitawa Power Stations between 1929 and 1948. The project greatly altered the area and was met with protest, particularly in 1938, during the construction of Piripaua, which dammed the Waikaretāheke River, a traditional fishery, to divert its water into a new, artificial lake, Whakamarino. In 1948, painter Doris Lusk stayed with a friend who was an engineer on the Piripaua project. During her trip, she produced important paintings showing the concrete structures and pipes of the new hydroelectric scheme dwarfed by the distant rolling hills. Although other artists, particularly colonial photographers, had turned a sceptical eye towards industry, Lusk's approach was distinctive. The raw earth bulldozed for construction appears in her work like an unnatural scar on an otherwise untouched valley.

In 1944, the Crown appeal was finally heard in the Native Land Court. The original decision that the lakebed was Māori customary land was upheld. Despite this, and further opposition from iwi, Lake Waikaremoana and much of Te Urewera were designated a National Park in 1954. In 2013, a land settlement with the Crown was finally ratified by Tūhoe. In the settlement, the iwi received financial, commercial, and cultural redress valued at approximately $170 million, a Crown apology, and a correction of the historical record. Under the Tūhoe Claims Settlement Act 2014, Te Urewera was granted legal personhood. It is the first natural resource in the world to be awarded the same legal rights as a person.

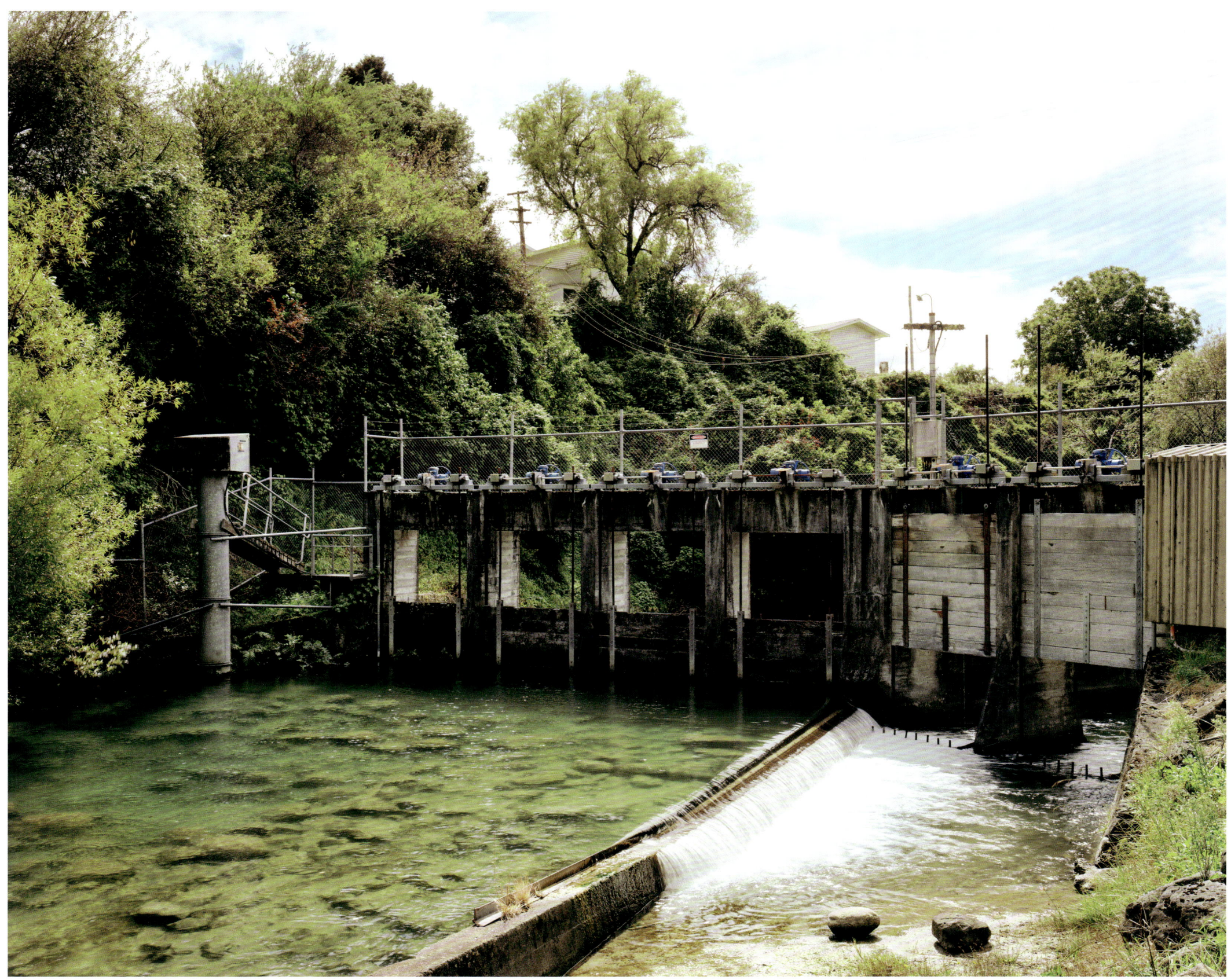

Manager's Office, Waipaoa Freezing Works, Outside Gisborne, 2016

North of Gisborne, State Highway 2 follows the muddy Waipaoa River through a valley of densely cultivated orchards, vineyards, and agricultural land. As the valley narrows and the foothills of the Raukūmara Range draw closer, the orchards and trimmed hedges recede and the land stretches into the wide pastures of sheep and dairy farms. Eventually, across the river, the concrete ruins of the Waipaoa freezing works appear, 'looming against the sky like some relic of bombed Berlin … a crumbling monument to an industrial enterprise which didn't work out', as the *Gisborne Photo News* described them in 1956.

The Waipaoa Freezing Works was instigated and funded solely by a collective of local farmers who felt that the larger works of the region were taking an unfair percentage of their earnings. A 1915 article in the *Poverty Bay Herald* describes a meeting at which 'upwards of seventy representative farmers unanimously endorsed the establishment of a new freezing works' and notes that 'at the close of the meeting there was a ready application for shares … no less than £8,730 worth of shares were actually applied for, and a "big effort" is being made to raise £30,000 (£2.6 million today) within a week in order to enable the provisional directors to start placing orders forthwith'. The importance of the project was such that 600 people turned out for the laying of the foundation stone, after which construction was completed in just six months.

In *Cast in Concrete: Concrete Construction in New Zealand 1950–1939*, Geoffrey Thornton writes, 'From the outset the Poverty Bay Farmers' Meat Company wished to develop a direct trade with United Kingdom ports, especially Bristol, and in 1919 purchased its own vessel, the *Admiral Codrington* … to ensure its independence of shipping companies.' Bought for an inflated post-war price with further money still required for a refrigeration fitout, the vessel proved the project's undoing. It required nearly fifty tons of coal per day to operate, and its entire cargo was spoiled on the first voyage after the refrigeration system failed. In 1923, the business and its ship were sold to British meat and shipping company Vestey's, exactly the kind of conglomerate it had been founded to circumvent. Local farmer investors lost their land or were forced to mortgage their homes, a number declared bankruptcy, and, in 1931, the freezing works were stripped and decommissioned. The stress of the collapse is said to have played a part in the early passing of one of the directors, George Witters, who died in 1934 at the age of 58.

Today, the voids left by Waipaoa's collapsed roof and vanished handmade windows blur the distinction between inside and outside, while chickens roam over a layer of hay and bird shit on the ground floor. Near the factory is the former manager's office. Blackberry vines crawl through the broken windows, and a swarm of wasps loudly buzzes behind the building's barred doors. At first, the delicate wrought iron and timber work seem incongruous with a slaughterhouse, as does a Venetian courtyard and fountain, now blocked by a fallen tree and the decayed roof. But the care and pride of the construction begins to make sense when it is understood as symbolic of a community's dreams.

Beyond the sad conclusion of the Waipaoa Freezing Works is a local legacy left by Witters, who was also a conservationist. During his lifetime, he planted thousands of trees, including natives, on his properties. Just ten kilometres from Waipaoa is Gray's Bush, one of the last blocks of untouched kahikatea and pūriri lowland coastal bush in the country, which Witters successfully petitioned to have gazetted into the public domain in 1926.

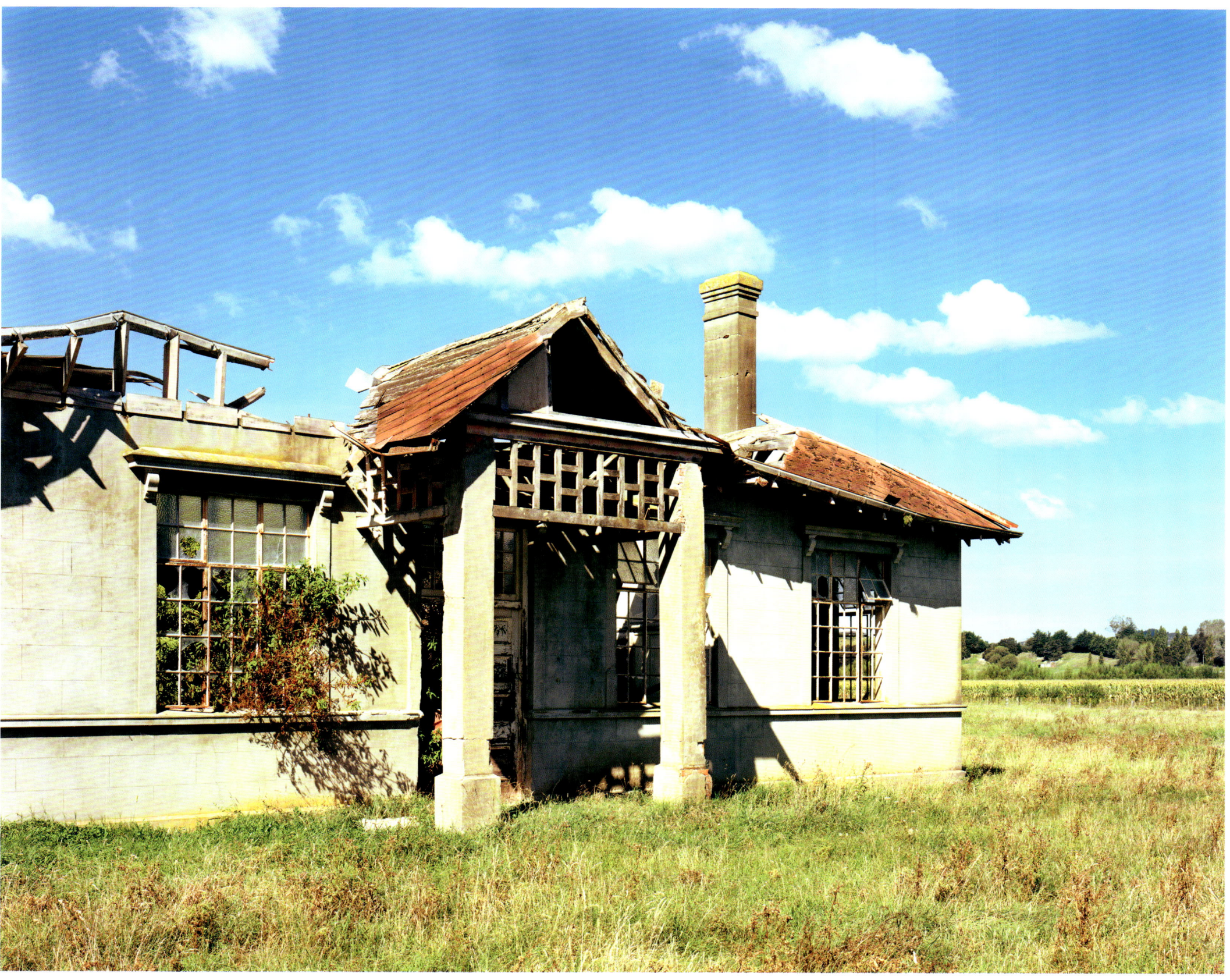

Sawmill at the Lane and Brown Shipyard, Whangaroa Harbour, Tōtara North, 2016

A black-and-white photograph taken by Northwood Brothers in the early twentieth century looks across Whangaroa Harbour, near the top of the North Island, to the shipbuilding yard and sawmill at Tōtara North. Beneath darkly exposed, denuded hills, the mill appears almost white, a cloud of smoke rising from the shipyards, echoing the form of the mountains beyond. The lower hills around the coast towards Ōkura Bay are dotted with a handful of workers' houses and boat sheds reflected in the still water. The photograph was once captioned, with an optimism characteristic of the colonial project, 'Totara North, in Whangaroa Harbour, One of New Zealand's Loveliest Fiords, Rivalling the Southern Sounds.'

In 1872, William Brown and Thomas Lane established the Lane and Brown Shipyard and Sawmill on the Whangaroa Harbour. Further south, near Kerikeri in the Bay of Islands, Brown's father had begun shipbuilding as early as 1850, utilising the Northland forests, as the crews of European whaling ships and other vessels came ashore to fell kauri for repairs. Tōtara North, under Lane and Brown, operated on a new scale, and by the turn of the nineteenth century their shipyard was said to be the largest in Australasia, boasting nearly 1,400 square metres of floor space and buildings large enough to accommodate two 350-ton ships.

Whangaroa was also the site of an early and tragic encounter between Europeans and Māori. In 1807, the sealing ship *Star* entered Whangaroa, and the young Māori chief Te Ara joined the crew for the vessel's journey back to Sydney. The following year, the brig *Commerce* visited the harbour with Bay of Islands chief Te Pahi on board, and the captain demonstrated his chiming pocket watch to locals. Unfortunately, in the wake of this visit, an illness carried by the Europeans wiped out a large number of the people of Whangaroa, including the chief Kaitoke. The disaster was presaged by the captain accidentally dropping his watch in the harbour, which Māori conceptualised as unleashing an atua whiro (malignant spirit).

In December 1809, the brigantine *Boyd* anchored in Whangaroa to add kauri spars to their cargo and to return Te Ara after his stay in Sydney. Perhaps because of an illness, or a failure to realise that deck work was beneath his status, the chief had been tied to the capstan for hours during the journey, flogged, and later denied food for several days. These acts represented an unforgivable attack on his mana (spiritual power and reputation) and, coupled with the recent epidemic, they necessitated utu (the righting of a wrong). Under the guise of leading Captain Thompson and his men to a stand of kauri up the Kaeo river, Māori took their revenge, killing and eating the group. Then, using their uniforms to board the anchored *Boyd* at dusk, they killed the seventy remaining members of the crew.

The next morning, chief Te Pahi, who supported European trade, arrived and tried in vain to rescue survivors clinging to the masts. Three weeks later, as news of the attack spread around the world, he was mistakenly blamed for it. In retaliation, the crews of five European whaling ships killed Te Pahi and between fifty and 200 innocent people at Rangihoua village in the Bay of Islands.

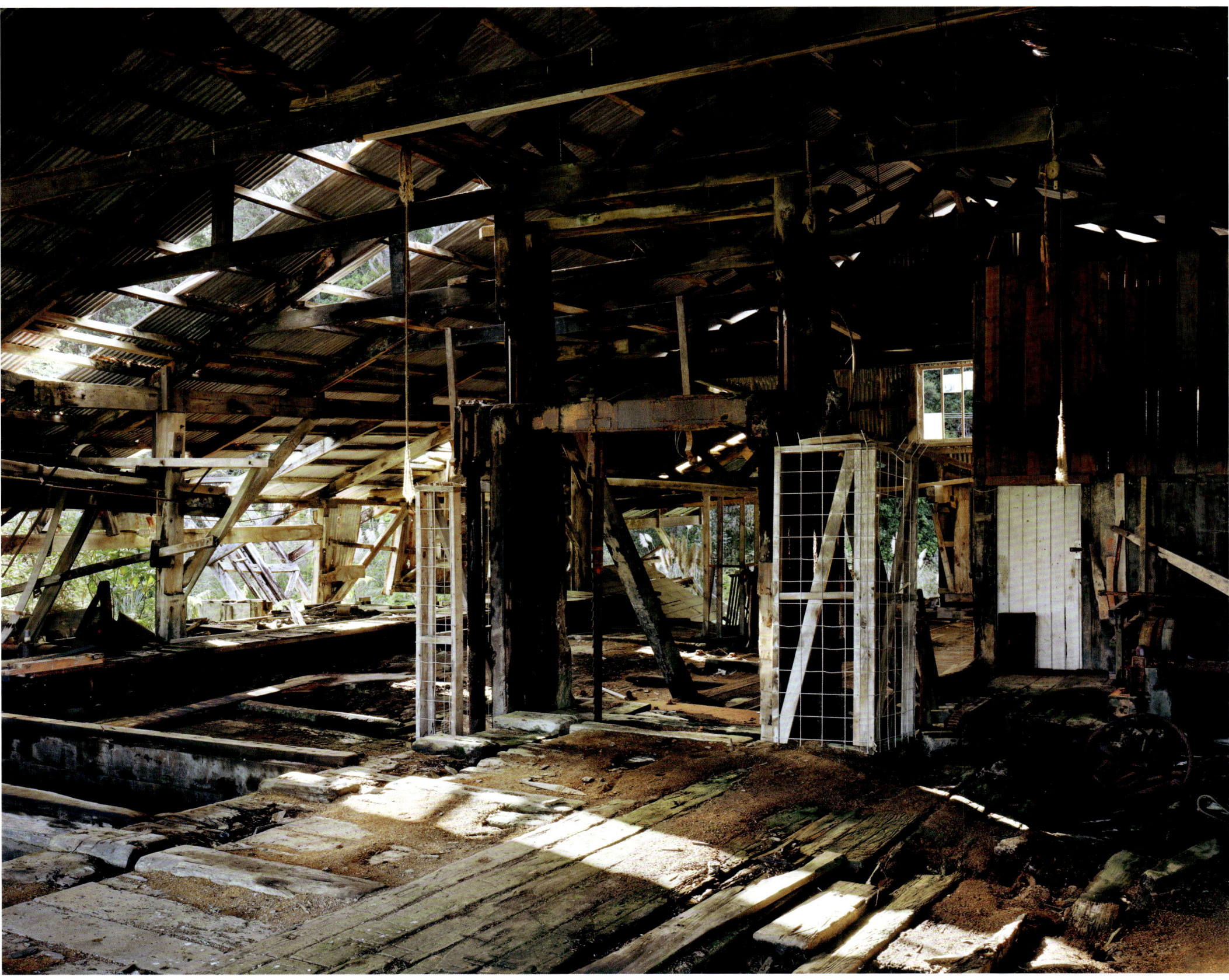

Wildflowers in a Development, Katikati, Near Tauranga, 2015

In 1861, after a stint of almost seven years as Governor of Cape Colony, South Africa, George Grey returned to New Zealand and resumed his former position as governor of this country. In the meantime, the Kīngitanga (Māori king) movement had emerged as a means of retaining sovereignty in the face of colonial expansion. Composed of a confederation of tribal groups from the central North Island and centring on Tainui on the Waikato River, the Kīngitanga saw differences set aside in the name of solidarity. The colonial authorities, however, saw Māori unity as a threat to imperial authority, and in July 1864 Governor Grey invaded the Waikato, beginning the Waikato War. After several bloody battles, heavily armed British soldiers defeated vastly outnumbered Māori. The invasion then spread to the coast, and 1,700 British troops, with artillery and naval support, attempted to take the harbour of Tauranga, which Māori had fortified at Gate Pā. After surviving the largest artillery barrage of the Waikato War, a group of just 230 Māori successfully repelled the British forces, inflicting over 100 casualties in ten minutes of combat and driving the British from Tauranga.

Two months later, though, the colonial forces attacked again, this time at Te Ranga, where a reconnaissance party had discovered a new Māori fortification being built. Invading before it was completed, the British killed 100 of the 500 defenders. The loss led to a surrender, and soon after the Tauranga district of around 290,000 acres was confiscated by Governor Grey as part of a 'proclamation of peace' in 1865. Among the areas confiscated was the region of Katikati, thirty-five kilometres north-west of Tauranga, which has been subject to a complex history of raupatu (confiscation), return, and exploitative purchase. Between 1864 and 1866, the Government obtained the 90,000-acre 'Te Puna–Katikati block' by entering into an agreement with a small number of chiefs from a single tribe. Other chiefs and other tribes were not consulted and did not agree to sell their lands, yet the Government insisted that the purchase was legitimate. Eventually, a small compensation was paid, but the land was not returned and a key clause of the Treaty of Waitangi (1840) promising that Māori could retain their land was broken.

With Katikati and surrounding land now in Crown hands, in 1874, George Vesey Stewart, an English farm and mill owner from Ireland, reached a deal with the Crown to reserve 10,000 acres at Katikati for a 'special settlement of not less than forty families of Irish farmers with adequate capital'. In 1875, the first of the settlers arrived from Ireland aboard the ship *Carisbrooke Castle*, the *Auckland Star* newspaper recording a contingent of '363 people including 122 healthy-looking, clear-complexioned Irish lasses'. A further 451 Irish settlers arrived in 1878 aboard the *Lady Jocelyn*, after an eighty-eight-day voyage from Belfast. Katikati then became a farming centre and a hub of the kauri-gum-digging trade, as the region's forests were cleared for pasture.

During the century that followed, horticulture—primarily kiwifruit and avocados—became the town's main industry, and in 2018 it was named the 'Avocado Capital of New Zealand'. In the 1990s, to revitalise tourism in the area, colourful murals celebrating the colonial heritage of the town were painted on the exterior walls of businesses along the main street. Today, it is a favoured retirement location with 34.4% of residents aged sixty-five and over, compared to the regional average of 18.5%.

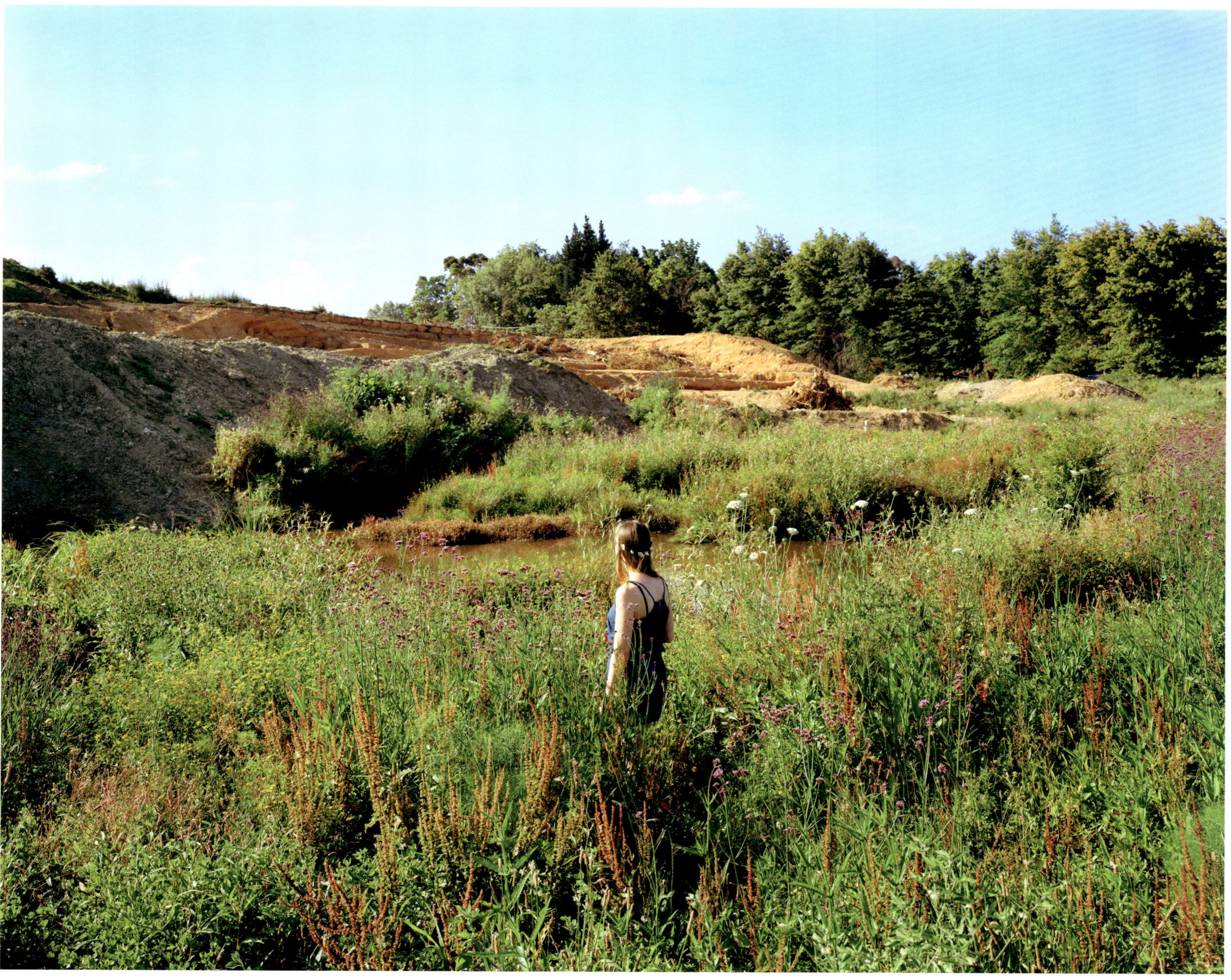

Limeworks, Frenchman's Gully, Near Te Manunui Rock Art Site, Canterbury, 2016

From above, the east coast of the Te Waipounamu (the South Island) is a mosaic of green and ochre fields, which stretch hundreds of kilometres between the Pacific Ocean and the foothills of the Southern Alps. West of Timaru and into the hills, the terrain becomes more dramatic as white limestone outcrops separate the fields, twisting and pulling from the ground like tectonic plates in motion. Before the arrival of Europeans, the fields were part of a vast forest of tī kōuka (cabbage trees), a kind of forest that no longer exists. Like the pōhutukawa, kauri, and kōwhai, the tī kōuka is endemic to New Zealand and one of the country's iconic species—its limbless trunks ending in a bouquet of sword-like leaves between which small white flower clusters bloom in summer.

Most cabbage trees seen today at public parks, beaches, and on the side of motorways are in their youth, perhaps only five metres high. At Pakawau in Golden Bay, however, a tree believed to be nearly 500 years old stands seventeen metres tall, hinting at the scale and beauty of the vanished tī kōuka forests. For the Māori people of the region, Ngāi Tahu, the tree was an important food source, with its roots, shoots, and stems all edible. Roots were cut, cleaned, dried, then cooked in hāngī (pit ovens), becoming a sweet food that could be stored. Gathering these roots was one of several reasons for Ngāi Tahu's lengthy expeditions to remote inland areas.

During summer nights on these journeys, people would camp beneath the limestone outcrops of what is today South Canterbury, and they would sometimes create rock paintings. Made using a combination of charcoal, iron oxide, animal fats, and vegetable gums, these figurative and semi-abstract images have survived outside for hundreds of years. Though the original intention behind them is unknown, today they are considered to be among the earliest artworks made in Aotearoa. Of the nearly 350 rock-art sites in the region, Te Manunui (meaning 'the great bird') is one of the most sacred. Painted on the underside of a limestone overhang (now protected behind metal cages), the eponymous image shows a pouākai (Haast eagle), a bird that went extinct approximately 600 years ago, around the same time as its prey, the moa, once the world's largest flightless bird.

In 2007, Te Manunui was gifted its name by tangata whenua (people of the land) as part of a project that made the site made accessible to the public, and gave it Category 1 heritage protection in 2014. When I visited, driving the dusty clay road the back way towards the outcrop, I was surprised to find a limeworks, separated from Te Manunui by only a handful of cabbage trees and a macrocarpa windbreak. Behind the quarry buildings was a vast open-cast pit—the lime it produces enabling the unnaturally green pastures of the area. The quarry's limestone hill has been almost removed in just a few decades, while beside it, the drawings on the outcrop remain, hundreds of years after their creation.

The Ngāi Tahu artist group Paemanu, which translates to 'the perch of the birds', credits their name to the imagery found in rock paintings throughout Te Waipounamu. Founding member Areta Wilkinson explains, 'Te Manunui is a vital source of inspiration from which the group draws its creative spirit'.

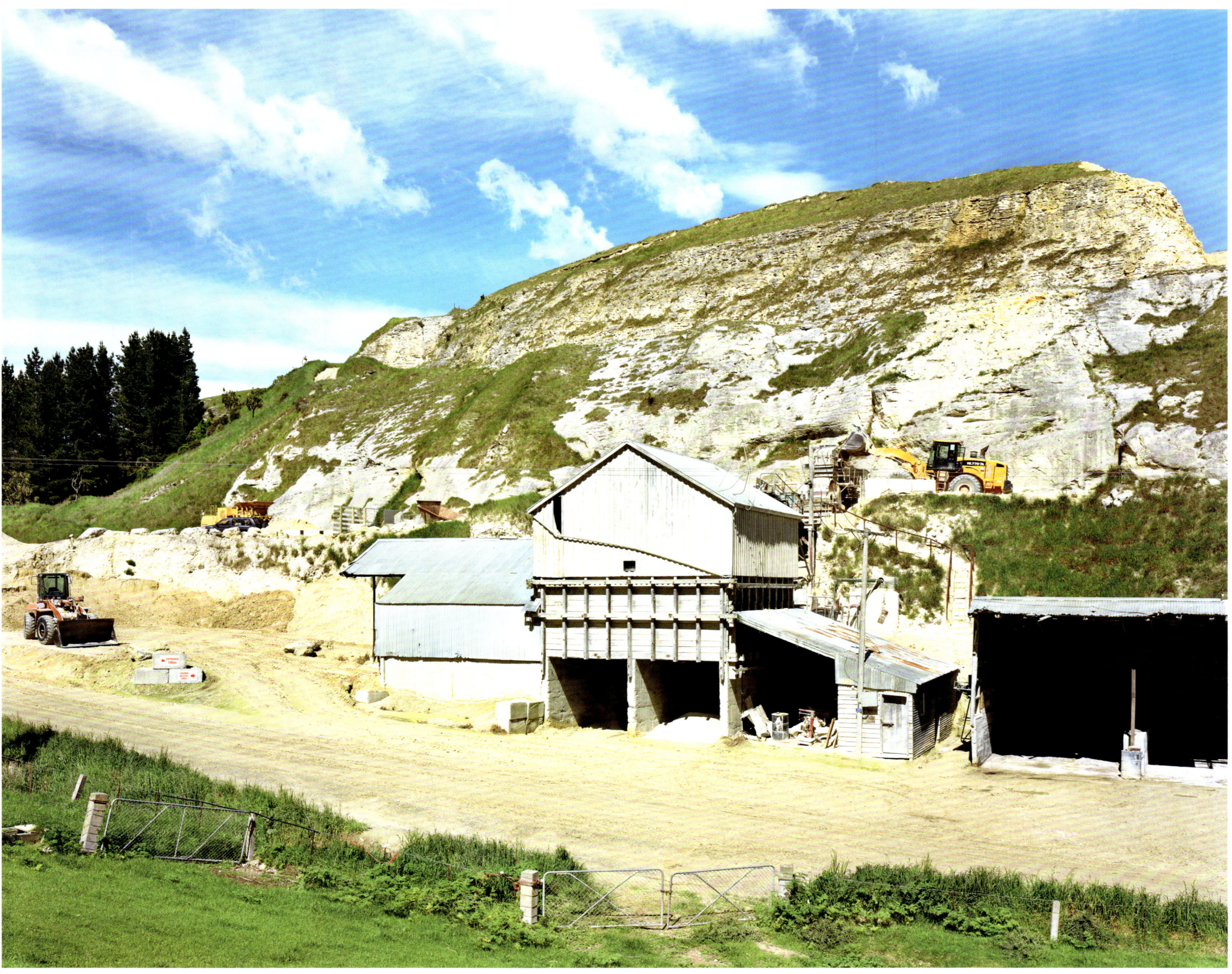

A West Coast Sawmill Relocated to the East Coast, Temuka, 2016

In a 1907 report on the New Zealand Timber industry, the Department of Lands wrote, 'Westland is now one of the largest timber districts in the colony, both in production and future supply. It only needs further development to witness a large increase in the sawmilling industry, and it appears probable that in the future a great proportion of the timber used in the cities and towns of New Zealand will be derived from this district.' The report proved accurate, the 1960 *Encyclopedia of New Zealand* noting that over 20% of New Zealand's timber came from the West Coast from 1910 to 1911.

Before milling began on the West Coast, the dominant tree in its rainforests was rimu (red pine), and this soon became its most logged, the Department of Lands stating, 'following [rimu] comes the kahikatea (white pine), whilst silver pine (manoao) and black pine (mataī) are also cut for certain purposes and tōtara is much in demand'. Rimu was used for housing and furniture, kahikatea for housing and roof shingles. The giant tōtara became fence posts or wharfs, and much of the mataī, which would have been over forty metres high, was merely burnt for heating and cooking.

Between 1874 and 1885, the New Zealand Government passed a number of acts to protect forests from burning and clearing, although their aim was not to preserve but to ensure a supply of native timber. In 1887, however, the State Forests Department was dissolved, and the Department of Lands became responsible for managing forests as well as farmland. The new department began to offer settlers incentives to clear the forests on their land as quickly as possible, by burning or logging, to encourage farming and settlement; by March 1907, according to the official register, there were 441 sawmills in operation across New Zealand, many of which were partially owned by farmers fulfilling the incentives.

In 1920, an investigation by the New Zealand Forest Service revealed that the total area of the West Coast's remaining native forest suitable for milling was much smaller than expected. Despite this, profit was once again held above conservation, and much of the West Coast region—New Zealand's largest area of old-growth native conifers like rimu—was designated a state forest, as a future source of timber. By 1980, the Forest Service listed over 600 sawmills in operation in the West Coast of the South Island alone. Over the decade that followed, though, national protest movements centred on places like Whirinaki Forest gradually caused a shift in public opinion on native logging. Finally, between 1987 and 1996, large areas of the West Coast were protected for conservation, with much of the region's best forest covenanted into the now beloved Paparoa and Kahurangi National Parks. In 1990, the designation of Te Wāhipounamu, the Southwest of New Zealand, as a World Heritage Area provided a level of protection to all the forests in South Westland, finally bringing the era of native logging to a close.

Today, over 80% of the West Coast region is conservation land, maintained by the Department of Conservation. Comprising 19,000 square kilometres of mostly regenerating rainforests which span mountain ranges, lakes, and rivers, the area makes up 25% of all conservation land in New Zealand.

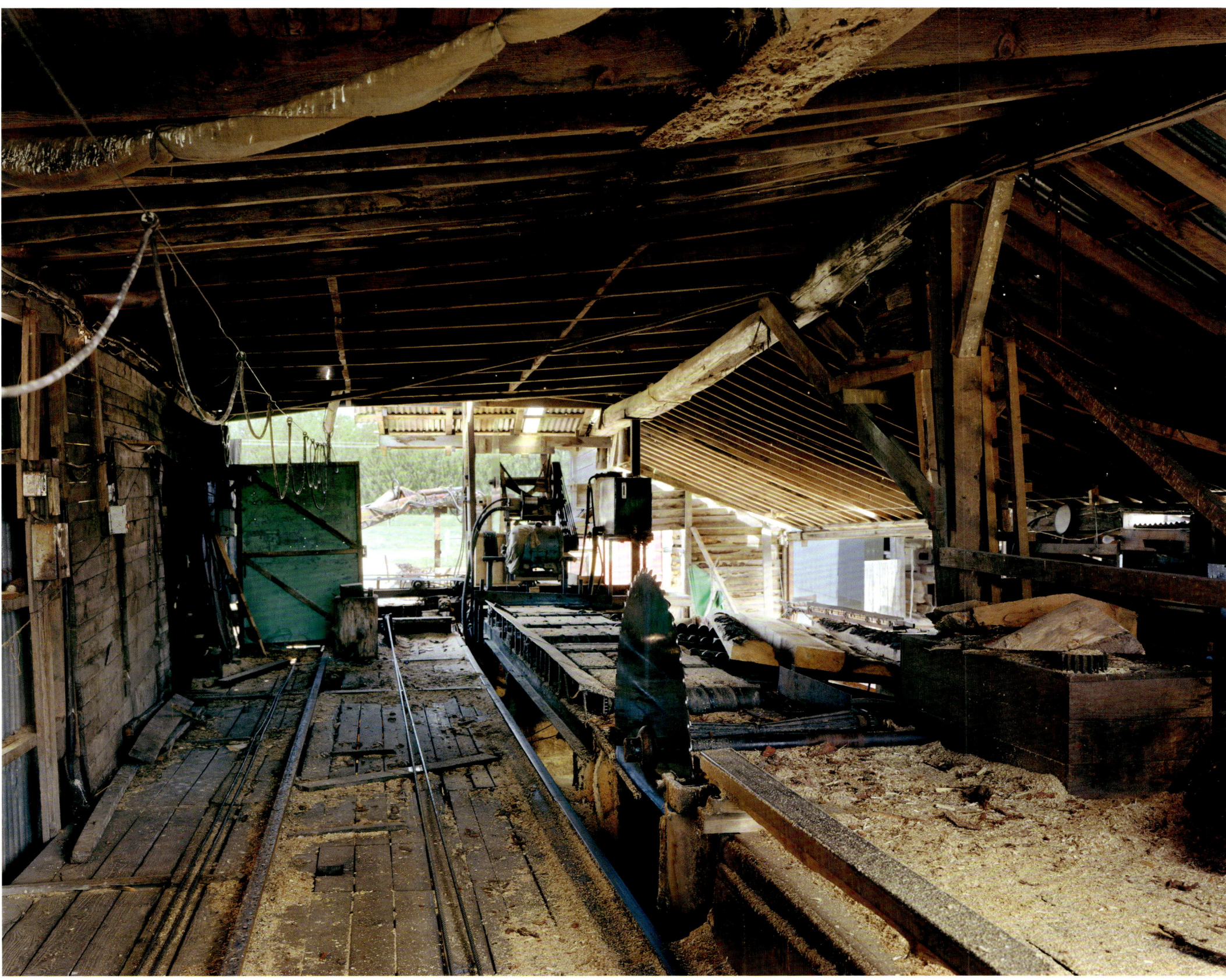

Henry Simon Purifier, Former Aero Flour Mill, Temuka, 2016

On the South Island's east coast, Temuka sits beside a wide, braided river and State Highway 1, in a place where coastal wetlands once met the forest's edge. Long before Europeans ever dreamt up 'New Zealand', Waitaha, Kāti Māmoe, and then Ngāi Tahu lived here, because it was abundant with natural resources and a place where the Opihi and Te Umu Kaha Rivers could be forded. At this time, the ancient forest Arowhenua still stretched hundreds of kilometres across the land, and, beyond it, flax and cabbage trees covered vast coastal wetlands and lagoons. In 1853, Europeans arrived, set up camp, and evicted Māori, surveying for a township in 1863. Originally called Te Umu Kaha ('the strong oven') for Arowhenua's importance as a place of food gathering and preparation, it was renamed Temuka, an anglicised version of the Māori name.

Following the first European settlers came loggers. A 1911 article from the *Christchurch Press* notes that Arowhenua was 'a splendid piece of native forest … which for some years gave employment to a number of pit-sawyers, in providing building material for Timaru and Temuka settlers' homesteads on the plains, and in splitting fencing material'. With the forest gone, other industry emerged. After it was found that wheat grew well on the South Canterbury plains, the first flour mill in the region opened six kilometres upriver from Temuka in 1864, with another following a few years later in Winchester. By the 1870s, large flax-milling operations were rapidly turning Te Umu Kaha's wetlands into rope for sailing ships; the same *Press* article observes that 'on the rich alluvial soil flax made a prolific growth that is now never seen, at least in the South Island, for such land has all been found well worth cultivating'.

Temuka's success was such that by the turn of the century its central King Street was lined with ornate brick and stone buildings—the town now able to boast New Zealand's first boiling-down and tannery works, a cheese factory, and a pottery works, among other industries. But, by 1923, letters to the *Temuka Leader* described farmers being 'at the mercy of the miller and grain Speculator'. Out of this situation emerged the Temuka Flour Milling, Grain, and Produce Agency Company. Its first shareholder meeting in 1925 stated that their product was 'equal to any other flour on the market … the West Coast spoke well of it, and in Dunedin it was quoted among the very best'. For the next five decades the Temuka flour mill flourished, producing Aero Flour, which was touted as yielding baked goods 'as light as the proverbial feather' in a 1928 advertisement.

With the downturn of the 1970s, economies of scale finally caught up with the small wheat-growers mill. The building lay shuttered on the main trunk line until it was purchased by the independent Coupland's Bakery, which closed operations there for good in 2001. Today, a contractor's yard and workshop operate out of the former grain stores and loading dock. Above this, narrow flights of hand-cut wooden steps climb the building's five floors. Between perilous holes cut in the floors to remove equipment, machines over a century old, manufactured by Henry Simon and Thomas Robinson and Son in the English villages of Rochdale and Cheadle Heath, lie still beneath a layer of flour dust.

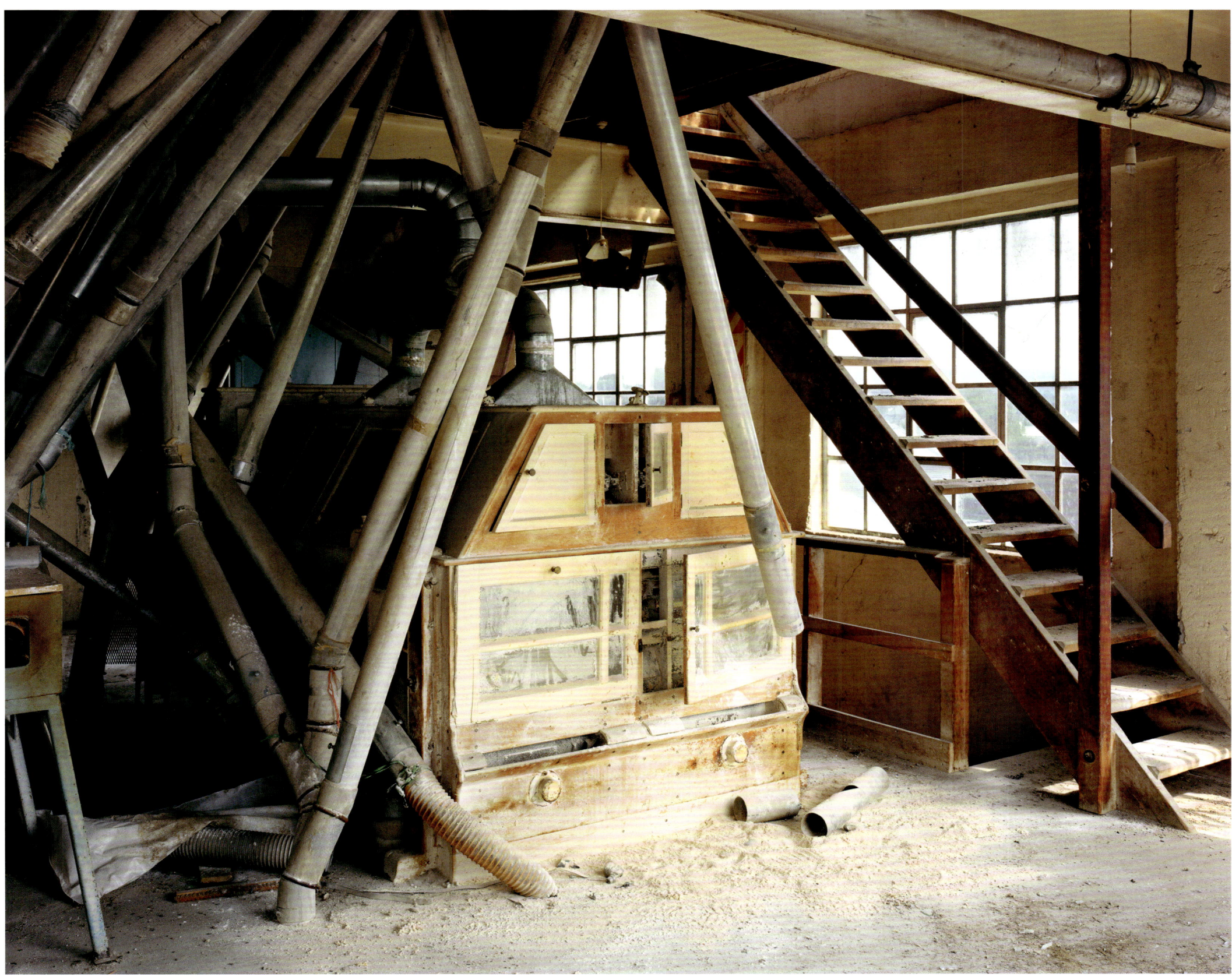

Loading Fertilizer, Former Empress Flour Mill, Waimate, 2016

Halfway between Christchurch and Dunedin, and ten kilometres inland from the coast, Waimate sits beneath the Hunter Hills in what was once the Waimate Forest. In 1855, the first European settler in the area, Michael Studholme, negotiated rights with Ngāi Tahu for a pastoral licence, and, by 1859, his station, known as Te Waimate, had grown to about 98,500 acres. After centuries of Māori habitation, Waimate was still home to more than 3,000 acres of native forest before Europeans arrived. However, by 1877, when the railway reached town, five sawmills were in operation; most of the forest was soon logged, and the following year, a bushfire wiped out what little remained.

With the forest cleared and the region growing, flour milling became a major industry in Waimate, as in the nearby towns of Temuka and Timaru. In 1892, the Empress flour mill was established near Waimate's new railway line. It produced 300 tons of flour annually for local consumption, and a further 1,000 tons was exported by rail. In 1903, the proprietor's son, Robert Nichol, returned to New Zealand from Canada, where he had studied cutting-edge milling operations, and the mill was remodelled and rebranded as Nicol and Sons. Now a modern roller flour mill, they produced what they billed as 'the finest of Canterbury wheat', and their product won awards at the 1910 Anglo-Japanese Exhibition in London, the 1911 Festival of Empire in London, and 1912–14 Auckland Exhibition.

In 1921, the mill was expanded again, adding four thirty-five-metre-high concrete grain silos, which were inaugurated by Prime Minister William Massey. To fund the upgrades, the company went public, becoming the South Canterbury Co-operative Flour Milling Company. But before most of the new equipment could be used, the business was in trouble. New Zealand's flour market had become oversaturated, and, in 1936, the Government introduced regulations, including quotas on output, in an attempt to protect the industry. At Waimate, this came at exactly the wrong time, and, despite an attempt by the Timaru Milling Company to save the business, the mill closed for good.

Sometime later, the premises were purchased by the Waimate Transport Company, which has remained its owner. To the shock of many, in 2008, plans were made to demolish the historic buildings and construct a warehouse. As the building had only limited heritage protection, its owners were acting within their legal rights, but the news was met with opposition from Waimate residents as well as national heritage groups. The sense of loss is encapsulated best by a simple statement from a heritage group director: 'We would ask that if the building is demolished, that the heritage plaques attached to the building are removed carefully.'

By 2018, the Waimate Transport Company had decided to save the complex, where a father and son team once boasted, 'a home and foreign record unique to the dominion'. A local artist was commissioned to decorate the silos with a mural of famous figures from the town: former Prime Minister Norman Kirk, the settler Michael Studholme, Second World War–hero Eric Batchelor, the first female doctor in New Zealand, Margaret Cruickshank, and Chief Te Huruhuru of Ngāi Tahu. The silos are now a visitor attraction and icon of Waimate.

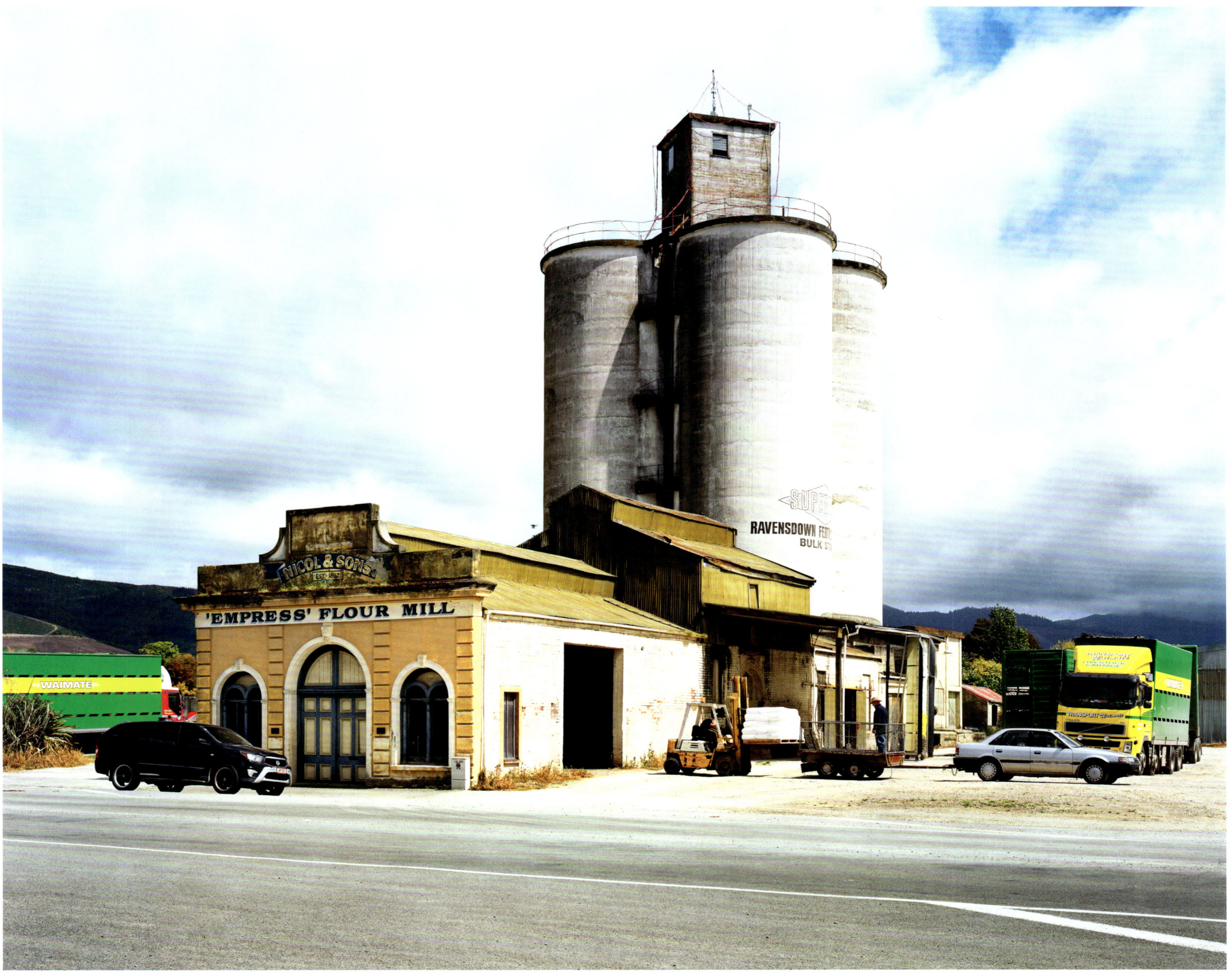

Collapsing Kiln, Mākareao Limeworks, Blue Mountains, Otago, 2016

North of Dunedin, the mouth of the Waihemo, or Shag River, is a site of Māori settlement that dates to the twelfth century. Beneath the sand dunes, archaeological digs have found the remains of an estimated 6,000 moa, once the largest flightless birds in the world. Heavily relied upon as a food source, moa were extinct by 1445, along with their only natural predator, the pouākai or Haast's eagle. In 1830, early European whalers also established themselves on the Waihemo river mouth, which by then was deserted. Above it, on the slopes of the former Matakaea pā, later settlers discovered the first bituminous coal in the country, and, in 1863, they opened the Shag Point Coal Mine, which dug into the hills for a century to follow.

For generations, the Waihemo river was also a navigational route for Ngāi Tahu, Waitaha, and Kāti Mamoe Māori, who journeyed hundreds of kilometres inland. Starting in the 1850s, European farmers slowly cleared the river valley for pasture, and turned the Māori river trail into the Palmerston-Dunback Road. A decade later, as miners swarmed the route in the Otago gold rushes, the Otago Witness newspaper wrote, 'It is no use fighting against fate; we cannot resume our Arcadian simplicity; greatness is forced upon us, and we must adapt ourselves to the time.' Today, though, a stone arch bridge across McCormick's Creek is one of the last physical remnants of their toil. It sits opposite Limekiln Road and beside State Highway 87, which bypasses it.

Leaving the highway, Limekiln Road winds towards the Blue Mountains, which the Mākareao Limeworks has been gnawing away at since the 1860s. Lime is one of the world's oldest industries; evidence of stone furnaces for lime burning dates as far back as 2,450 BCE in Khafaje in Mesopotamia. In the Middle Ages, huge amounts of lime were used in the construction of the churches, castles, and palaces of Europe. But it was not until the seventeenth century, when brick became a primary building material, that use of burnt lime as mortar became common. The first lime kilns in New Zealand were small and operated locally, but, in 1898, the Government established the Inch Valley Lime Quarry at Mākareao, partly to promote the use of agricultural lime by farmers. The works' importance was such that the main trunk railway line even branched off the coast from Palmerston to reach it.

Initially, the coal-driven limeworks failed to find its feet, and, in 1901, a new gas-powered kiln was commissioned. But during its construction, the death of three workers in a cutting collapse became a nationally reported tragedy, and the still-struggling business was sold to the Milburn Lime and Cement Company in 1909. Enthused after visiting the engineer Ernest Schmatolla in Germany, Milburn's new manager, Frank Oakden, secured the Australasian rights to his Elliptical Schmatolla Kiln and had one constructed at Mākareao. The gas-fired design still burned coal but achieved almost twice the efficiency by trapping and recirculating smoke. The works finally successful, the Schmatolla Kiln remained in use at Mākareao until 1952, when it was superseded by the modern limeworks below it.

In 1963, Milburn Lime amalgamated with New Zealand Cement, and, in 1971, Switzerland-based Holcim bought a 42% stake in the company. In 1989, Holcim divested the lime business to subsidiary Taylor's Lime, which ran the plant until its purchase by the Canadian multinational Graymont in 2015.

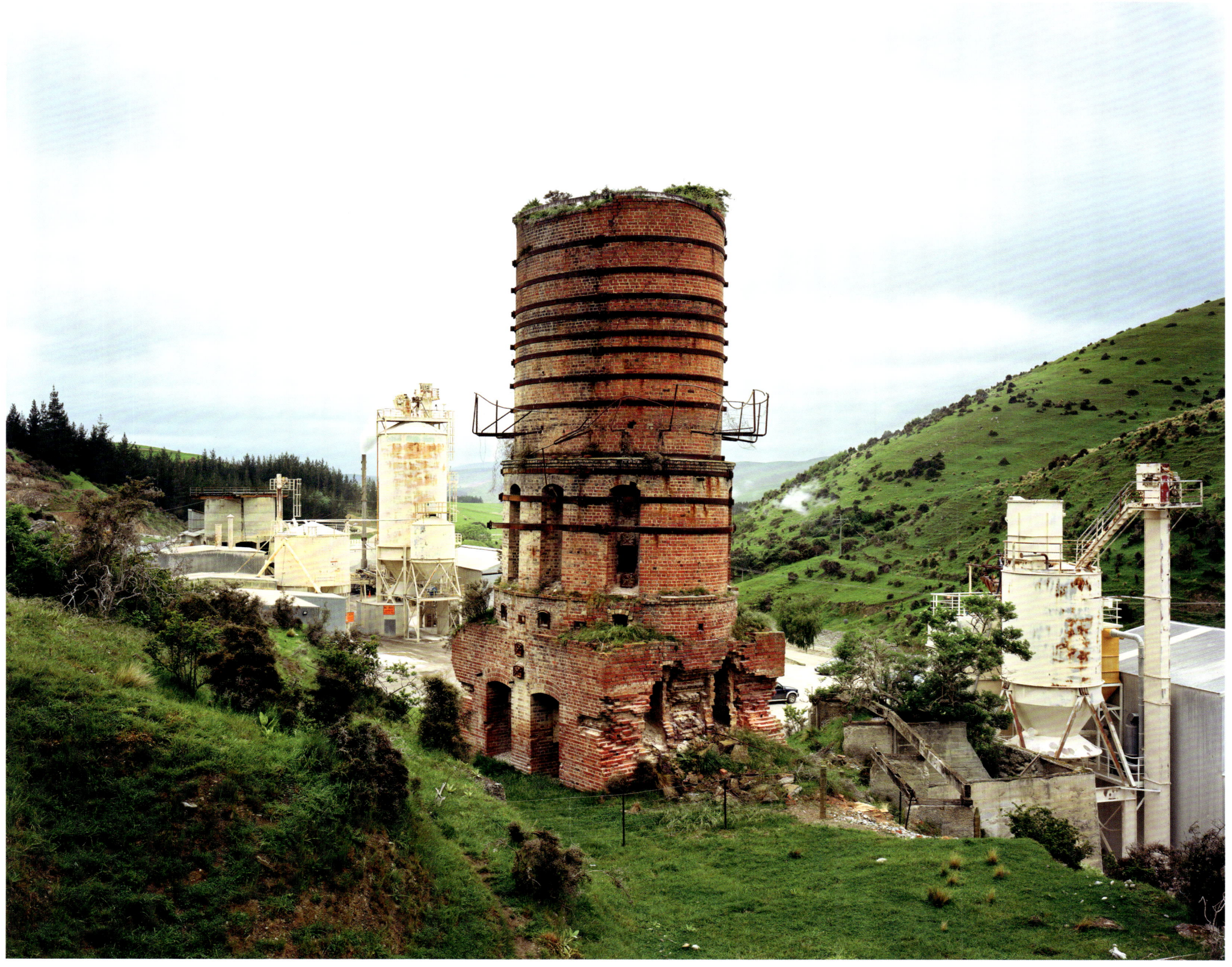

Boiler Room, Former McGill's Flour and Oat Mill, Milton, 2017

The farming settlement of Fairfax was established in 1850, sixty kilometres south of Dunedin (founded just two years earlier) on plains above the Tokomairiro River and beneath the hills of the Otago Coast Forest. Before the construction of railways, travelling to such settlements was a major undertaking, so those who lived in them needed to be self-sufficient. Many of the European settlers of New Zealand—including my great-great-grandfather, who arrived at Fairfax in the 1850s—were recent arrivals from Ireland or Scotland. There, many had been tenant farmers, working land at times almost barren from centuries of use, whereas here they found alluvial soils productive beyond imagining. Shaped by severe hardships like the Irish potato famine, which claimed over a million lives between 1845 and 1852, they arrived hoping to be freed from class restrictions and to finally prosper through hard work.

Experimenting with different seeds and crops in each region, they found that the South Island's east coast was perfect for growing wheat, and by 1852, Otago's first flour mill was operating north of Dunedin on the Ōwheo stream (renamed the Water of Leith). Peter McGill helped to build the mill, then worked there for four years before constructing the second mill in the region in 1857, using timber he milled himself. The mill was situated near Fairfax, capitalising on the abundance of water from the Tokomairiro River. Other industry soon followed McGill, and within a few years a new township called Mill Town (later Milton) had sprung up, eclipsing the earlier settlement.

McGill's operation grew rapidly. In 1878, the *Otago Witness* described a substantial complex, featuring a chimney over fifteen metres in height, a cutting-edge boiler made in Dunedin, an engine imported from Edinburgh, and mills for flour, oatmeal, and barley. In May 1886, there were reports of the mill being totally destroyed by a fire during the night, 'the insurances barely cover[ing] the loss on the grain and flour in the mill, which was packed from floor to ceiling'. Nevertheless, the *Otago Daily Times* observed in July, 'Within a few weeks McGill will sail for Great Britain, where he intends to obtain machinery for a plant which will be second in completeness and all modern improvements to none in New Zealand.' The new building was also to be made from brick and concrete, and to be one of the country's first roller flour mills, greatly increasing its efficiency.

In 1918, two decades after McGill's death, Fleming and Company, the makers of Creamoata porridge, purchased McGill's mill to restore production after their mill in Gore was severely damaged by fire. Later, as the contours of industry shifted, the buildings were acquired by the Bruce Woollen Mill to be used as flow-over storage. When the woollen industry fell into decline, McGill's factory was left to decay for nearly five decades. Now the warehouses and grounds are home to a car-wrecking business. In September 2022, the building's owner, a Dunedin entrepreneur, began illegally demolishing the mill, despite it being considered an archaeological site because it was built before 1900.

The main building and its iconic chimney were temporarily saved, but McGill's boiler room was razed before Heritage New Zealand was notified of the demolition.

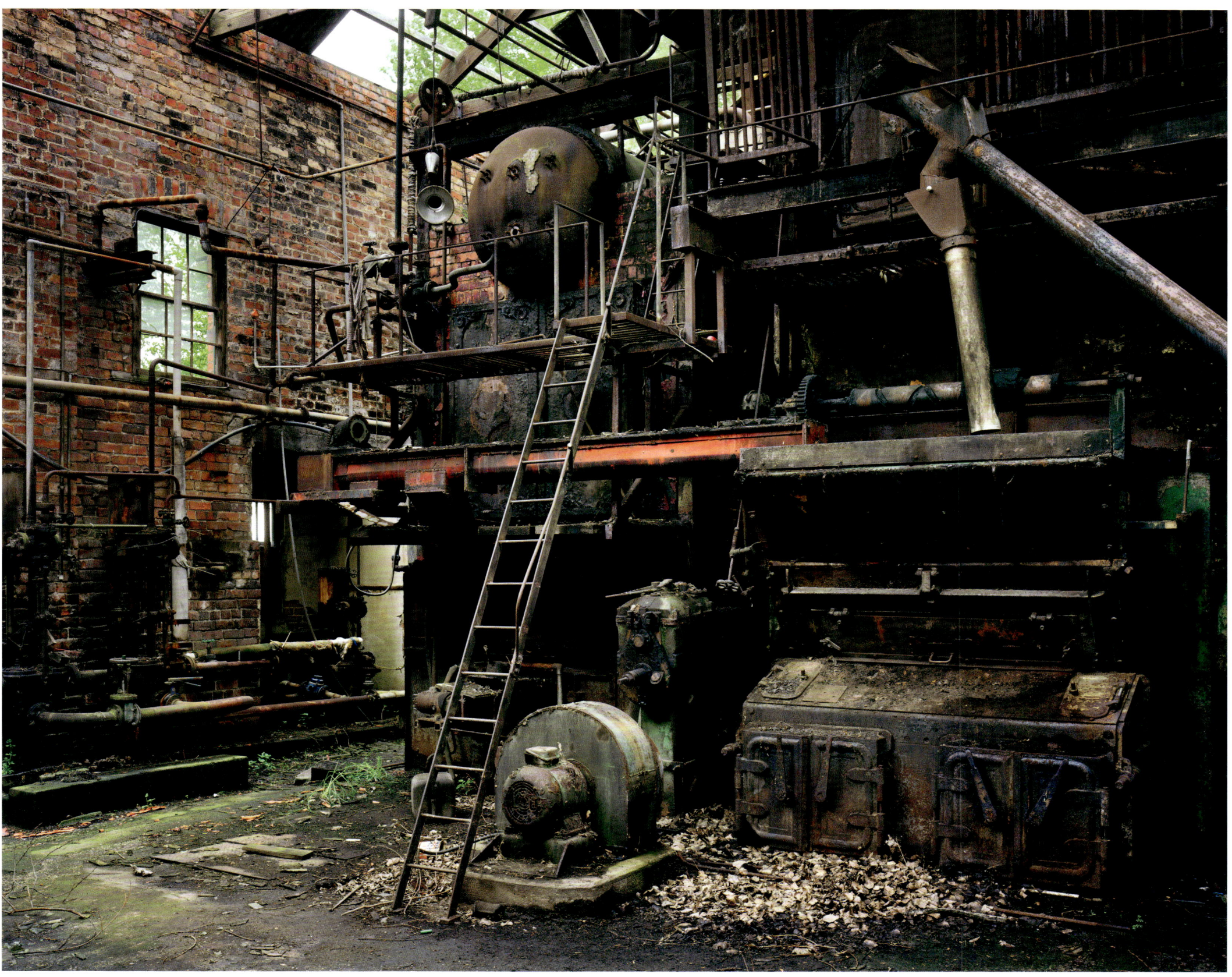

Boilers Behind the Bruce Woollen Mill, Milton, 2017

Mill Town might have remained a small settlement or even vanished were it not for the discovery of gold thirty kilometres away at Gabriel's Gully in 1861. Overnight, the town became a staging post for the gold rush, and its main street was soon lined with two-story brick and stone buildings to serve the miners flooding into the region from as far away as California. The name of the town was later shortened to Milton, calling to mind the famed seventeenth-century English poet John Milton. Various streets in the new town grid were also named for British literary figures (such as Abercrombie, Chaucer, Dryden, and Shakespeare), illustrating the town's ambition.

As with Baildon, Yorkshire, where my father was born, the woollen industry became the backbone of Milton. New Zealand's first woollen mill was built just north of the town in 1871, and, in little more than a decade, more were operating in the greater region—at Kaiapoi, Roslyn, Ōamaru, and Ashburton. Residents of Milton had petitioned for a mill since at least 1868, but it was only as the population grew in the 1870s—with help from assisted immigration schemes—that the prospect became viable. Fundraising efforts began, in which many locals purchased shares, and construction on the mill commenced in 1897. On 23 March that year (also Otago Day, commemorating the arrival of the first European settlers in the region in 1848), the town turned out to witness the mayor laying the first foundation stone. The *New Zealand Geographic* later wrote that the event would 'long be looked back on as a red-letter day'.

The construction of the mill progressed quickly, with manufacturing officially beginning on 19 November 1897. An initial staff of twenty-three quickly grew to over eighty, and the mill won a gold medal for blankets, wheeling yards, and hosiery in its first nationwide competition at the 1898 Otago Jubilee Industrial Exhibition. Needing to grow to meet new demand, the mill's board went to its local shareholders, asking them to forgo dividends and to contribute extra capital to fund expansion. At the same time, however, almost without warning, the price of raw wool increased dramatically and the demand for worsted yarn, Milton's main product, fell. The dire situation saw the mill left with over £2,000 (£218,500 today) of unsold goods, and by the end of the year it faced the first of several insolvencies.

On the morning of 28 April 1901, a fire ripped through the mill's recently expanded buildings. A neighbour, Miss Gibb, told the *Bruce Herald*, 'The task [of fighting the fire] was hopeless in the face of the primitive methods that had to be resorted to, and the flames, fanned by the strong wind, which was blowing at the time, rapidly spread to the ceiling. It was then plain to all that the mill was doomed.' The fire left most of the cutting-edge machinery a write-off and destroyed stockpiled product. The buildings had covered more than an acre and a half of the city, but now, apart from some red brick walls, only smouldering ruins remained. After the loss, the *Bruce Herald* reflected, 'The scores of young people, formerly employed at the mills, who are now compelled to wander aimlessly about the streets, is perhaps the most lamentable feature about the disastrous fire.'

Not long afterwards, though, the board called a town meeting. Rousing pledges were made to 'Stand by Bruce', and—with 172 staff and locals taking up some £10,500 (£1,084,000 today) of further shares, and an insurance payment forthcoming—rebuilding began.

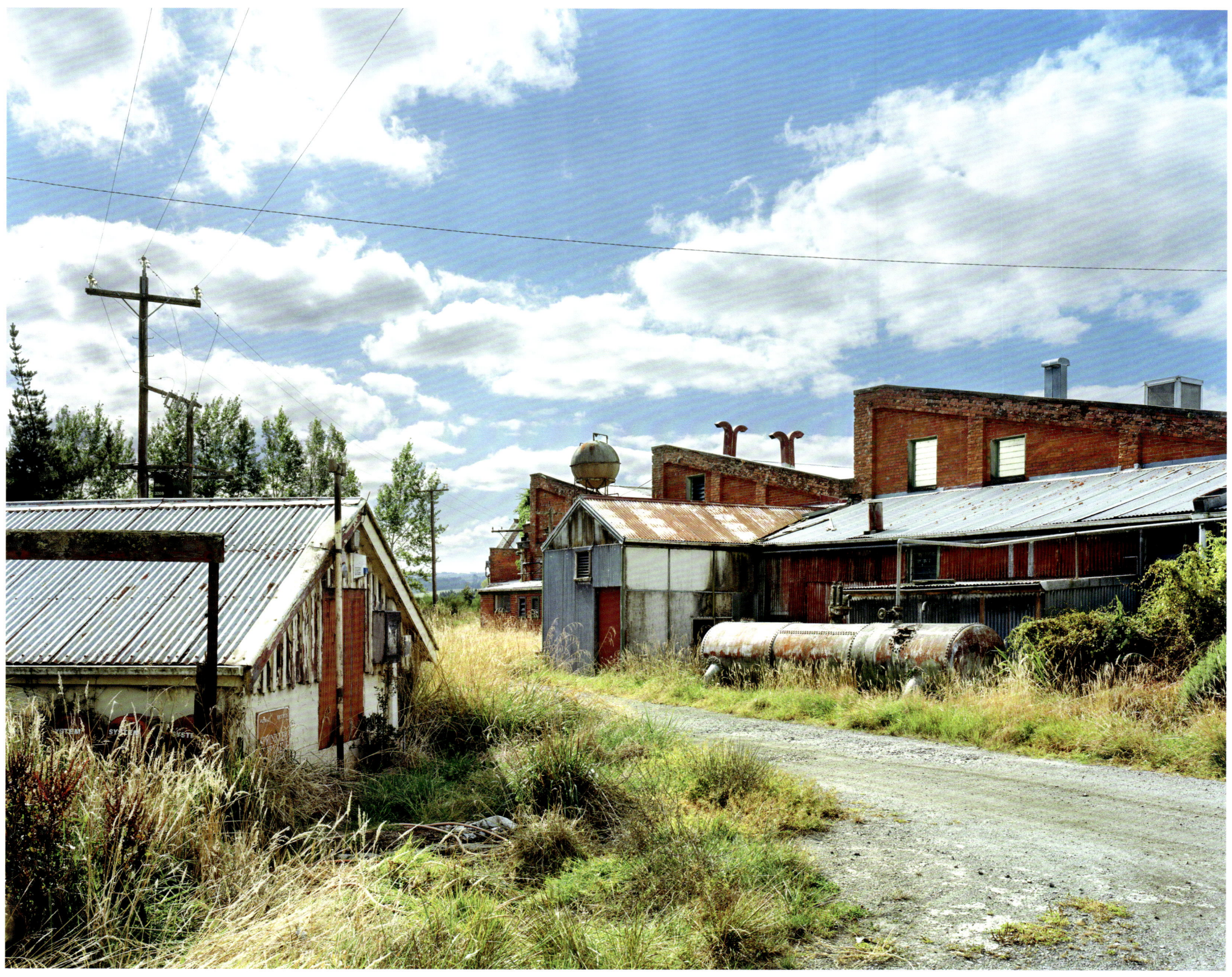

Spinning Machines, The Bruce Woollen Mill During Receivership, Milton, 2016

Following the devastating fire at the Bruce Woollen Mill in Milton in 1901, the workers began rebuilding it themselves. By the middle of 1902, the mill was again operational. For the next thirty years, production ran smoothly, until the Great Depression of the 1930s. Facing a large decrease in sales, shifts were reduced to a 'soul-destroying' two or three days a week, and even the directors took pay cuts of 36%. In 1933, William Moore—who had been the chairman since 1896 while continuing to work as the local grocer—died and was replaced by Peter McNish McSkimming of McSkimming's brick and pipe works. Under McNish, the mill became one of the first in the country to directly market to consumers (the marketing push even extended to the inclusion of products in the 1934 Canadian National Exhibition in Toronto). Within just a few years, Milton had outlet stores in many of New Zealand's largest cities and had established a popular mail-order programme.

With the outbreak of the Second World War in 1939, many of Milton's male staff volunteered to serve and the town's women had to be brought on as workers. Further women were bussed in from Balclutha, and the mill produced large quantities of khaki clothing for the army, along with air force uniforms and other products for the war effort. However, maintenance and innovation lagged, and, further hindered by post-war labour shortages and a lack of spending power, the mill entered a decade-long slump. By the late 1950s, a post-war boom saw business thrive again. Over 100 staff were added to the hosiery department in Dunedin along with a weaving section in Lawrence. But the recovery did not last, and, a decade later, the woollen industry was struggling again, with dire consequences for independent regional operations like Milton.

Overseas manufacturing had introduced synthetic fibres, which were poorer in quality but significantly cheaper to produce. Meanwhile, the cost of raw wool and production was rising locally. To compete, mill machinery constantly needed to be upgraded, creating a huge financial burden and risk. For these reasons, the Bruce Woollen Mill board accepted a buyout by Alliance Textiles of Ōamaru in 1962. The following year, the *New Zealand Financial Times* wrote that Alliance had 'drawn up their blueprint for integrating the operations of the three big textile mills and perfecting a scheme of rationalisation that must make the group the most influential in the textile field in the country'. However, the overseas tide was too great to stem, and the next decades at the mill saw a sequence of redundancies, closures, strikes, and buyouts. In 1999, it finally closed. Between 2012 and 2015, an attempt was made at a relaunch, but this also failed and receivership began.

Today, the railyard on the main South Trunk Line behind the mill lies silent. Past a graveyard of abandoned cars, overgrown with gorse and weeds, and beside a gravel lot where the train station once stood, tracks still turn off to the complex. Ivy growing on the crumbling brickwork obscures what used to be doors to the loading bay, from which the factory sent out its product for nearly 100 years. Inside is a man who worked there decades ago. His job is now to sell the once state-of-the-art machines for parts and scrap. In one room, a homespun Hi-Fi system connected to a web of speakers sits next to old spinning machines—soul tracks like "Never Can Say Goodbye" echoing through the dark, deserted mill.

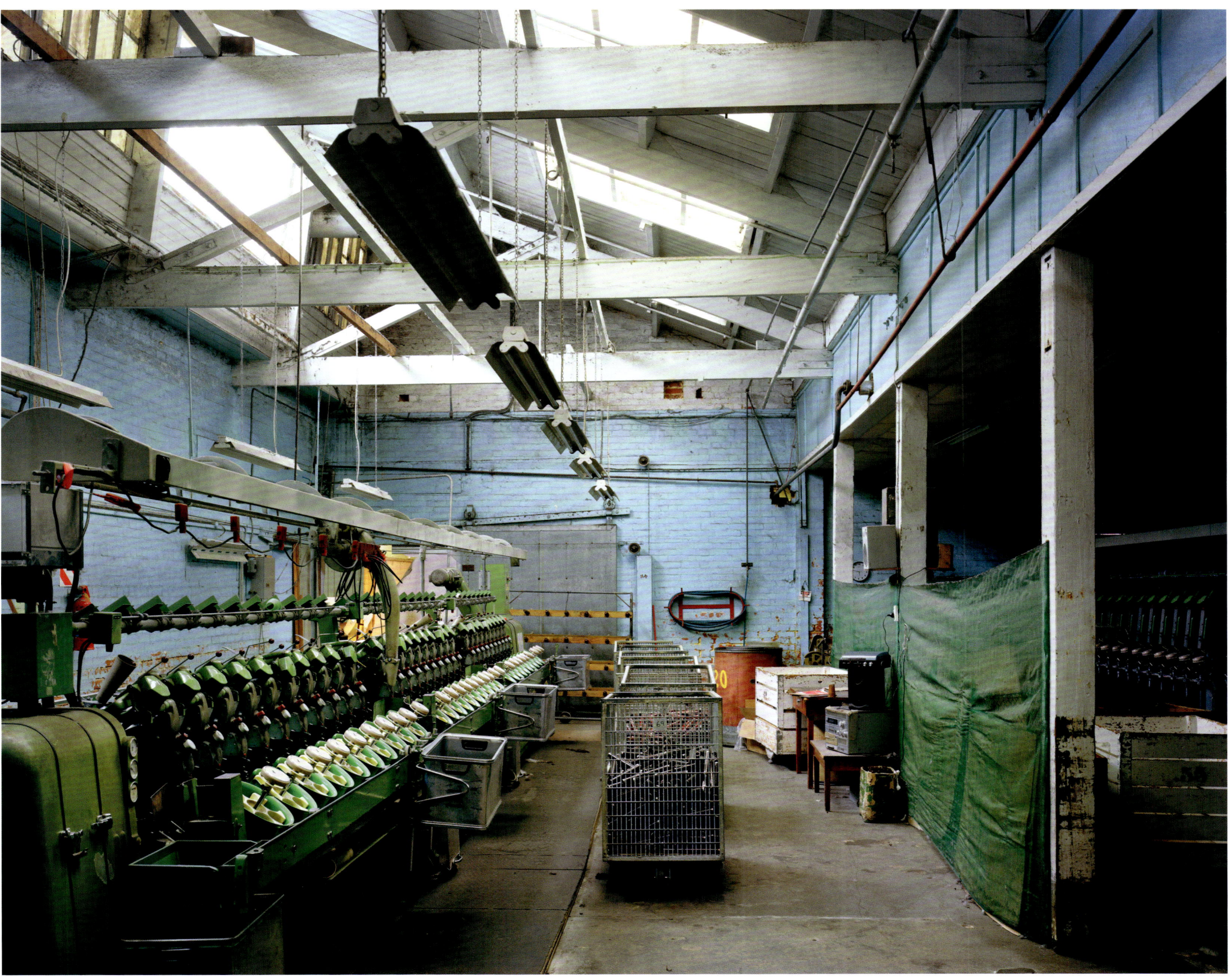

Gregg and Company Chicory Kiln, Clutha River / Mata-Au, Inch Clutha, 2016

Although the Waikato River is New Zealand's longest, the Clutha River / Mata-Au is the swiftest and carries the most water. Forming in Mount Aspiring National Park above Lake Wānaka, the Clutha flows nearly 340 kilometres through Central Otago before splitting into two branches at Balclutha and following the ten-kilometre-long Inch Clutha delta to the sea. A seasonal Māori settlement once lay at the river mouth, and later, the first European whalers and sealers established Port Molyneux there. In 1844, the New Zealand Company seriously considered Molyneux as the main port for Otago, in place of Dunedin, but later subdivided and sold the fertile land of Inch Clutha and its surrounds in 1852.

The settlers who bought the land drained the delta's wetlands to establish farms, and the Inch Clutha School opened in 1854. By 1863, the ferry *S.S. Tuapeka* was regularly travelling a route fifty kilometres up and down the river between Molyneux and Tuapeka. In 1878, though, the Clutha was hit with one of the worst floods in the nation's history. In early August, a late snowfall half a metre deep covered most of Otago, with even more on the mountains and a snowdrift said to be twenty-five metres deep in the Carrick Range. A warm north-westerly then moved in, melting the snow as torrential rain also began. Farm buildings across Otago were submerged, hundreds of thousands of sheep and cattle were killed, and timber from destroyed structures flowed downstream, levelling bridges and buildings. The town of Balclutha lay a metre under the floodwaters and the settlement and schoolhouse at Inch Clutha were washed away. When the water finally receded, the delta was almost two metres higher than it had been and the river was no longer navigable and with its course changed.

Farmers began rebuilding at Inch Clutha, and the residents of Balclutha constructed flood banks along the river. In the wake of the flood, Gregg and Company coffee, spice, and starch manufacturers (founded in 1861) began offering free chicory seed to anyone who would grow for the company, and a Mr Baird of Inch Clutha began growing the crop, the root of which was a substitute for coffee beans before the invention of instant coffee. Chicory grew so successfully on the flood-enriched soils that Gregg and Company bought out Baird's farm and began planning the construction of a processing factory.

An *Otago Daily Times* article from 1881 notes, 'On Inch-Clutha, immediately opposite the Balclutha railway station, Messrs Gregg and Co. are erecting a chicory-kiln. … These works when completed will, it is believed, be the largest of their kind in the Australasian Colonies … and we are assured that the class of root now growing will when manufactured be superior to anything hitherto grown in the Colony. We heartily wish Messrs Gregg and Co. every success in the promotion of this new industry.' The article goes on to describe the factory's most impressive features, including 'patent drying tiles … specially imported for the purpose'.

The Inch Clutha chicory farm became New Zealand's primary 'coffee' producer. By 1905, it covered an area of fifty-six acres, and, in 1926, the three-story concrete factory was doubled in size. The business thrived until 1956, when the New Zealand Government lifted protective tariffs, rendering the local production of chicory unviable.

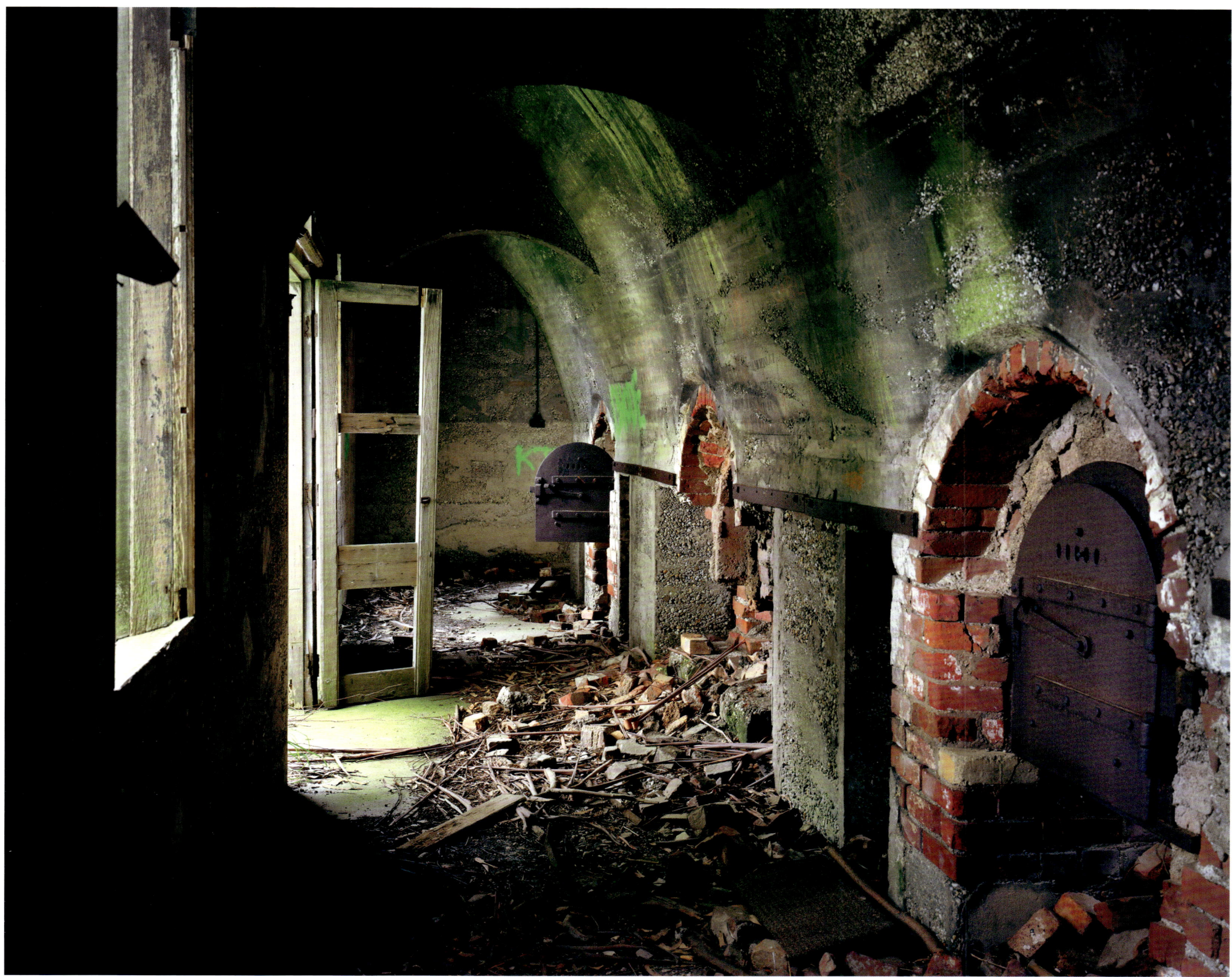

Winter Morning, Marawera Flour Mill, Near Tapawera, 2016

As many as 5,000 years ago, in the region of Khorasan in ancient Egypt, bread was being made from wheat, barley, and emmer—the grains crushed by hand with rocks, before being kneaded with water into loaves and cooked over open fires. The practice did not change significantly until about 500 BCE, when the development of hand-driven grinding stones gave rise to the first dedicated flour mills in ancient Greece. By the time of the Roman Empire, mills were being driven by water wheels, which dramatically improved the scale and speed of production. Mills rapidly spread throughout Europe, and in the nineteenth century, they made their way to New Zealand, where flour became a key industry of the colonial period.

One of the first mills was built in the early 1870s at Marawera, which lies in a lush alluvial valley beneath the Wharepapa Range and the 1,795-metre Mount Arthur. Through the valley, a two-lane road follows the bends of the Motueka River. A few remaining wooden hop and tobacco kilns on small farms and lifestyle blocks dot the landscape. Further on, near Tapawera, a gravel driveway lined with century-old oak trees leads to a homestead and assortment of farm buildings, and in the distance sits the Marawera Flour Mill. Now lying unused, the mill once anchored a community by creating a local supply. Although records say that it opened in 1871, its origins are earlier. In the 1860s, parts of an original structure at Wickham Market in Suffolk, England, were dissembled and exported to New Zealand.

Cutting-edge technology at the time of its construction, the Marawera Mill was driven by a water-turbine below ground, fed by ceramic pipes that connected to a holding tank on the hill above. Owing to the creation of a railway connection, use of the mill at Marawera had rapidly declined by the early twentieth century when it became cheaper to purchase flour made in city factories. After this, subsequent owners of the farm sometimes used the mill to produce small amounts of flour well into the 1950s, but it was no longer a necessity. Over the following decades, the building then became little more than a barn, storing farm implements, and sometimes hay.

Despite the farm changing hands several times since the 1870s, most of the mill's workings have remained intact, each owner seeing some value in its history. Even today, inside the mill, beneath the claustrophobically low ceiling of the ground level, a blacksmith shop dating to the Great Depression remains—the tools covering the hand-sawn benches almost rusted together and buried beneath layers of dust. In the corner of the room, and nearly invisible in the dark, an impossibly narrow staircase twists towards the upper level, and as I climb the creaking steps, rats scurry across the floorboards back to their nests. In the dim, dusty, and constricted upstairs room, beneath a small window, sits a large grinding stone. Although the mill hasn't been used for over sixty years, everything remains in its place, as if the staff left at the end of the day and never returned.

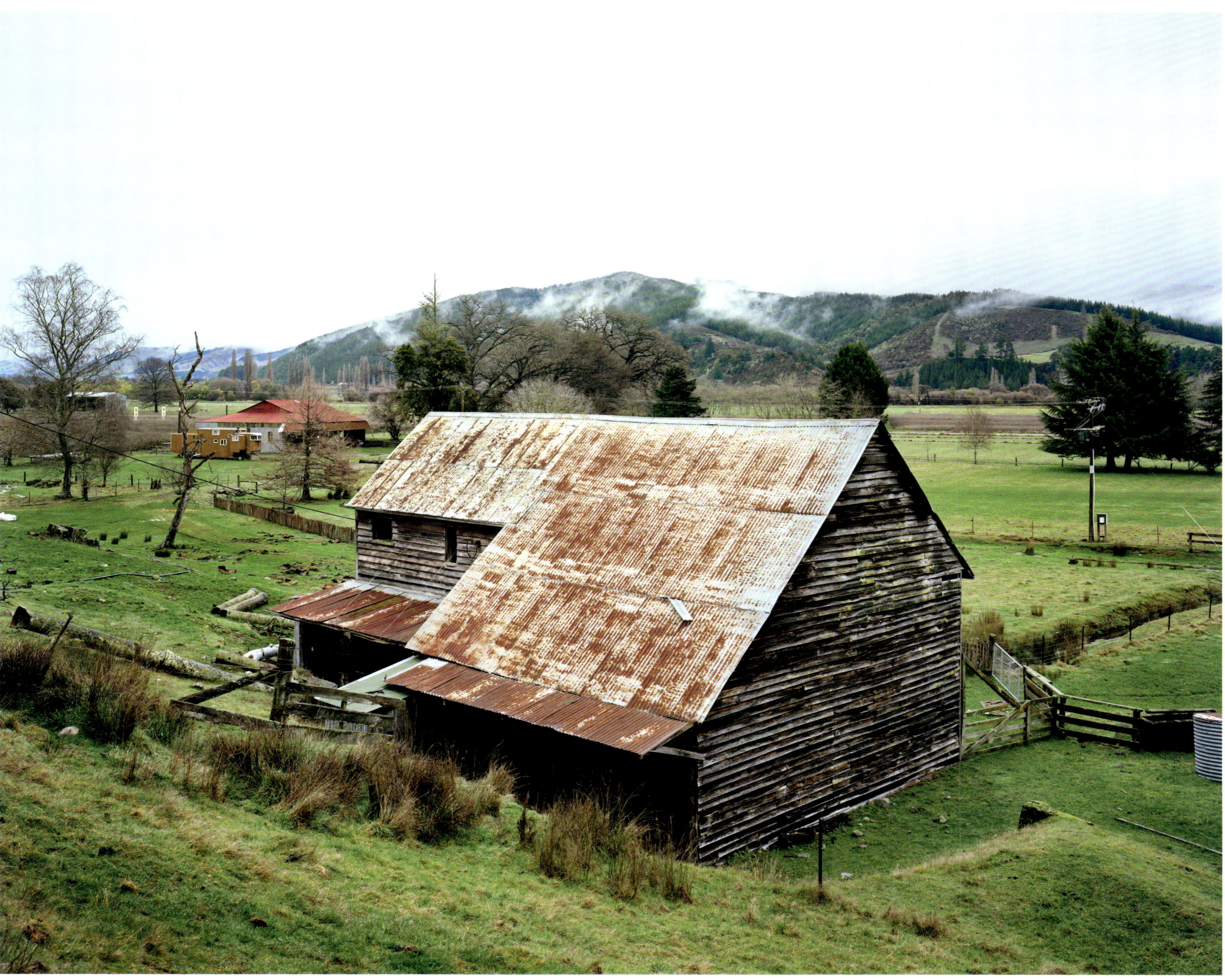

San Pedro Drying in the Upper Level of the Hoffman Kiln, Former McSkimming Brickworks, Benhar, 2016

Coal was first discovered near the mouth of the Clutha River during a land-surveying expedition in 1844. Twenty years later, the Benhar Coal Company opened five kilometres east of Balclutha. Deposits of good clay were found, too, and within a decade the company was also making ceramic sewer pipes, which were in high demand in the developing region. A year after the works opened, Archibald Anderson, who owned an adjacent 750-acre block, surveyed land three kilometres from the factory for a service town he named Stirling. By threatening to force the railway around the large block, he convinced the Government to divert the Main South Railway Line—then expanding south—to his yet-to-be-built town, and Sterling thus gained a railway station. Proximity to the rail line proved a boon to the Benhar pipe works, and by the 1890s, it had over fifty staff and had begun making bricks, tiles, and garden vases.

Around 1894, the company's owner, John Nelson, decided to lease the pipe-making business to former employees Peter McSkimming and his son, Peter McNish McSkimming, and the pair later purchased it outright. Among their first actions as management was the construction of a Hoffman kiln. The German-designed kiln type was a breakthrough in brick manufacture, its multiple chambers allowing bricks to be produced continuously. Having more than tripled their output, and continually expanding, Benhar became perhaps New Zealand's only true 'English factory town'. By 1903, it had the production capacity to supply half of the stoneware pipes for Dunedin's new sewerage scheme. In the 1905 *Cyclopedia of New Zealand*, the entry for Stirling—where most of Benhar's workers then lived—notes, 'It has an Athenæum [library], public school, dairy factory, one hotel, and two smithies; and across the Matau branch of the Clutha River is the pretty village church, with its pointed spire, which forms a conspicuous object for miles around the district.'

In the early 1900s, McSkimming's son-in-law Parker McKinlay made research trips to England to acquire clay and glaze recipes for sanitaryware, and, in the following decades, Benhar became New Zealand's sole manufacturer of the same. Upon his return from a trip in 1920, he brought ceramicist Thomas Lovett into the company and Benhar began producing a wide range of domestic ware and other ceramics. Lovett later went on to found Te Rona pottery in Temuka. In this golden period, Benhar had eight muffle kilns, three large bottle kilns, and used 10,000 tons of coal a year, drawing clay from an area of nearly 500 acres. The Hoffman kiln, however, now mostly remained inactive, because its continuous firing went against the Presbyterian beliefs of the McSkimming family, and it was later converted into a boiler house.

In 1980, McSkimming was sold to Ceramco Limited, which owned Crown Lynn, the country's main producer of dinnerware. In 1989, though, a relaxation of regulation allowed the import of mass-produced ceramics, and Ceramco went out of business. The makers of Fowler Bathroom Products bought Benhar that same year, but just a year later, a fire gutted the works leaving only the Hoffman kiln and manager's office standing. The new owner of the damaged factory began clearing the site in 1992, demolishing the Hoffman kiln's iconic chimney until he was blocked by locals, who formed a human chain around the building. The kiln is now protected by a heritage order, but the structure remains in a state of decay.

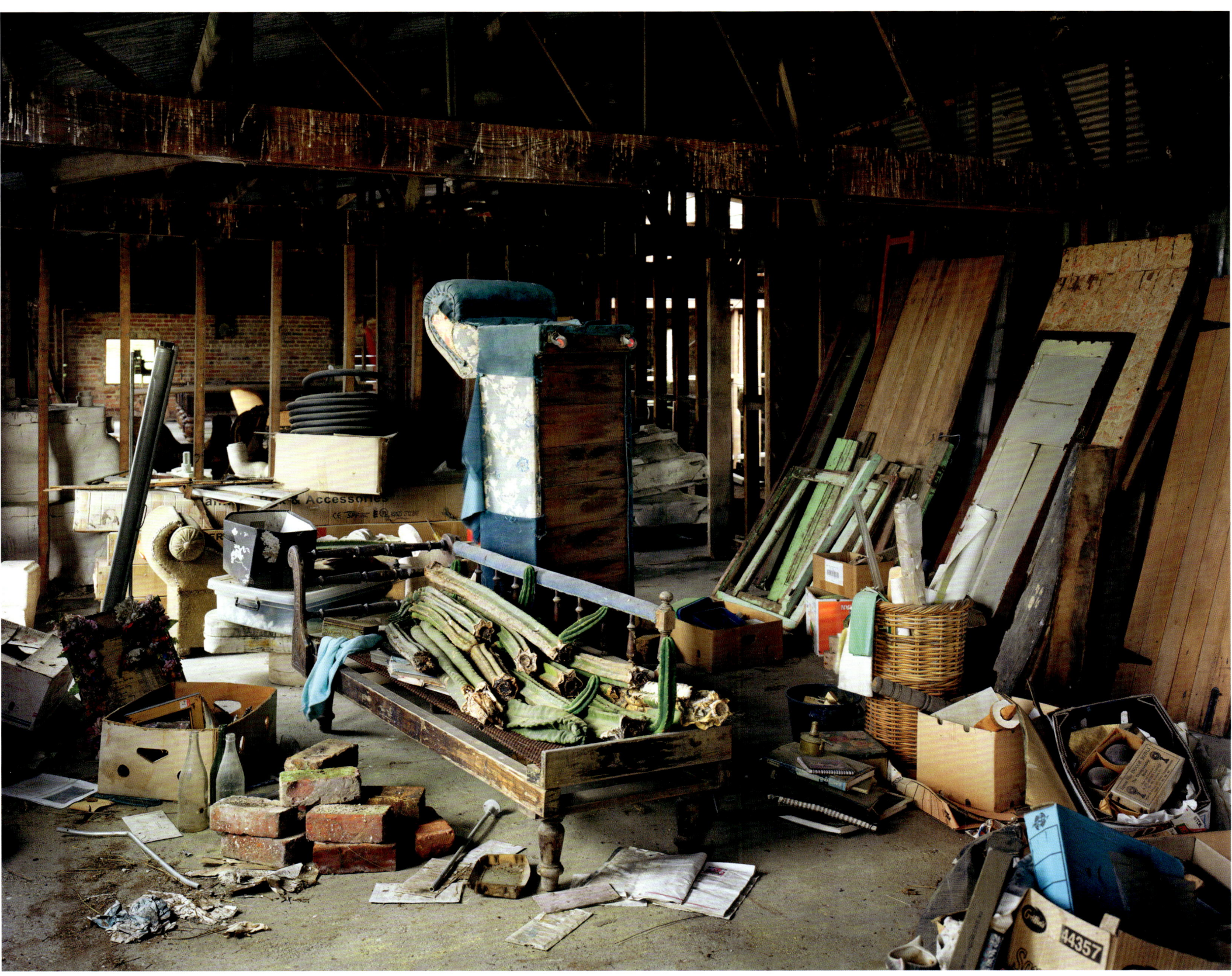

Remains of McCallum's Mill, Ōpārara, Karamea, West Coast, 2016

Karamea sits on the northernmost plain of the West Coast region, beneath the vast rainforests of the Tasman Mountains, which run nearly 100 kilometres to Golden Bay at the top of the South Island. It is one of the earliest known settlement sites on the West Coast, archaeological evidence showing that Māori were occupying sites on the Heaphy River, some twenty kilometres north of Karamea, as early as 1350. There was extensive pounamu (greenstone) gathering on the river, while south, and beyond Karamea, midden remains have been found at nearly every river mouth, indicating myriad settlements and extensive travel up and down the coast. The original name of the Karamea River is Kakara Taramea ('sweet-smelling taramea'), referring to the taramea (speargrass) that once grew on both banks, its leaves heated to extract resin, which was mixed with bird fat to create perfume.

The Karamea River provided one of the West Coast's few natural ports, but as Europeans arrived, initial colonial surveys found little gold or coal, and so the place went largely untouched by the first waves of settlement and industry. Its isolation was such that when a group from England and the Shetland Islands began building the settlement of Karamea in 1874, it was still accessible only by ship, and for decades, farming functioned purely at the level of subsistence. The area remained separated from the greater coast until 1911, when a cooperative butter factory opened and a road south over the Radiant Range connected Karamea with the rest of the West Coast.

Now Karamea buzzed with industry. Flax from the swamps behind the beach was milled, and at least five sawmills logged the vast beech forests that stretched across the mountains behind the flats of Karamea. A 1918 survey plan of the district shows the land along the coast subdivided into small farming blocks, while native forest owned by the Crown was divided into blocks and leased to the many sawmilling companies. In this period, a port still operated from the mouth of the river exporting timber, but after the 1929 earthquake at Murchison to the south, the waterway permanently silted up and became unnavigable.

Despite the industrial activity, Karamea has remained a modest settlement due to its remote location and the relatively small land area between the coast and the mountains. In 2002, logging of the West Coast's native forests was finally banned by the Government, and much of Karamea's forest is now decades into regeneration, the only obvious markers of the history of extraction being former logging tracks and the remains of McCallum's Mill. Beyond the gravel road on which McCallum's sits are the Ōpārara Arches, a series of breathtaking limestone formations that span mirror-like pools deep within the forest. The road once built to log the forest is now a path used by tourists. Owing to increased use, the winding and narrow way has over the decades led to several fatal accidents, and it is soon to be widened and sealed.

To the north of Kamamea is the area's other major tourist attraction, the Heaphy Track, one of New Zealand's most popular 'Great Walks'. Building on the former pounamu trail and nineteenth-century expeditions, the track runs for eighty-two kilometres; after four to six days, hikers emerge at Tākaka Hill near Golden Bay at the top of the South Island. The track is walked by thousands of people each year, and booking fees for the Department of Conservation's huts along the route generate revenue of over $1 million per annum.

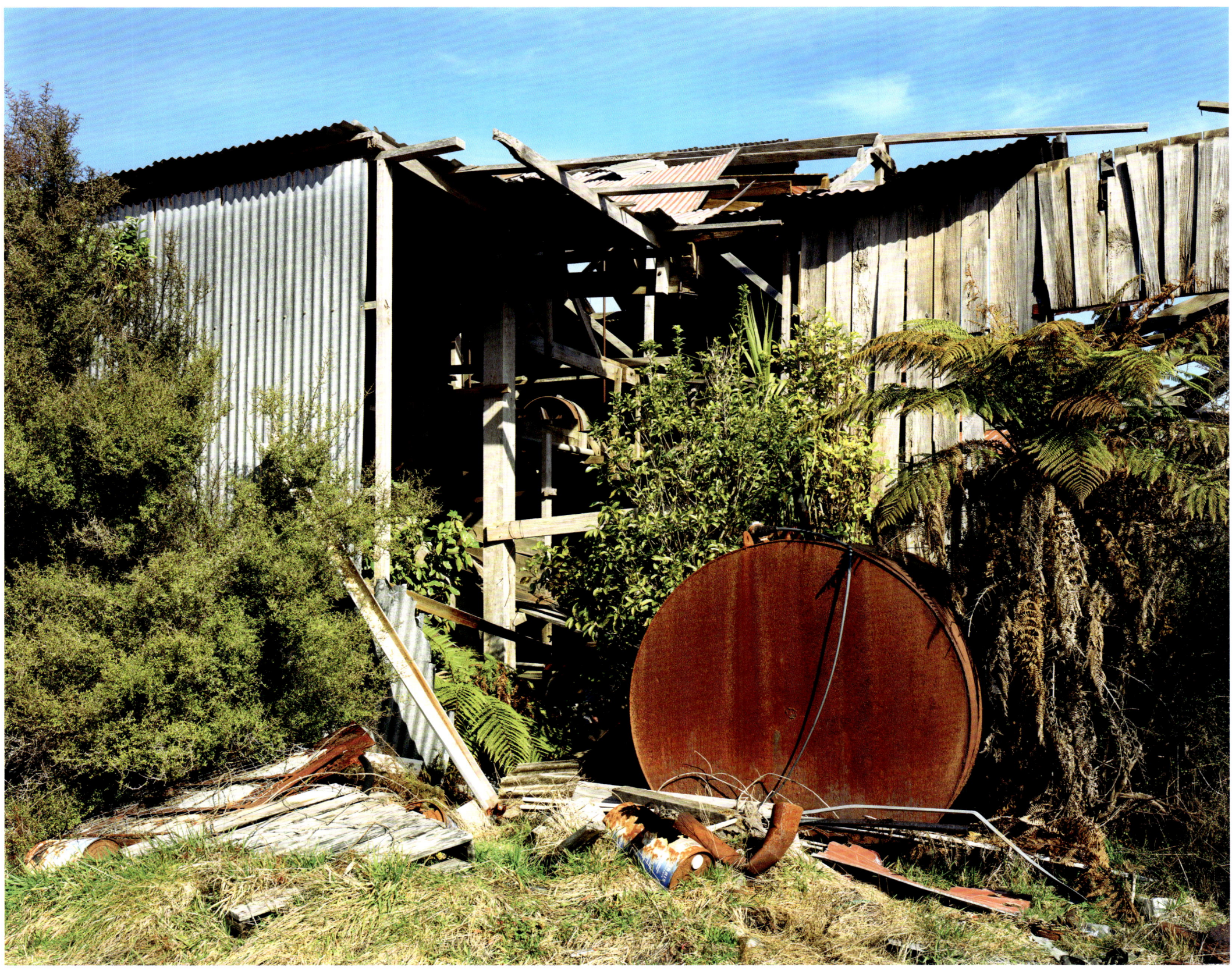

A Poet Writing Before the Falls and Freezing Works, Mataura, 2016

Known as Te Au Nui, meaning 'the big swirling waters' or 'the great current' in Māori, for centuries the Mataura Falls have been an important mahinga kai (source of food and resources) for Ngāi Tahu. Although there was no permanent Māori settlement in the area before European arrival, the place was well-known for being abundant in kanakana (lamprey), which swam upriver between October and December. In a good year, the fish numbered in their thousands, and people came from as far away as Ōtautahi Christchurch to catch them. The falls also indicated an area, a bit further downstream, where the swift-flowing Mataura River could be safely forded, and as Europeans arrived in the region in the early 1850s, this drew them to the site as well.

In 1853, the entire southern part of the South Island—nearly seven million acres stretching from Fiordland to Stewart Island to Gore and Mataura—was purchased from Ngāi Tahu by the Otago Provincial Government for £2,600 (£274,500 today). Just 4,588 acres were set aside as 'reserves for the resident natives'. Below the Mataura Falls, a ferry was established to get horse-drawn vehicles across the river, superseding a perilous route around the eastern coast. In 1859, the Provincial Government constructed a thirty-metre wooden truss footbridge across the river, the central support of which rested on a large rock in the middle of Te Au Nui. However, the footbridge was constantly slippery with spray from the falls, and after continued complaints, the forwardmost part of the falls was removed with dynamite. Just two years later, a flood washed out the bridge, and a new suspension bridge was built downstream where the present bridge remains.

By the early 1880s, Mataura had become an industrial hub for Southland, powered by two stalwarts: a freezing works on one side of the river and the Mataura Paper Mill on the other. The industries changed the river further and radically. A weir was constructed across its width above the falls to supply hydroelectric generators that then impeded the migration route of the kanakana. The freezing works has continued to expand and is still in business. The mill was bought by Carter Holt Harvey in 1991. Citing intense pressure from Asian competition and over $1 million per annum in losses in the late 1990s, the Australian multinational closed the mill in August 2000 resulting in 155 redundancies.

Sifting through boxes of photographs at the Mataura Museum, I find a collection of fading Polaroids of staff from the mill. In the pictures, young people smile optimistically on their first day of work, and as I spread the Polaroids out, I realise the same people appear again at retirement parties, posing with cakes and farewell gifts of watches or dinnerware. Two decades after the closure of the mill, the pain of its loss can still be seen in Mataura's boarded-up shops as much as in the vast complex of buildings, now derelict and collapsing. In 2021, it was revealed that the new owners had been using the space to store 40,000 tons of water-soluble toxic aluminium dross from the Tiwai Point Aluminium Smelter, before the company folded and left the Government and aluminium industry to pay around $1 million in environmental remediation.

In 2006, a ten-kilometre stretch of the Mataura River encompassing Te Au Nui was approved as the first freshwater mātaitai (marine reserve) in New Zealand.

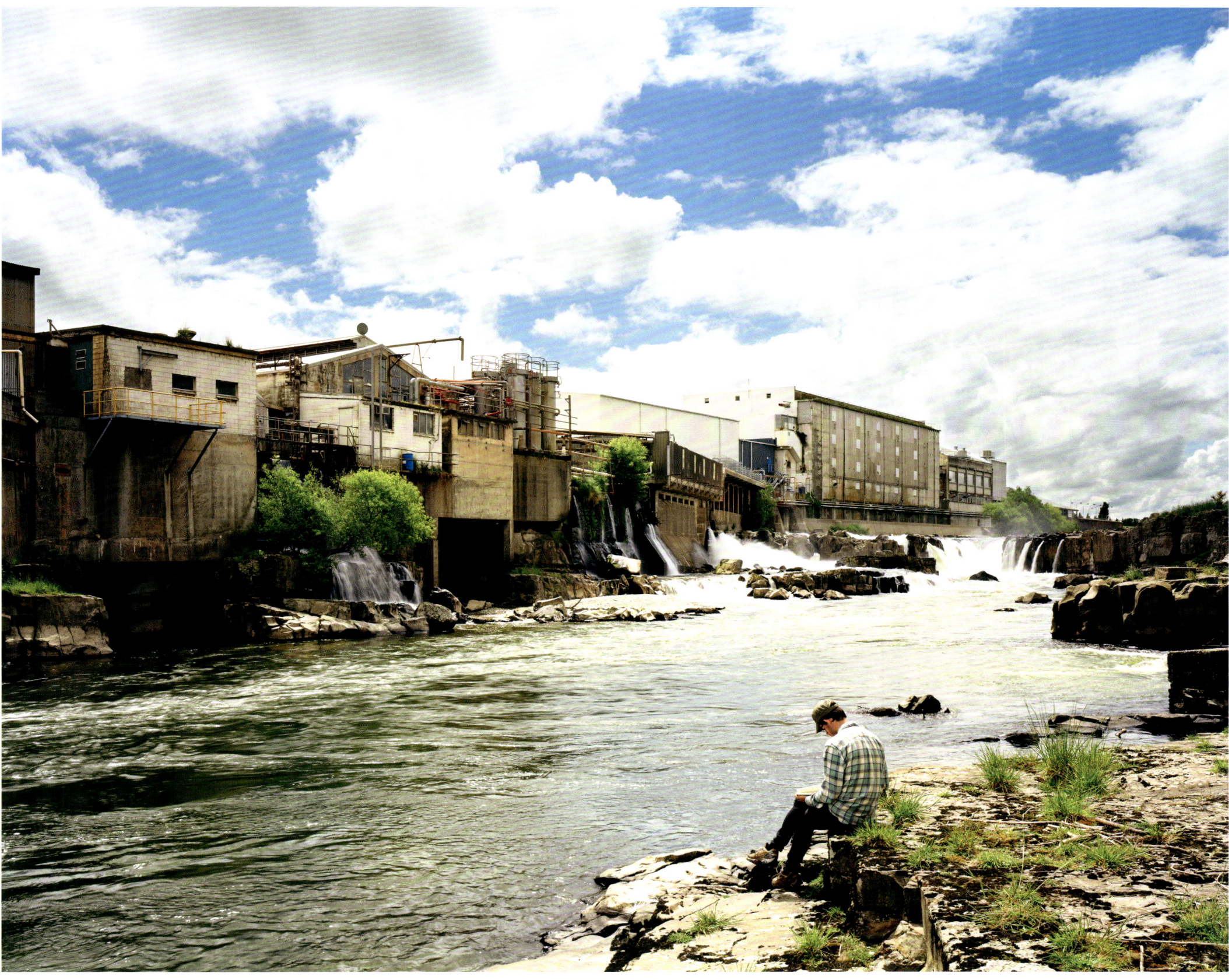

Winter, Powerhouse at the Old Escarpment Mine, Denniston Plateau, 2016

Coal mining began on the West Coast's Denniston Plateau in 1878. Of all New Zealand's coal-mining sites, it was Denniston that would become the best known—thanks to the technical triumph of the Denniston Incline, the popular 2003 novel *The Denniston Rose,* and the Department of Conservation's recent promotion of the area as a tourist attraction. Although it is perhaps a singular mine in the collective imagination, Denniston was in fact an ever-expanding network of mines, both public and private, of vastly different scales and configurations. In the nineteenth century, the first mines on the plateau—Banbury, Coalbrookedale, and Ironbridge—sat near the Denniston township and Incline, which carried coal down the mountain twenty-four hours a day. But as coal seams were exhausted, new companies moved to the area and mining spread to the most distant reaches of the plateau, over its cliffs, rivers, and valleys.

During the Second World War, mining operations at Denniston shrank due to a shortage of workers and the economic hardships of the period. A fire (which still smoulders underground today) saw the closure of the Ironbridge Mine in 1944, and the Whareatea Mine was left the sole large operator on the once-bustling plateau. Since Denniston was the major supplier of coal for New Zealand's railways, the drop in production exposed a national vulnerability, and in 1948, the Government passed the Act for the Nationalisation of Coal Mines and took over the Westport Coal Company. At Denniston, the State Mines Department reopened, improved, and expanded mines, while also pushing further onto the plateau. In 1954, activity reached its apex with the construction of an expensive aerial cableway that ran kilometres across the rugged terrain, from the new mines on the remote edge of the plateau to the Denniston Incline.

One of the last and most distant of the state mines to open was the Escarpment Mine, set just beneath the plateau's southernmost edge, which began operation in 1964. On one side of the mine, cliffs drop almost vertically 600 metres to the valley below, and on the other, rocky outcrops climb another 400 metres to the plateau's summit, Mount Rochfort. Like its forerunners in the area, the Escarpment Mine initially employed traditional underground mining techniques, the bulk of its workforce tasked with moving coal and debris from the coalface one wagon at a time. In 1979, though, it was redeveloped as the first state hydraulic mine. In hydraulic mining, shafts are dug at a slight uphill angle and pressurised water and gravity combine to wash coal and debris out of the mine and along metal fluming to coal-filtering screens below. The system reduces the quantity and intensity of labour required and dramatically improves mine safety.

Having exhausted the economically viable parts of its coal seam, the Escarpment Mine closed in 1982. A few kilometres away, the Sullivan Mine lasted a decade more thanks to hydraulic mining, before a global collapse in coal prices brought an end to mining on the plateau for good. Today, a small and decaying bright blue shed, once the powerhouse for hydraulic pumps that ran twenty-four hours a day, is—along with a decaying coal bin—the most tangible remnant of the Escarpment Mine. In the decades since work ended, the site has sat frozen in time, its fluming, buildings, dams, and native-timber coal bins left to moulder in the West Coast's endless wind and rain.

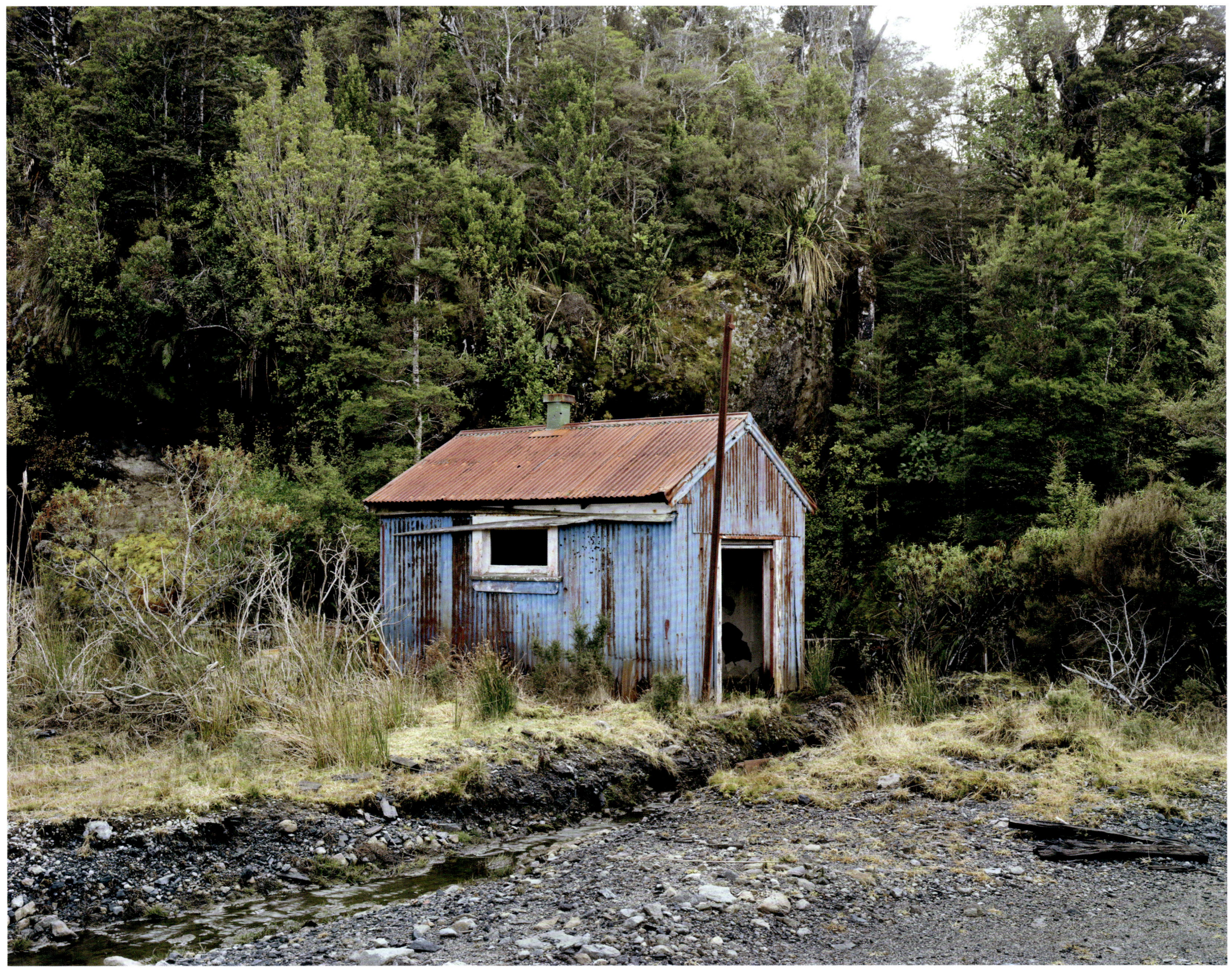

Collapsing Coal Bin, Escarpment Mine, Denniston Plateau, 2016

By the new millennium, new technology and an increase in coal prices had made mining on the Denniston Plateau viable once again. In 2005, New Zealand—owned L&M Coal Limited acquired a council permit for a mining exploration across more than 46,000 acres of the plateau. The company found more than forty-five million tons of unmined, high-quality coking and thermal coal, with over five million tons at the shuttered Escarpment Mine alone. Many of Denniston's early mining areas have heritage protection; however, the land itself is classified as stewardship land by the Department of Conservation, and, unlike national parks and conservation areas, it remains available for new mining. In 2008, L&M began negotiating with the Department for access for construction and hauling the coal, and in late 2011, the local and regional councils granted mining permits for the Escarpment Mine Project to the company, now known as Buller Coal Resources, following its acquisition by Australian conglomerate Bathurst Resources.

Conservation groups like Forest and Bird and the West Coast Environment Network mobilised national campaigns against the project, and within a month of the consent being issued they had filed appeals in the environmental court. Their case stressed that the project threatened rare landscapes and habitats for endangered species, and that in the face of climate change mining should cease. The conservation groups were supported in their opposition by Pure Advantage, a 'green capitalism' advocacy group composed predominantly of Auckland CEOs, of which Buller and Grey district mayors commented in a joint statement: '[They] talk about branding, but they run airports, airlines, bus [tour] and car companies, Chinese-based manufacturing, and spirit and wine companies—some of the world's most resource-intensive industries. All these industries need steel, and steel is made with hard coking coal, the type of coal that's found on the Denniston Plateau. This is high quality coal, not coal for use in power stations.'

Complicating the situation further still, Bathurst Resources had reached a deal to pay $22 million over seven years to the Department of Conservation, which would fund an estimated sixty years of pest and predator control across over 30,000 square kilometres of the Heaphy River catchment area in Kahurangi National Park, along with pest control and care of historic projects on the plateau itself. In October 2013, the Environment Court decided to allow the Escarpment Mine Project to proceed, and Forest and Bird elected not to appeal, instead reaching an agreement with Bathurst to create a 'Denniston Permanent Protection Area' exempt from future mining. In late 2014, Bathurst Resources purchased assets from Government-owned Solid Energy, then in receivership, and work on the project began.

The first stage took place adjacent to the Escarpment Mine, at the former Whareatea Mine. Before this, the mine was perhaps Denniston's best preserved historic site, but by 2015 it had been blasted into a series of opencast pits and lakes. The Escarpment Mine was to meet the same fate. However, the closure of the nearby Cape Foulwind Cement Works—one of the main buyers of its coal—in early 2016 led the project to be paused. A 2024 shareholder's report from Bathurst Resources notes that they have 'completed conceptual design options for the Upper Waimangaroa haul road, including assessment of a slurry pipeline option'. This would once again make the Escarpment Mine economically viable for the price of a wide gravel road or pipeline being carved through tens of kilometres of pristine wilderness.

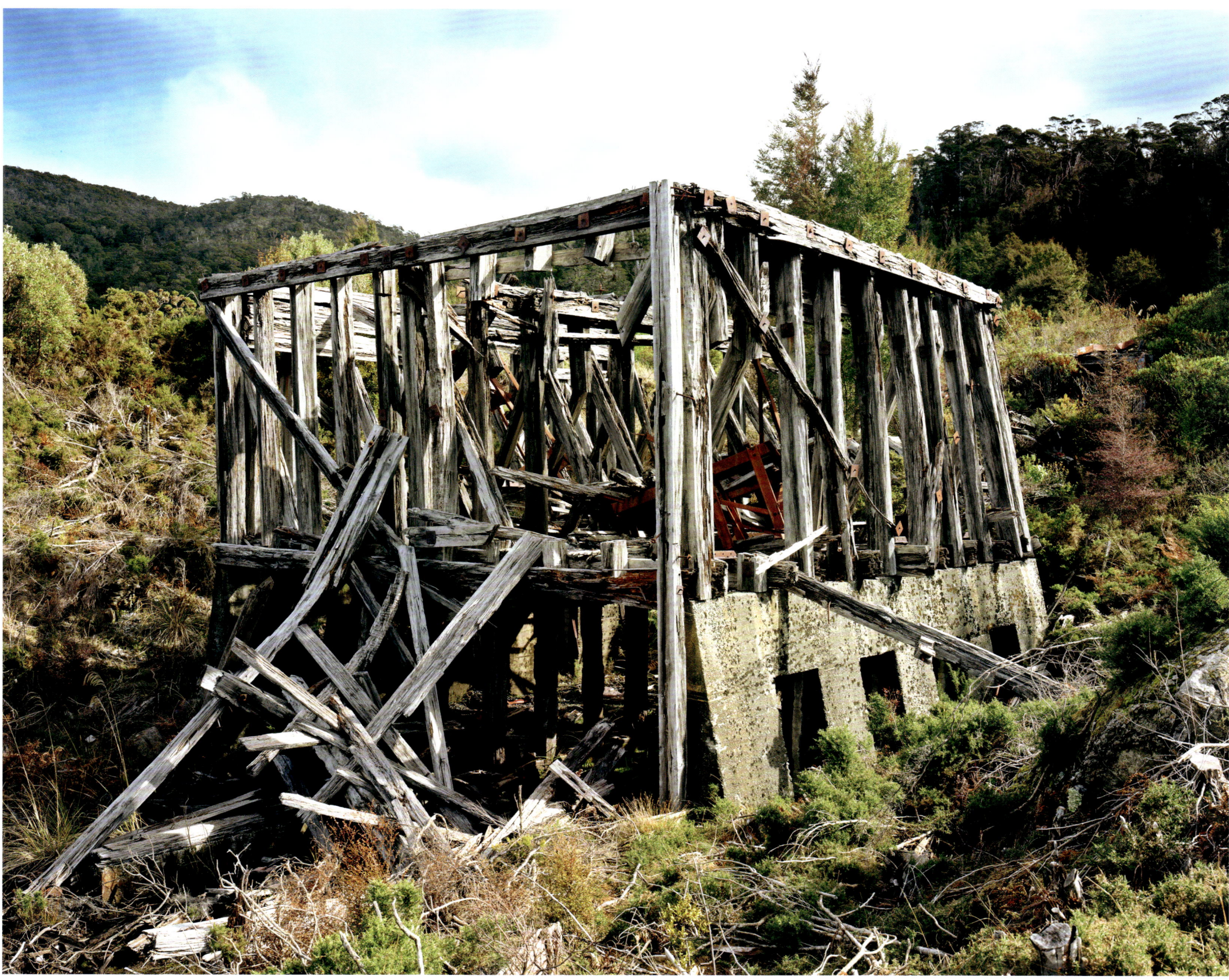

Saplings Growing Among the Sawmill (After Cleveland), Kopara Village, West Coast, 2016

A two-lane back road winds from Greymouth through pastures that stretch across vast river basins and over hills clad in dense regenerating kahikatea forest. Far into the hills, it passes Nelson Creek, where, in 1865, an early and short-lived gold rush saw 1,200 miners venture into this remote part of the West Coast. Still following the road, as it narrows and becomes gravel, the trees and mountains close in. Despite the beauty of the winter light filtering through the forest, I think of *Deliverance* (1972) and wonder what lies down the overgrown clay tracks, behind gates or assertive 'private property' signs. The area still has the feeling of being a frontier—its private sawmills, gold dredges, coal pits, hunting grounds, and possibly more nefarious endeavours concealed amid the dense forest.

As I descend into the Haupiri Valley, I find black ice lurking on hairpin bends where the light fails to break through the canopy. Emerging from the forest, the darkness lifts and, a short while later, the scattered, derelict remains of Kopara Village come into view across a small bridge and down another muddy track. The former settlement sits on the plains of the Haupiri River, beneath giant forest-clad mountains. In the twentieth century, it sprang to life around a sawmill where for decades men laboured, stripping the surrounding hills of the ancient kahikatea forest, which stretched for hundreds of kilometres. Today, the only movement at the sawmill, though, is the slow growth of saplings breaking through the collapsing frame.

In the 1950s, artist Les Cleveland—who was also a journalist, musician, and political science professor—worked as a lumberjack at this sawmill and took a series of photographs published in his 1966 book *The Silent Land: A Pictorial Record of the West Coast of the South Island of New Zealand*. Framed as a 'documentary photographer', in this country where the term is somewhat pejorative, Cleveland clearly intended his work to have poetic meaning (indeed, the publisher of the book, Caxton Press, was at the time the country's premier poetry imprint). Lest there be any doubt, beside the photographs are his words, which make the poetry of his vision clear:

> Are cracked timbers and sullen weeds
> A fitting epitaph to tragic failure?
> Can the land display no terms of settlement
> Except those of complacent pillage?
> Are its monuments an ironic tribute
> To a crippling smallness of vision,
> A mean and fatal economy of imagination,
> On the part of those now rotting in hurried graves?
> Or could there be further significance
> In this morbid confusion?
> Could it reflect the unpretentious philosophy
> Of those who care simply for present expediency
> Rather than the wreckage of the past?
> Are such squalid realities
> A belated, comic glimpse behind the façade
> Of vanished Victorian Arcadia?

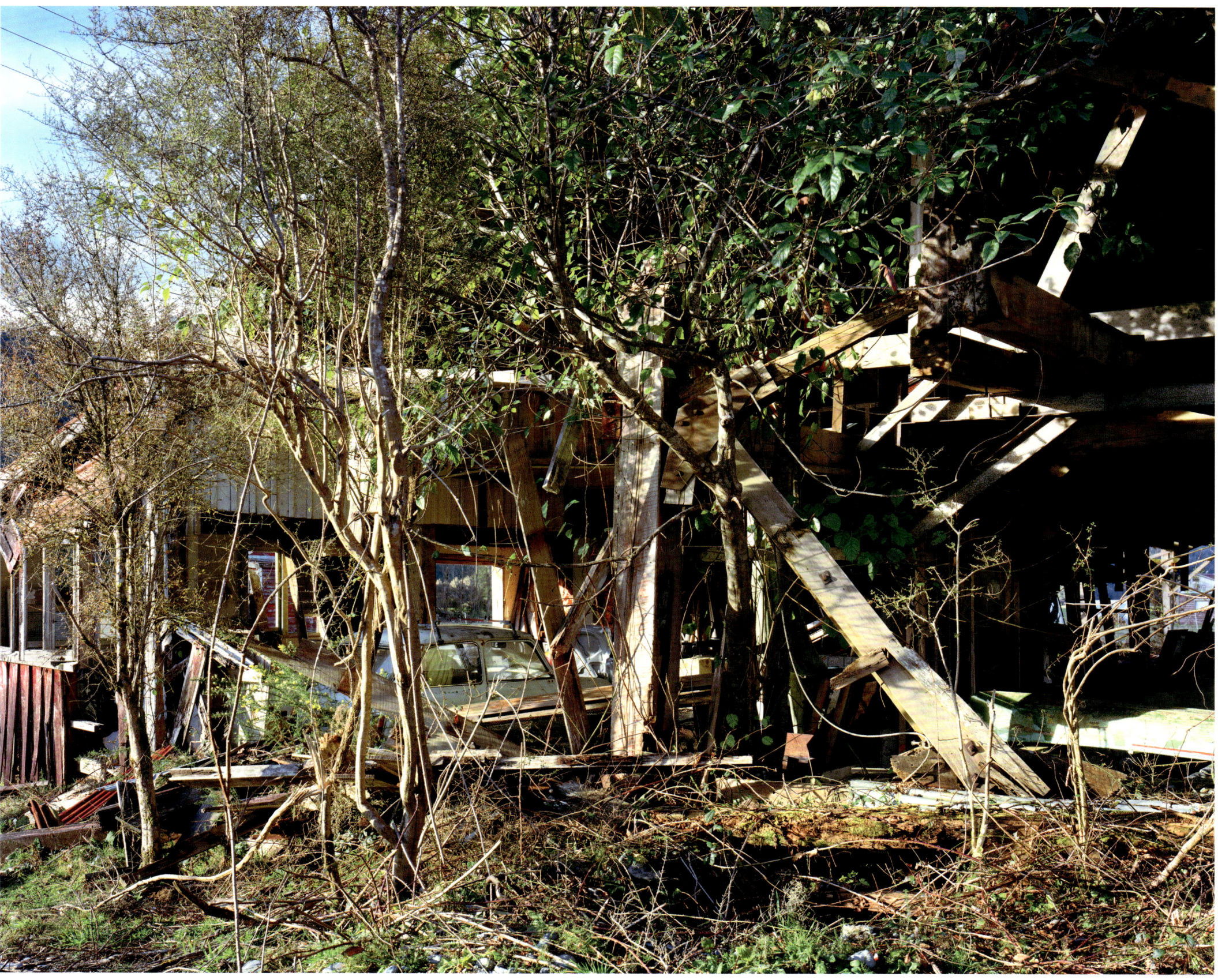

Late Evening, Looking North Towards the Limeworks, Clifden, 2017

In the middle of the nineteenth century, when European activity began at what would become Clifden, the swift and perilous Waiau River formed a natural boundary limiting colonial expansion into Southland. Some sixty kilometres north-west of Invercargill, near the bottom of the South Island, the area was first logged for ancient beech and tōtara that had been untouched by Māori. Next, through back-breaking labour, vast sheep stations were established upon the ruins of burnt and clear-felled forest. The endeavours required the crossing of the Waiau, and for a time, a punt service was used. But in 1899, Clifden's now-famous suspension bridge opened allowing settlement and industry to rapidly spread inland.

The entry for Clifden in the 1905 *Cyclopedia of New Zealand* records that a school, telephone bureau, and post office had all appeared since the construction of the bridge. In the typically aspirational, colonial tone of the period, the text describes 'large areas of bush country which have yet to be exploited for sawmilling purposes'. Meanwhile, the region became an early example of tourism in the country, well known for 'its bush-clad limestone cliffs, far-famed caves and trout-stocked waters, well worth a visit from a sightseer or a sportsman'. The *Cyclopedia* waxes lyrical about Clifden's cave system, too, one of the few in Southland, which formed in the Miocene Epoch from the gradual accumulation and compression of shell fragments, sand, and pebbles in a shallow sea: 'Whatever feeling of fatigue or annoyance may have been caused by the difficulty of crawling in, that vanishes completely under the spell of the beautiful scene, with its magical effects, as of glow-worms sparkling from the snow-white stalactites.'

Across the road from the cave entrance, Clifden's geology meets a different end in the quarry of the Clifden Limeworks, a rare industrial stalwart that has been in continuous operation since 1915. A simple website states that the plant's production consists of agricultural lime; nap rock for dairy lanes, forestry roads, and tracks; big rocks for flood protection; and grey rock for roading. It was in large part the availability of locally produced agricultural lime that jump-started the farming industry in the nineteenth century and became New Zealand's economic mainstay. Here in Clifden, the ancient limestone is carved from surrounding hills, crushed, and burned into a calcium-rich dust for spreading on pastoral fields to reduce soil acidity and increase the yields from livestock.

Today, few buildings remain at Clifden; the settlement is now little more than a rural school and golf club. But it is still a magnet for tourists. In addition to the caves, visitors come for the suspension bridge. Spanning 111.5 metres, it is the longest in the country and a Category 1 historic place. Designed by county engineer Charles Henry Howorth, also an early Southland artist, it features tall concrete pillars limewashed to look like local stone and thick steel cables, the latest technology when the bridge was built. Its trusses of tōtara and planks of Australian hardwood were praised at the time for the unusual care of their craftsmanship. Now, though, the striking pillars rise above an almost-empty landscape. A meagre campsite flat sits to one side of the structure, and a bland modern bridge on State Highway 99, a few hundred metres down river, has since bypassed its predecessor.

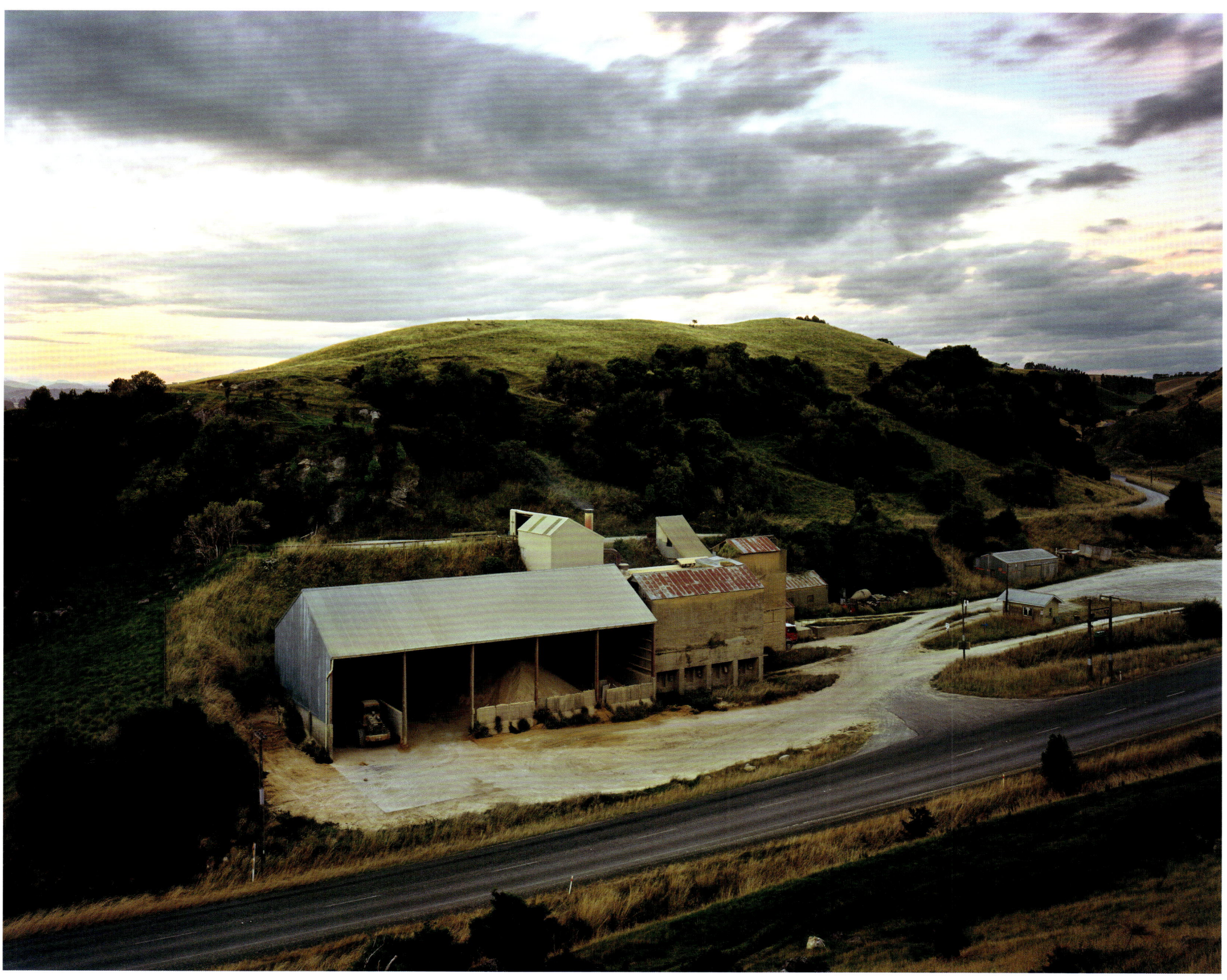

Bridge at Middle Break, Denniston Incline (After Lock), West Coast, 2016

East of Westport, a two-lane road traces the coast's flat alluvial plains, above which the Denniston Plateau rises steeply to nearly 700 metres. Then, 300 metres higher still, is the plateau's summit, Mount Rochfort, from which on a clear day it seems as though Denniston floats above the world and the Tasman Sea stretches west forever. The mountain was named by the German geologist Julius von Haast (also the first director of the Canterbury Museum) during an expedition funded by the Nelson Provincial Council in honour of John Rochfort, the English surveyor who first found coal in a creek near Denniston in 1859. After this, surveys by von Haast and James Burnett established the abundance of coal on the plateau, and in 1878, the Westport Colliery Company was formed to begin its exploitation.

Initially, the plateau was only accessible via a pack track that climbed a gruelling 600 vertical metres. This left the company with the puzzle of how to move the huge quantities of coal they anticipated extracting from the area. Their solution was the most audacious engineering project of all those dreamt up on the West Coast: the Denniston Incline. Traversing more than two kilometres and rising over 500 metres, the system relied on gravity alone to operate, with full coal wagons descending from the plateau on one track and their weight hauling empty wagons back up on another. The only measure of control was a rudimentary steam braking system, located halfway up the hill at 'middle break'. When the Incline opened in 1879, it had taken nearly two years to construct. With an angle of around 38 degrees, it was among the steepest railways ever built, and it became known locally as the 'Eighth Wonder of the World'.

Despite the frequency of derailments and runaway wagons, the miners used the Incline as transport to and from the plateau. In her book *The Hill*, published in 1971, Cecilia Adams—a long-time resident of Denniston—observes, 'The Incline was its official name, but for the first fifty years of its existence it could as aptly been called "the lifeline" for that, in fact, was what it was to the many souls who populated that black plateau at the summit of the mountain. ... Every item for the maintenance of life and work had, of necessity, to be carried up that set of rails which seemed to rise perpendicularly right up to the sky.' She goes on to recount how everything from grand pianos to full-sized billiards tables 'crept up the rails to bob safely over the brow at the top and on to the platform'. But it is the following passage that I find most memorable:

> Sunday afternoons saw many couples taking a walk down this delightful path, sometimes to branch off on a shortcut out to the Incline. ... There was a mite of strategy and some foresight in this arrangement, as after climbing the first few sleepers it was found to be much easier climbing if the couple held hands and stepped up together. ... After a time of holding hands a measure of guile was introduced with the suggestion that an arm of each round the waist of the other would make the effort easier still, and so in this manner the steepest steps to the top were mastered, with the pair arriving breathless, but laughing at the summit; which usually meant falling into each other's arms in a triumphant kiss of victory; a subtle and cunning way to encourage an otherwise shy or bashful girl- or boy-friend.

After eighty years of continuous operation and the movement of more than thirteen million tons of coal down the mountain, the Denniston Incline finally closed in 1967, when it was superseded by truck access via a sealed road.

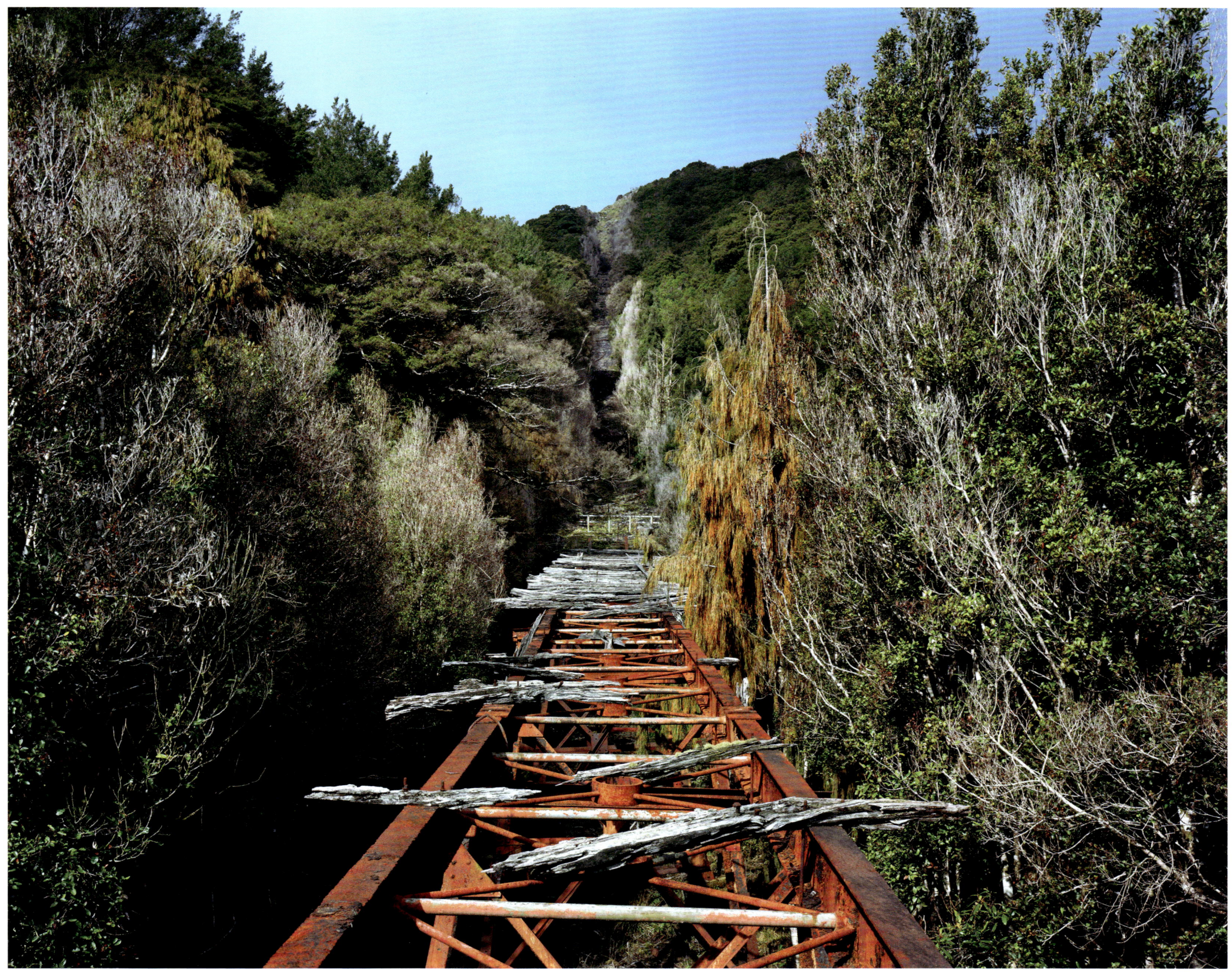

Winter Morning, Remains of the Coal Barge S.S. Lawrence, *Mōkihinui,* 2016

Located in the north of the West Coast region, just before the road ends at Karamea and the Tasman Mountains, Mōkihinui feels exceptionally remote. The Mōkihinui River, the third largest of thousands that criss-cross the region, draws from a nearly 700-kilometre basin, forming deep in the vast mountain ranges of the Mōkihinui Forest, descending through countless gorges, and finally flowing through the lush valley around Seddonville towards the Tasman Sea. Unfazed by its remoteness, and the challenging rainforest landscape surrounding it, prospectors still found their way to the area, where they located a large coal seam on the river in 1862. They established a coal mine and, with no road or rail access, built a wharf for small vessels to get coal down the river. But despite their investment, in little time the venture failed, the difficulty of transporting coal from the site rendering mining unprofitable.

In 1885, the Mōkihinui Coal Company formed to make a second attempt on the coal seam, this time with a larger capital outlay which they believed would make the operation viable. In addition to a new mine near the original one, they established a second further upstream at Coal Creek or Parenga. Then, at great expense, a railway line was constructed to connect the entire operation. It ran from the mines high in the mountains down to the valley, where it followed the river, winding around cliffs, bridging tributaries, and tunnelling through the dramatic landscape until reaching the dock near the river mouth. After a year, the operation was described as 'thriving', and, in 1889, the company invested in a dedicated coal barge, *S.S. Lawrence*, a 1,000-ton, 160-foot iron steamer built in England in 1884.

By 1891, the Mōkihinui Coal Company had won a much-coveted contract to supply coal to the New Zealand Railways. Success seemed inevitable, but it would continue to prove elusive. On the night of 28 April 1891, the *Lawrence* became lodged on the sandbar at the mouth of the Mōkihinui River. Struggling in the dark through violent waves, it eventually managed to break free, but its propeller blades had been damaged, and, without control, it drifted onto the south side of the river entrance. The next morning, bad weather continued breaking the ship's back, and the company had no choice but to abandon it and declare a total loss. As their only vessel, its loss meant the railway contract had to be forfeited to a competitor, and the business, like the boat, went under.

More than 2,500 ships have been recorded wrecked since the early days of colonisation in the 1850s. Of this vast number, fewer than 200 have been accurately located. Many sunken vessels were constructed of timber and so quickly broke into pieces beneath the powerful waves of Aotearoa's coastline. Often buried and almost invisible under the shifting sands of the West Coast, the remnants of the *S.S. Lawrence* remain on the Mōkihinui coastline, a monument to faded colonial dreams.

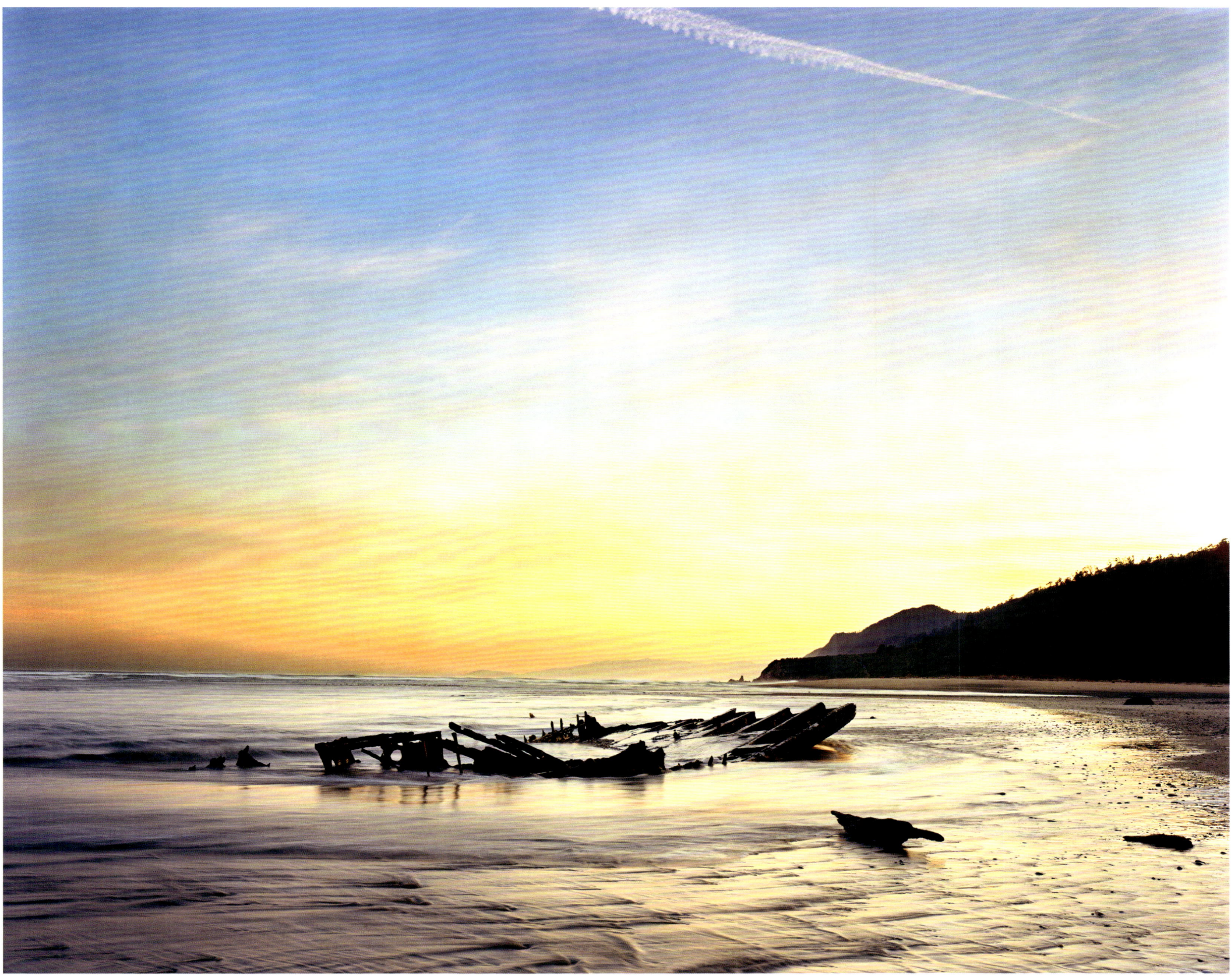

Ngarua Limeworks (Looking Towards Abel Tasman), Tākaka Hill, 2017

Near the top of the South Island, Tākaka Hill rises over a kilometre above the region's low plains, towering over the Motueka Valley and separating it from Golden Bay to the north. From a summit on the Pikikirunga Range, on which Tākaka Hill lies, dense rainforest falls through steep gorges to Abel Tasman National Park and the Tasman Sea, both named for the Dutch explorer who anchored in Golden Bay and was the first European to sight New Zealand in 1642. On the coast beneath the rainforest, a famous sixty-kilometre track winds around golden-white beaches, shallow inlets, and a string of granite caves, pillars, arches, and reefs. The picturesque scenery has made Abel Tasman National Park one of the most popular tourist sites in New Zealand, drawing more than 250,000 mostly overseas visitors, along with their cars and campervans, each year.

It was in 1843 that a small party led by Charles Heaphy, a British explorer and surveyor today best known for his topographical watercolours, became the first Europeans to cross the Tākaka Hill to Golden Bay, an area previously accessible only by sea. On their return, Heaphy espoused the virtues of creating a road over the Hill so that 'the whole of the upper part of the Tākaka Valley would become available for addition to the surveyed lands of the settlement, and about 7,000 or 8,000 acres would be added to the 27,000 acres already laid out'. In the 1850s, several gold rushes hit Golden Bay, and, to service them, a foot track was cut and later upgraded to a bridle track. Not until 1888 did this become a coach road, though, and it was then proudly announced that two buggies had crossed Tākaka Hill—the journey 'taking three and a half hours to ascend the hill from Golden Bay and another two to descend to Riwaka'.

With road access, industry soon followed, and, from the early 1900s, quarrying began on the dramatic limestone and marble fields that run along the Pikikirunga Range. In 1911, a Government architect selected marble from Tākaka's Kairuru Quarry for its 'high creamy lustre' to use in construction of the Parliament Buildings in Wellington. By the time they were completed a decade later, more than 5,000 tonnes of stone had been quarried from Tākaka. The same marble was subsequently used for other prominent buildings, including Christ Church Cathedral in Nelson and the Massey Memorial at Point Halswell in Wellington.

Today, the booming industry in the area is tourism, part of which is connected with the *Lord of the Rings* and *Hobbit* films, with numerous operators offering tours of caves, forests, and remote parts of the hill by helicopter. Driving across the hill now, little of the current road still follows the old trails, save for 100 metres near the summit and the Ngarua Limeworks, which almost exactly matches the route laid out by Heaphy more than 180 years ago. Near the summit and the limeworks, it is easy to imagine him stopping and looking over the limestone outcrops and forest towards Tasman Bay.

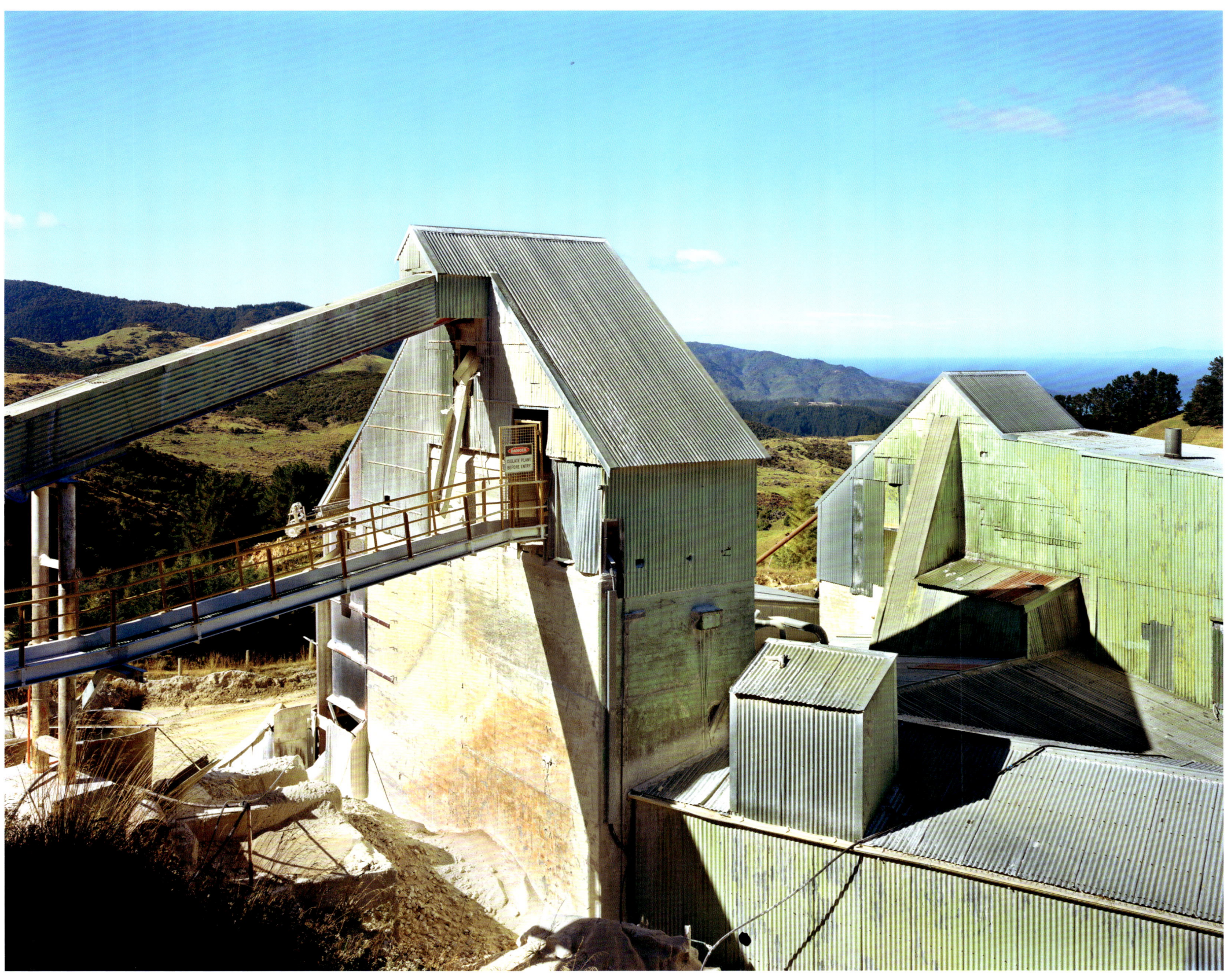

Hop and Tobacco Kilns, Beneath Tākaka Hill, Near Riwaka, 2017

North of Riwaka, a road snakes ten kilometres through a narrow, sleepy valley at the base of Tākaka Hill, heading towards Mārahau and Abel Tasman National Park, to which it carries thousands of tourists every year. Hidden down a gravel side road, and beside an old farmhouse, are two of the best examples of the hop and tobacco kilns that uniquely shaped the history of the region. The 1906 *Cyclopedia of New Zealand* calls Riwaka 'the head centre of hop-growing in New Zealand', noting, 'There are about forty growers in the district, and the yield is over 250 bales each season. Being well sheltered by the hills from prevailing winds, hop cultivation is carried on under the most favourable conditions. … The whole place has an air which indicates prosperity, comfort, and contentment.'

In the mid-nineteenth century, European immigrants found that the Nelson region provided an ideal climate for growing hops, the main ingredient in beer, and large farms were soon established. The hops were mostly picked by women and older children, and, owing to the fact that fresh hops spoil quickly, nearly every farm had its own kiln of a unique style and construction method. Inside the kilns, on the second story, the hops would be laid across grids of wooden battens. A wood or charcoal fire beneath would heat the air and cause it to circulate through the turret-like towers, drying the flowers. Hop farming quickly became the region's primary industry, and between the 1890s and the 1970s, almost 700 acres were at any time planted with vines.

The history of the Nelson region's other key industry, tobacco, starts in 1910, when Gerhard Husheer immigrated to Hawke's Bay from Germany and established the New Zealand Tobacco Company. Ejected from the firm during the First World War, due to anti-German sentiment, Husheer later bought the company's assets and formed the National Tobacco Company in 1921. It began growing tobacco leaf in Motueka, near Riwaka. The tobacco and hop industries thrived, but overproduction threatened both, and so attempts were made to regulate production and bolster promotion. In 1935, the Government passed the Tobacco Growing Industry Act, and four years later the Hop Marketing Committee was established.

By the 1960s, the Nelson tobacco industry was supplying 50% of the national market. Meanwhile, in Riwaka, a Government-owned research station had developed the world's first seedless hops. However, the adoption of mechanised hop-picking in the early 1960s dramatically reduced the amount of local labour required and destroyed most of the smaller operations, and by the mid-1970s, the world market was in oversupply due to the availability of more potent strains of hop. Then, in 1987, the passing of the Tobacco Growing Industry Repeal Act left local tobacco growers unable to compete with cheaper production overseas and almost killed the industry overnight.

In 2003, the hop industry was also deregulated, and a handful of large companies now control New Zealand's production, of which nearly 80% is exported. However, as unsweetened craft beers have become popular, and as demand for organic and locally grown ingredients has increased, the local industry has been revived and is now thriving.

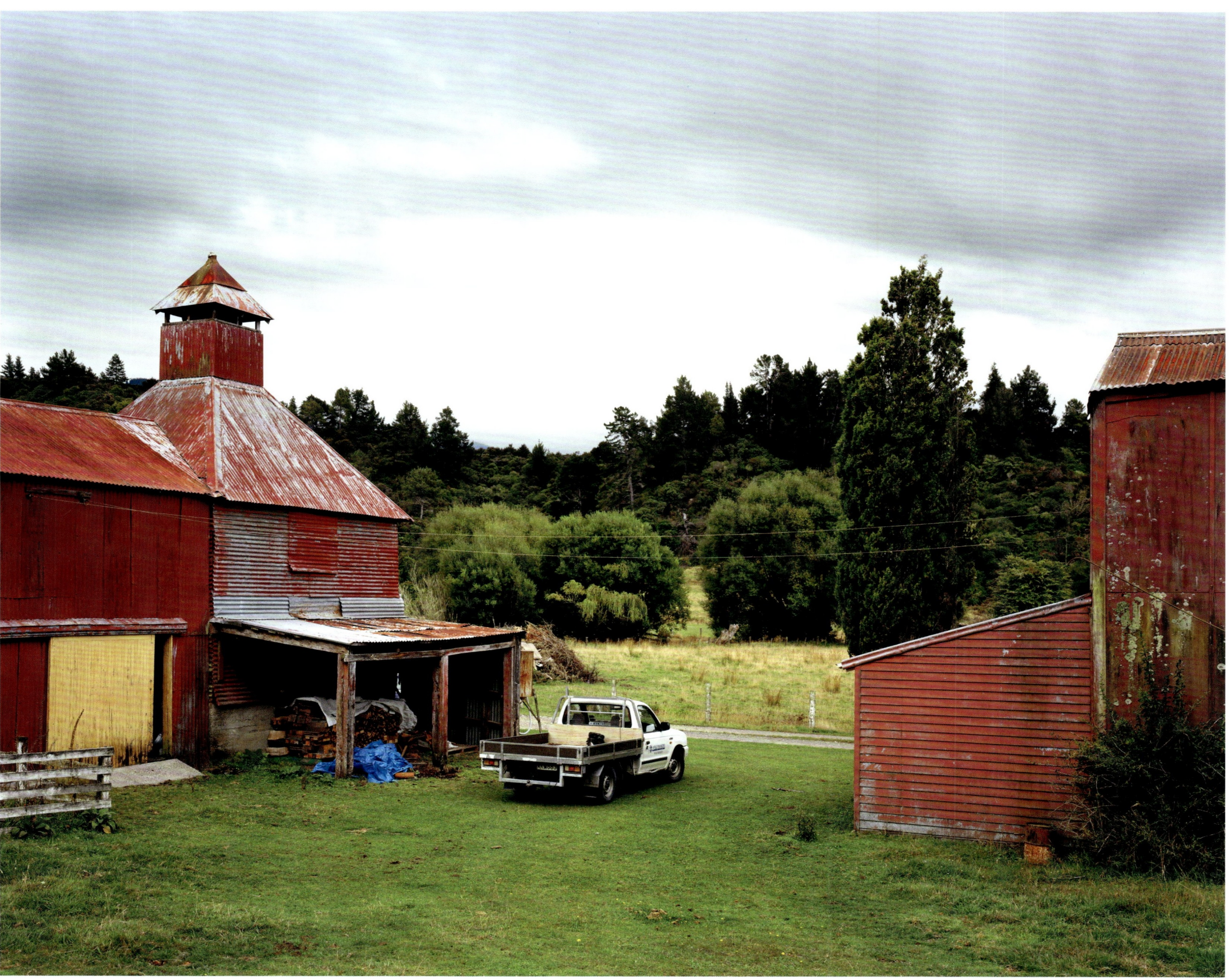

Hop Kiln and Barn, Stanley Brook, Motueka Valley, 2017

Inland from Nelson, the settlement of Stanley Brook lies in a valley on the plains of the Motueka River. As late as 1870, the valley was home to a vast and ancient forest, but this was soon logged and cleared by European settlers. The *Cyclopedia of New Zealand* from 1906 proudly describes Stanley Brook as 'a farming district with a population of about 200, with 3,000 to 4,000 acres suitable for grazing, and a fair amount of cropping also carried on', making note, too, of 'congregations of the Church of England and the Church of Christ'.

Today, the Nelson region is known for its tourism centred on coastal locations like Abel Tasman National Park. But in the early days of European colonisation, its sheltered inland regions, long, hot summers, and high winter rainfall made it attractive to horticulturists. Settlers from Germany and the south of England brought with them seeds of the hop vine, and soon found the plant thrived in the region. The flowers, called hops, have been a key ingredient in beer for centuries, providing it with its bitter flavour. Almost as soon as the forest was cleared, hop fields sprung up and with them hundreds of timber or cobb hop kilns to dry the hops.

Dating to about 1879, this wooden kiln at Stanley Brook is one of the best-preserved examples, and—with its slumping roof and tentacle-like grapevine—one of the most poetic. In *The New Zealand Heritage of Farm Buildings* (1986), Geoffrey Thornton writes of the building's life after its first decades as kiln: 'Having a strong interest in assisting immigrants [the second owner] Barker allowed two families to live in the building, one occupying rooms in the upper portion. [Then] over the years it was used in part for cutting chaff with a machine in the loft. ... In 1911 a Lister oil engine was installed in another lean-to for operating two shearing machines which provided a service to various farmers in the district.' Discussing the kiln's construction history, Thornton notes, 'The roof began as [wooden] shingles before their eventual replacement by corrugated iron. Beech saplings used as purlins are still in place, while the massive posts are of hand-hewn tōtara roughly squared. At ground level the floor rests on timber bearers bedded on river boulders.'

For more than 100 years, the farm at Stanley Brook has stayed within the Barker family. Remnants of buildings used in the production of hops and later tobacco, wheat, and wool, all on their farm, singularly chart the highs and lows of these industries in New Zealand.

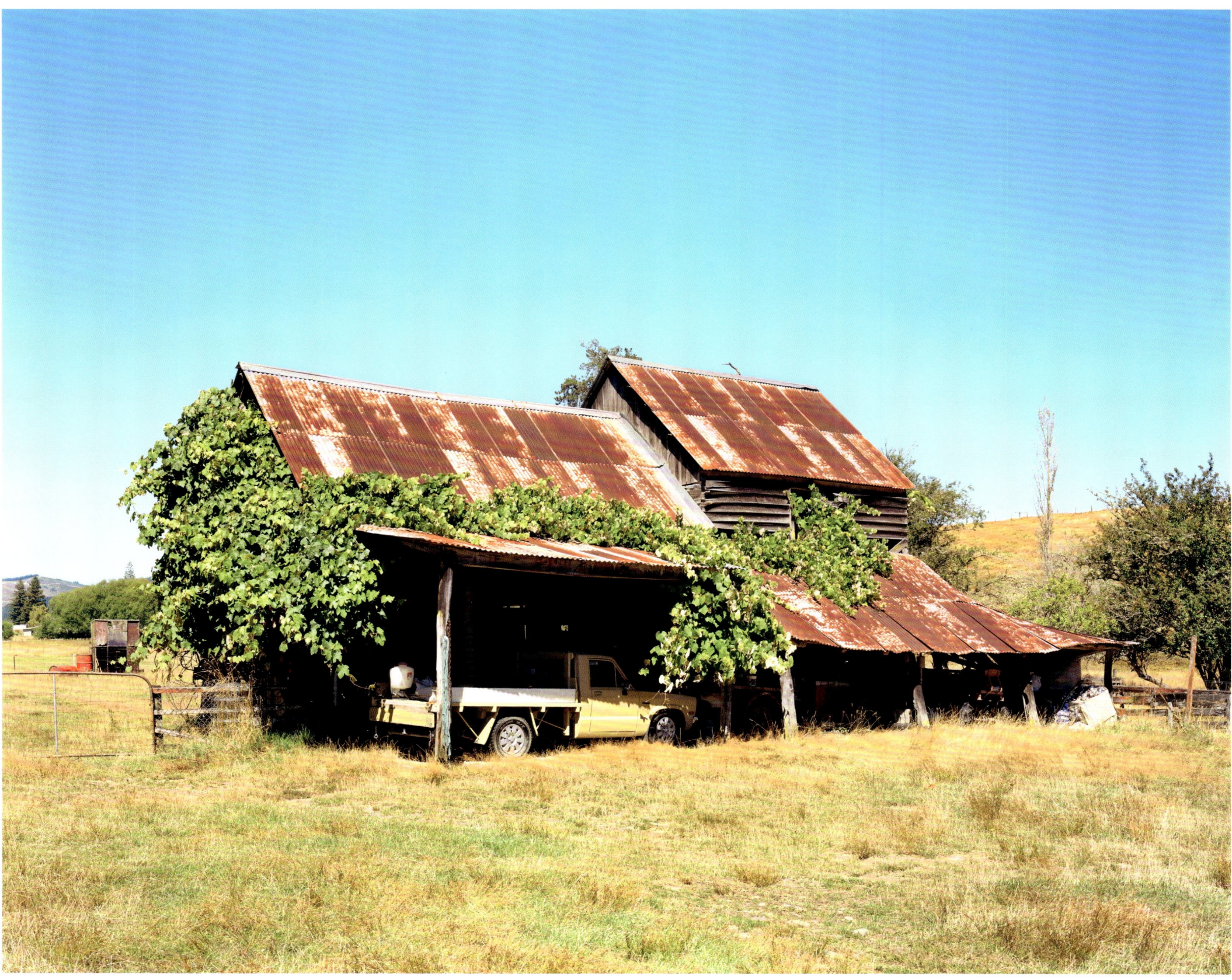

Chinese Miners' Hut, Illustrious Energy Mine, Central Otago, 2017

New Zealand's first major gold rush began in 1861 when the Tasmanian prospector Gabriel Reed discovered gold in what became known as Gabriel's Gully near Lawrence, Otago. Reed described the gold he found as shining in the gravel 'like the stars in Orion on a dark frosty night'. News of his discovery rapidly spread, and soon miners were pouring into the area from as far away as Victoria and California, where a gold rush had ended just a few years earlier. The gold found was alluvial, lying in waterways or among gravel relatively near the surface, from which it could be panned. By Christmas of 1861, over 14,000 people had swarmed upon Gabriel's Gully, and the accessible pickings were quickly exhausted. To continue working, the miners had to change to more costly and involved hydraulic mining techniques, employing pressurised water, or leave for new fields, like those along the Clutha River and the South Island's West Coast.

As new deposits were discovered in the region, tent cities known as 'canvastowns' sprang up, and with the miners came businesspeople of all sorts who established more robust townships, most of which ultimately vanished as rapidly as they had appeared. By the mid-1860s, many of the initial fields had been worked over and deserted, so the Otago Provincial Government began encouraging Chinese miners, who came primarily from the southern Guangdong province, to replace the Europeans as well as prop up the failing mining towns. Most of the miners came to New Zealand with the intention of earning enough to help their families, then return home, and they set out to work in some of the most extreme locations in the country, meticulously combing over riverbeds and piles of tailings abandoned by previous miners—literally leaving no stone unturned.

From the beginning of their time in New Zealand, the Chinese miners faced intense racism, and most gathered into self-contained communities. Men vastly outnumbered women to such a degree that in 1881, of the 5,004 Chinese migrants in New Zealand, only nine were women. That same year, Parliament passed the Chinese Immigrants Act, following similar legislation in Australia and Canada. This imposed a costly poll-tax on Chinese people entering the country and limited immigration, permitting only one Chinese passenger for every ten tons of cargo. By 1886, this already draconian law was deemed insufficient. The tax was raised to £100 (over $20,000 today) per person, with an even more extreme restriction of one Chinese passenger for every 200 tons of cargo. The generally held attitude is exemplified by Richard Seddon, Prime Minister from 1893 until his death in 1906, who once remarked, 'There is about as much distinction between a European and a Chinaman as that between a Chinaman and a monkey.'

In the 1920s, further restrictions on Chinese immigration rendered the poll-tax inoperative, but the legislation was not officially repealed until 1944. The miners had come to New Zealand in the hope of aiding their families, but, due to false promises and racist Government policies, few succeeded in their aim. Many died alone in harsh conditions, and were buried in unmarked graves, like those in Lawrence. In 2002, the New Zealand Government officially apologised to the Chinese community for the injustice of the tax.

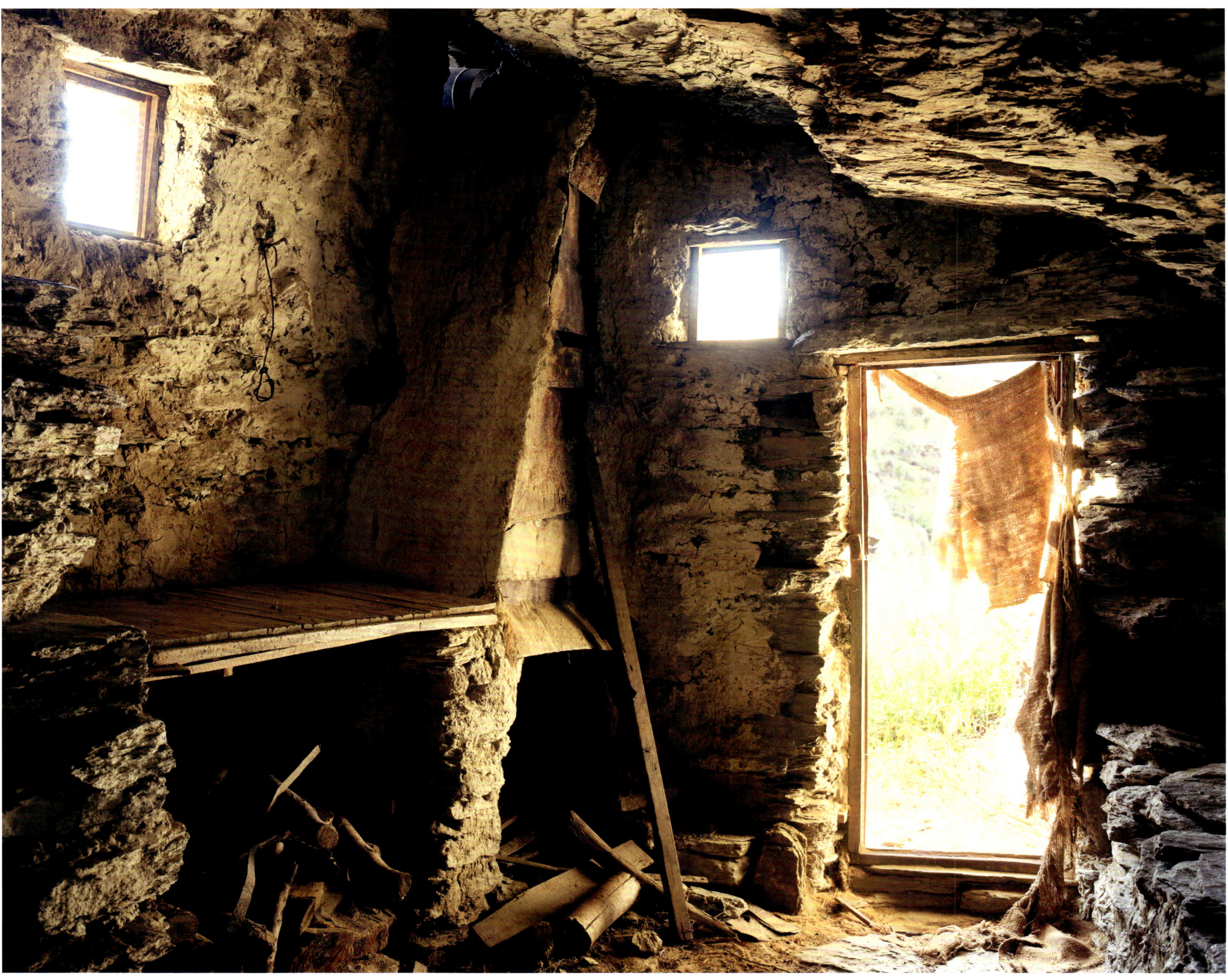

Scientists Performing Autopsies on Some of the 350 Pilot Whales that Beached and Died, Farewell Spit, Golden Bay,
2017

At thirty kilometres, Farewell Spit is the longest sandspit in the country, arching over the immense Golden Bay
below Cook Strait, which separates the North and South Islands of New Zealand. On the spit are vast sand
dunes, scattered lakes, and regenerating forest, while on the side sheltered by its curve, a narrow golden beach
runs for almost half its length before fraying into tidal pools, streams, and mangroves. As the tide goes out,
shallow mudflats appear, stretching as many as ten kilometres into the bay. In Māori, the spit is named Onetahua
(meaning 'heaped up sand'), but as Captain James Cook sailed away from New Zealand towards Australia at the
end of his first visit in 1770, he renamed it Farewell Spit.

The unique geography of Onetahua has been the cause of countless whale strandings, with Māori oral history
showing that such tragic events have occurred here for as long as people have been in Aotearoa. The most
calamitous stranding yet took place on 10 February 2017. According to the Department of Conservation, which
manages the area, 'Around 416 pilot whales stranded near the base of Farewell Spit overnight, of which 250 to 300
were already dead when the whales were discovered.' As many as 150 whales were refloated, but at least ninety
stranded again with the next high tide, and by the following day over 650 had beached. The timing of the event,
at the height of the tourist season, enabled a large rescue effort; more than 500 people aided and, ultimately, over
300 whales were saved. But, with 350 whales dying, the stranding became the second worst in recorded history.

The world's worst stranding also occurred in New Zealand, on the Chatham Islands, where 1,000 pilot whales
beached and died in 1918. Indeed, no fewer than six of the ten largest whale strandings have taken place in this
country. Despite decades of research here and overseas, the reasons for strandings are still not fully understood.
At Golden Bay, the leading theory is that the beach's gradual slope and soft sands disrupt the whales' use of
echolocation for depth sensing and navigation. Whales enter Golden Bay during high tides (and particularly
during king tides, as in 2017), believing the water to be deeper than it really is. Then, as the tide turns, they find
themselves too far onto the shallow mudflats. At many strandings, sharks have also been seen offshore, and so
another theory is that whales move towards the coast in search of safety. What is certain, though, is that as the first
whales strand, others soon follow to provide company and aid, acting on their strong social bonds—the whales'
sense of loyalty often leading to re-strandings after they have been re-floated.

Following the 2017 stranding, around 300 of the dead whales were carried with diggers further up Farewell
Spit, where they were buried in the sand dunes. In 2022, a new stranding became the second worst in history;
477 whales died on the Chatham and Pit Islands over a two-day period. Because of the likelihood of shark attack
to both volunteers and whales, the surviving whales were euthanised to prevent further suffering.

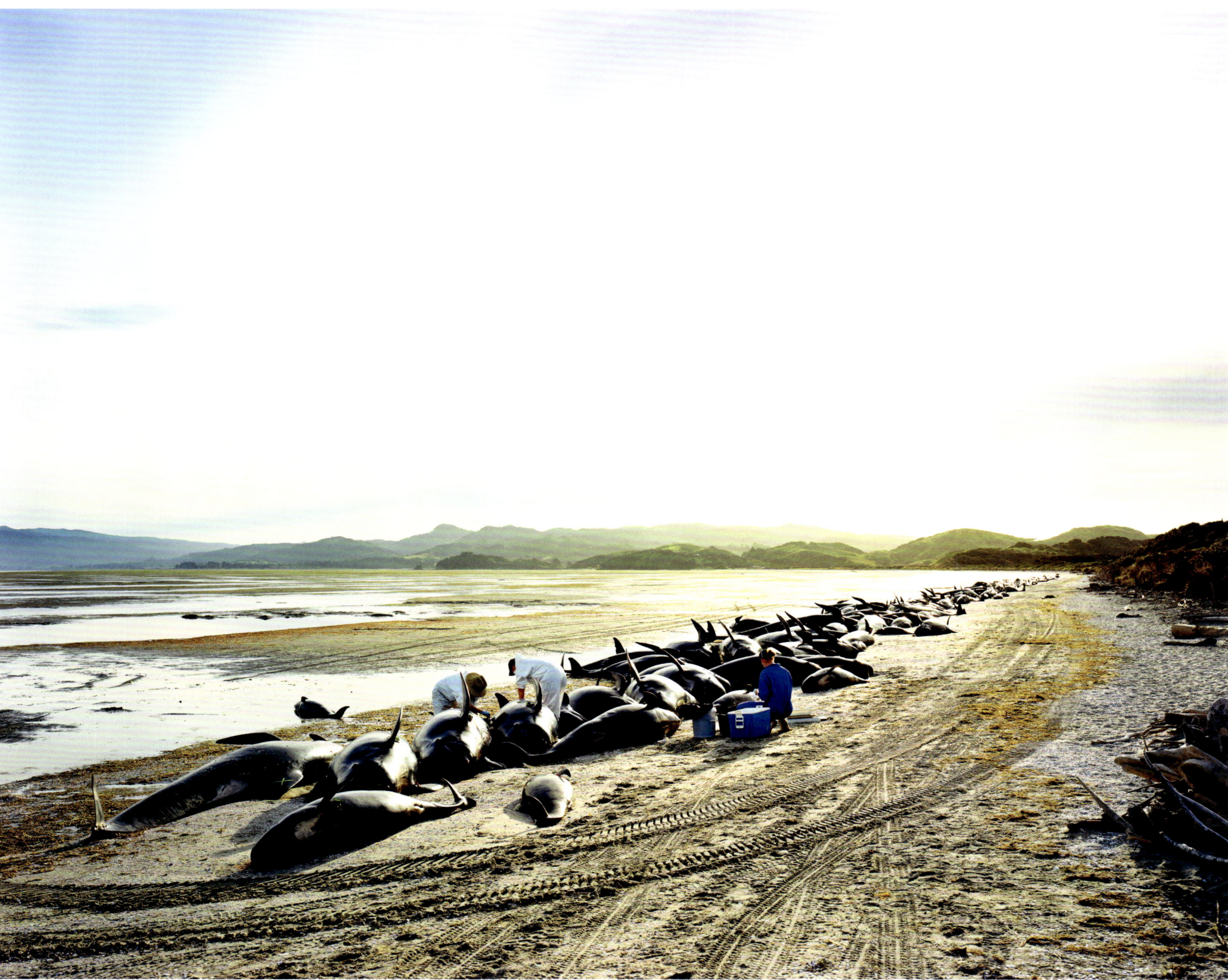

Musterers Quarters (After Barker), Lake Coleridge Station, Canterbury, 2018

Born into a well-to-do English family, Alfred Charles Barker graduated as a surgeon from King's College, London, before heading to New Zealand in 1850. His wife Emma wrote that he intended 'to purchase land and be the first doctor among the Colonists who are all well connected families'. The couple and their children arrived on one of the 'First Four Ships' sent by the Canterbury Association to establish a Church of England colony on the Canterbury Plains, and initially lived in a tent. For several years, Barker was the only doctor on the Plains, but apparently many settlers failed to pay his invoices, and, as other doctors arrived in the region, he lost interest in the profession.

In 1855, he established Lake Coleridge Station with two partners. Located in the Southern Alps, some 500 metres above sea level, the station has a uniquely striking location. It sits in the valley of the Acheron River, beside Lake Coleridge, with mountains rising dramatically on all sides around the homestead and station buildings. Accounts are hazy, but it seems that Barker quickly bought out his partners to become the sole owner. Sadly, in 1858, his wife died after the birth of their eighth child, and two years later he sold the station. The sale appears to have made him financially secure, and he increasingly turned his attention to amateur science and photography.

Today, Barker's fame rests chiefly on his photography. Beginning around 1857, he took some of the earliest pictures of Canterbury and documented the establishment of the South Island's largest city, Christchurch. Among his best-known works are portraits and self-portraits, which are formally posed but warm, and tableaux-like images of settlers in the emerging city and surrounding landscape. For me, though, his most interesting works are a series of pictures made around 1870, which show the interiors of churches, the Canterbury Museum, and his own home. At the time, the interior was an uncommon subject for colonial and pioneer photographers of New Zealand, who—like their contemporaries in the United States—focused their attention on lands being 'discovered'. The technology available to Barker would have also hindered his work, the 'slow' lenses of the day rendering the view through his camera's ground-glass dim, and the photographic emulsions requiring extremely long exposures to gather enough light.

Barker's interiors were among his last works. He died of meningitis at the age of fifty-four in 1873. Although it has changed hands many times since its establishment, Lake Coleridge Station has persisted through countless economic ups and downs and remains in operation.

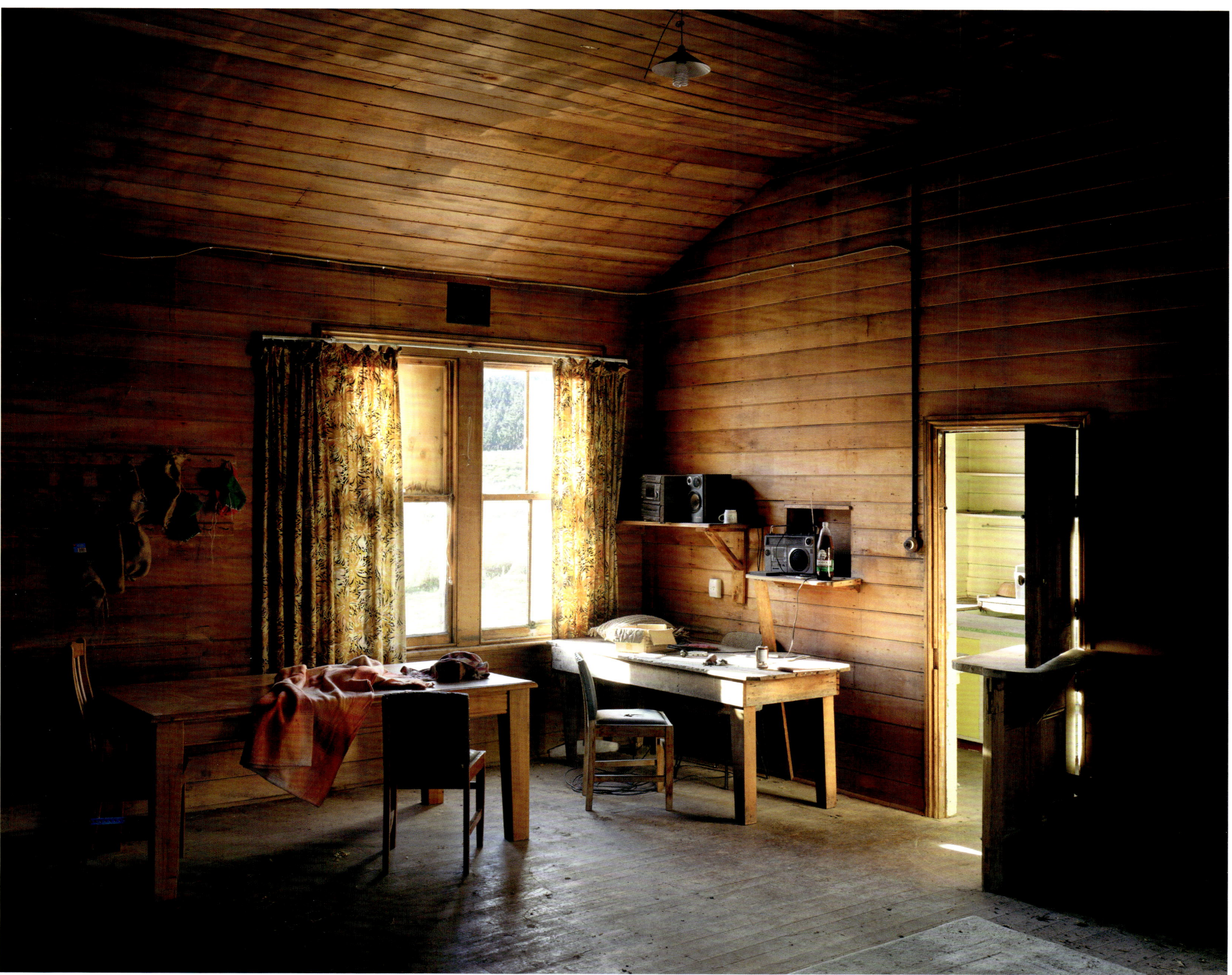

Overgrown Workshop, Elliotvale Coal Mine, Otago Coast Forest, 2018

Most of Aotearoa's ancient forests met their demise beneath the axes and sawblades of Europeans, but in some places, Māori, too, cleared vast areas of forest. On the low hills and alluvial soils of Otago's east coast, kahikatea, tōtara, and mataī once rose above a canopy of kōwhai and lacebark, before the forest was burned by the first people to arrive in Aotearoa, to ready land for settlement or to drive moa and other birds out for easier hunting. Large areas, too, are now thought to have vanished through accidental fires, which spread rapidly in Otago's dry climate. In 2022, a decades-long research project discovered that the region's endless plateaus—covered in tussock long believed to be the natural state—were almost certainly once clad in forests of kōwhai later claimed by fires natural and manmade.

When Europeans arrived in Otago, they quickly logged or burned what did remain of the forest to create pasture. Coal mining emerged as a major industry, and several of New Zealand's most productive mines outside the West Coast region were established along a seventy-kilometre stretch of coastal hills, which run from Dunedin in the north to the Clutha River in the south. Some of these proved enduring, such as the Kaitangata Mine, which opened in 1872 and operated for nearly 100 years (even today, Kaitangata remains a mining town; its Kai Point Mine opened in 1958 and is still in operation). Others, like the Elliotvale Coal Mine, came and went, sinking the fortunes of those who became entangled with them along the way.

Advertisements for coal from Elliotvale first appeared in newspapers in 1874, although the site seems to have been worked previously, perhaps even before the 1870s and the opening of the Kaitangata Mine. The Kaitangata Railway and Coal Company purchased Elliotvale in 1880, seemingly to kill competition. They invested money and dug new mine tunnels, but a few years later, coal prices hit a low once again, and further competition forced the operation to close. The mine was acquired by the London-based New Zealand Collieries, Railway, and Oil Syndicate (later the New Zealand Coal and Oil Company), which also owned the nearby Castle Hill and Kaitangata Mines. By 1901, the firm had spent £80,000 (more than £8 million today) installing cutting-edge mining equipment, but it seems that mining never recommenced. Following a failed shale oil prospect at Orepuki near Riverton, the company collapsed entirely in 1926.

The Elliotvale Mine is located about halfway between Milton and Balclutha, deep in the council-owned Otago Coast Forest. Turning off the Milton Highway, Moneymore Road heads south-east across kilometres of flat paddocks before it meets an intersection with Elliotvale Road. The rural junction is the kind a crane shot would reveal the main character in a Hollywood movie leaving for the city from, and beside it an abandoned schoolhouse sits behind a wrought iron gate that reads 'Moneymore School Centennial 1863–1963'. On the gate, the white paint has almost peeled away to golden rust, while in the hills beyond, all that remains of Elliotvale Mine slowly sinks beneath radiata pine needles.

Otago's lowland coastal forests are now the most under-represented of all prehistoric forest types in New Zealand. Their remaining area is estimated to be less than 1% of what existed before the arrival of people in Aotearoa.

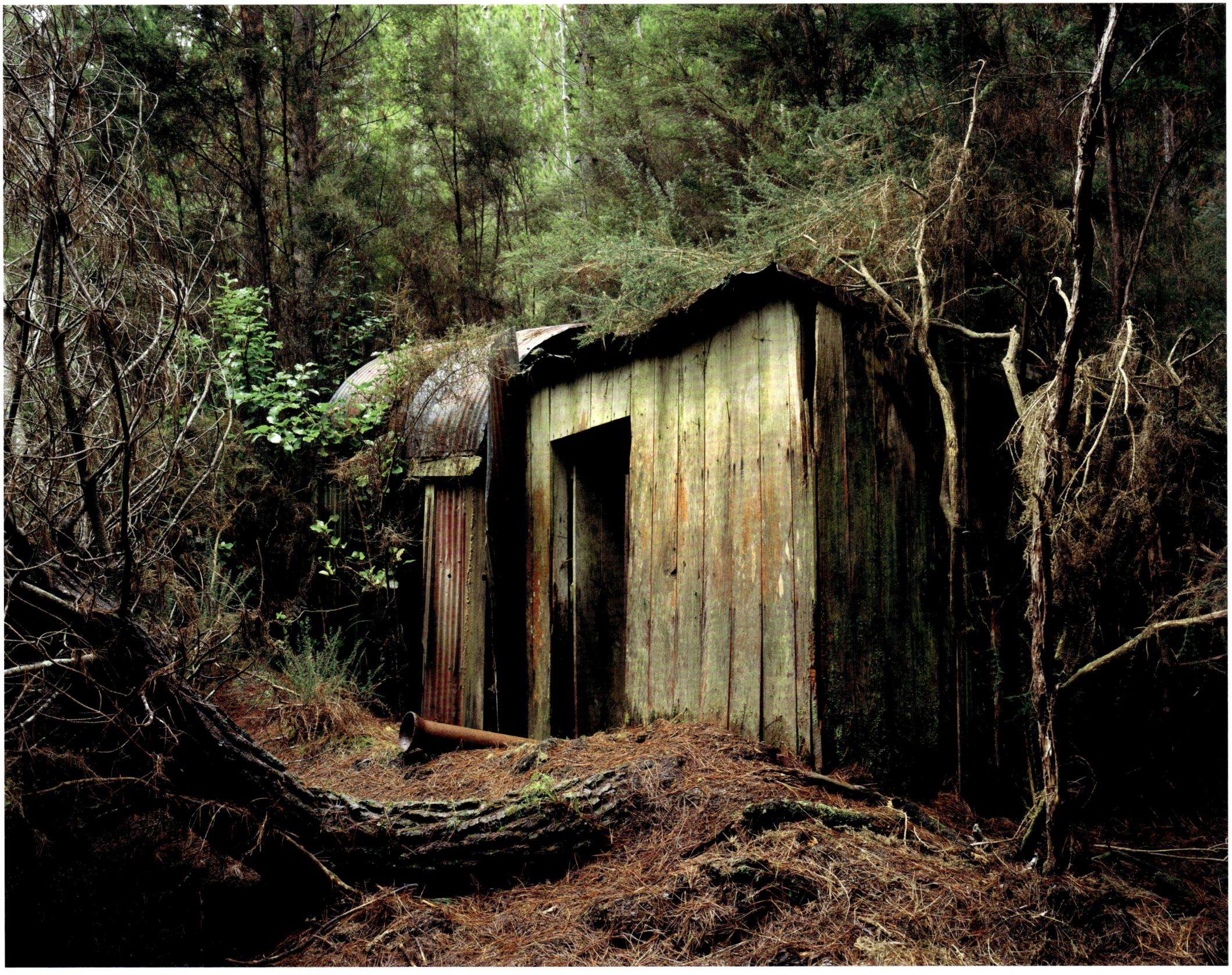

Winter, Sullivan Mine, Denniston Plateau, 2018

It often feels as though everything can be found online today, but beyond the tourist sites, and roads indexed by Google Street View, mysteries still remain. Before my photography trips, I spent hours poring over topographic maps, trying to align former mines marked on them to satellite images, in the hope of finding overgrown or under-documented locations worth uncovering. Most of the time, though, it was only when I spent time walking around a place—following goat tracks and dead ends—that anything was revealed. Such was the case when I visited the Sullivan Mine, which operated between 1952 and 1980 in the west of the Denniston Plateau—far from its well-known township and Incline.

In April 1949, the *Greymouth Evening Star* wrote, 'Big steps forward in the mechanisation of the workings on the Buller coalfields will be taken shortly, with the arrival from England of parts designed to modernise the coal haulage systems at both the big Stockton open-cast and Denniston workings. The plans for this work, which will shortly be implemented, envisage the spending of over £700,000 [£20,780,000 today], chiefly on aerial ropeways.' One of the largest Government investments ever made at Denniston, the ropeway was conceived to open new remote parts of the plateau to mining, the system of elevated coal buckets connecting the Denniston Incline to the Whareatea Mine, which opened in 1950, and then the Sullivan Mine, across the rugged plateau.

The first fully mechanised mine in New Zealand, the Sullivan Mine greatly increased mining efficiency, replacing much backbreaking manual labour of the past with a system of conveyor belts. By 1955, the *Press* newspaper wrote, 'The Sullivan Mine may well prove to be the most highly payable underground colliery in the Dominion. With the installation of new machinery at the face, production is confidently expected to rise to an average of five tons a day for all employees ... [whereas] the average production for all mine workers in underground pits in New Zealand is [just] a little more than two tons a day.' Yet despite the expenditure on the ropeway, owing to the cost of upkeep (and then replacement by trucks), after just eighteen years it had become redundant, and it was eventually removed. The mine itself survived until 1980, when, its coal seam exhausted, it closed, making way for the Sullivan West Mine a kilometre to the north-west.

In a black-and-white photograph published in the *Press* in 1955, the Sullivan Mine's vast corrugated iron coal hoppers float four storeys in the air upon steel trusses. From the elevated structure, enclosed conveyer belts descend in multiple directions above a sea of huts, workshops, and other buildings. Above it all, on a web of steel cables suspended upon giant winch towers, are the coal bins that then moved along the wires night and day. Visiting the site today, the mass and activity then frozen by the camera feels like a fever dream, the evidence of its existence reduced to little more than a handful of sealed mine and ventilation shaft entrances, a smattering of concrete foundations, and littered coal. Now almost reclaimed by the plateau's tussock and mānuka, the site is here further obscured by the severe weather that famously plagued generations of miners.

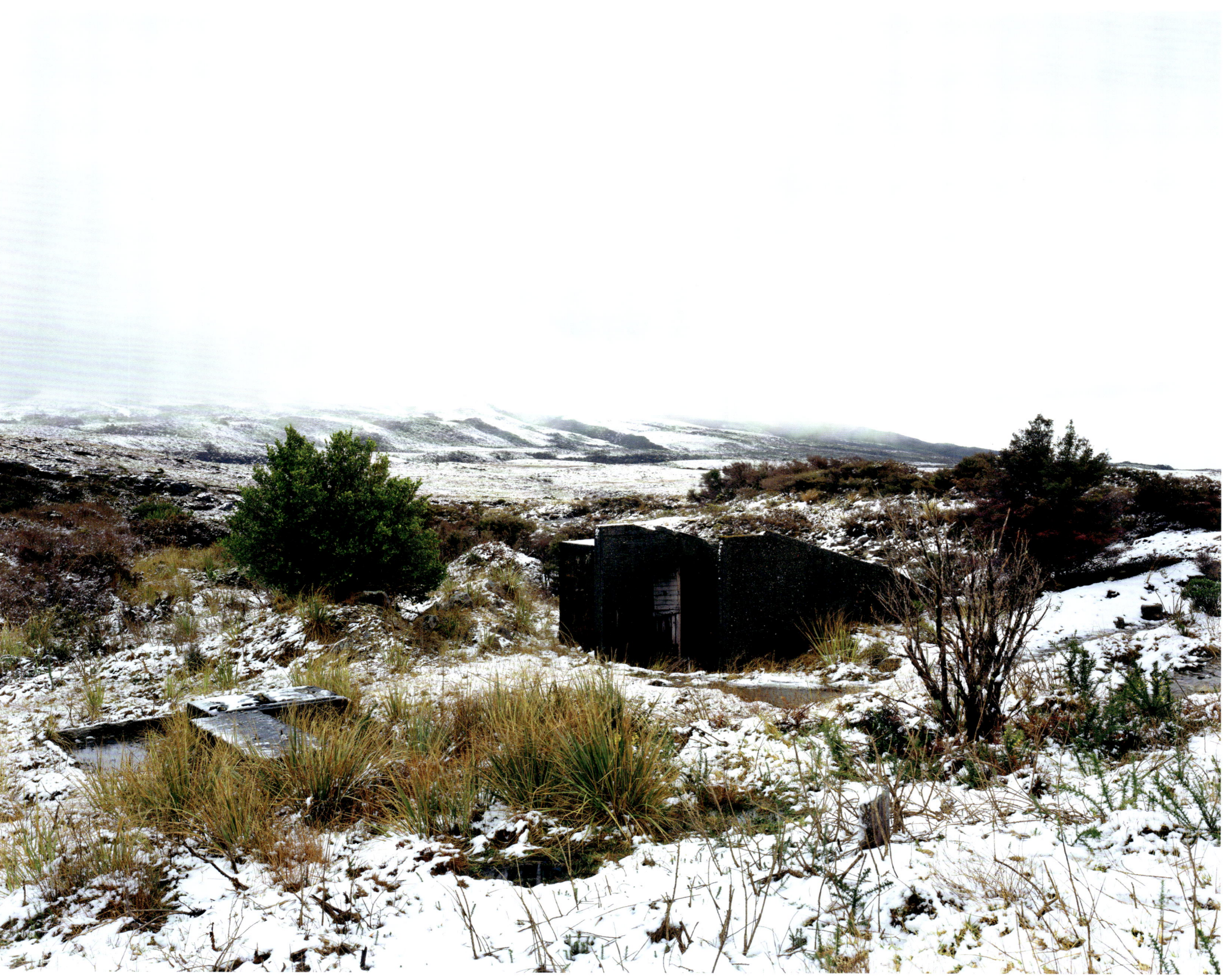

Fluming and Adit, Mt William North Mine, Near Stockton, West Coast, 2016

North-east of the Denniston Plateau, and across the deep gorge of the Waimangaroa River, the Stockton Plateau rises over 800 metres above the West Coast. As early as 1873, coal was found on Stockton's southern extent at Mount William Range, and in 1881 mining began just north of the plateau at Millerton, where the eponymous township quickly developed. Mining gradually spread from Millerton up the hill onto the Stockton Plateau, and in 1906 the Westport Coal Company established the Stockton Mine. During the Second World War it began struggling and was taken over by the State Mines Department. From 1964, coal exploration took place around Mount William North, finding over 2,700,000 tonnes of coal that was deemed ideal for the New Zealand Railways, and leading to the opening of the Mount William North Mine in 1969. Utilising new hydraulic mining techniques, it produced over 500,000 tonnes of coal a year, but as demand for railway coal ended, it closed after just eleven years of operation.

Greatly in debt, State Coal Mines restructured into CoalCorp in 1987, closing less profitable mines and making over 1,000 miners redundant. The scale of opencast mining on the ecologically sensitive Stockton Plateau—now New Zealand's largest and most productive coal field—dramatically increased, with the pits stretching over eight kilometres and as many as forty metres deep, and consuming the summits of Mount Augustus and Mount Frederick. At the time of CoalCorp's establishment, the threat of climate change was beginning to be more widely discussed, and the company commissioned Austrian environmental scientist Fred Singer—described by *Scientific American* as 'best known for his denial of the health risks of passive smoking'—to speak as a climate change denier to industry leaders around New Zealand. In shareholder reports throughout the 1990s, the company framed climate change as 'an unknown, and still debated phenomenon', and in 1997 it underwent rebranding and acquired the noticeably less coal-sounding name 'Solid Energy'.

In 2005, Solid Energy was granted consent to develop a new opencast mine along the Cypress Stream behind Stockton, after beating appeals in the environmental court by Buller Conservation Group, Forest and Bird, and Te Rūnanga o Ngāti Waewae, and after settling with the Department of Conservation and Ngakawau Riverwatch. In 2006, protestors formed the Save Happy Valley Coalition and began occupying the proposed mine site, delaying the project until 2009. During the period of inactivity, a cream pie thrown by a protester narrowly missed the Chief Executive Officer of Solid Energy at an annual general meeting, activists tied themselves to train tracks to block coal trains, and thousands of snails found to live only in affected areas were collected by hand and relocated to Department of Conservation fridges to be held until mining concluded.

In 2012, Solid Energy applied for further resource consent for a new opencast mine at Mount William North, adjacent to the Cypress Mine and Happy Valley, and proposed to produce around 500,000 tonnes of coal per annum over twelve years. These plans were put on hold in 2013, when Solid Energy went into receivership.

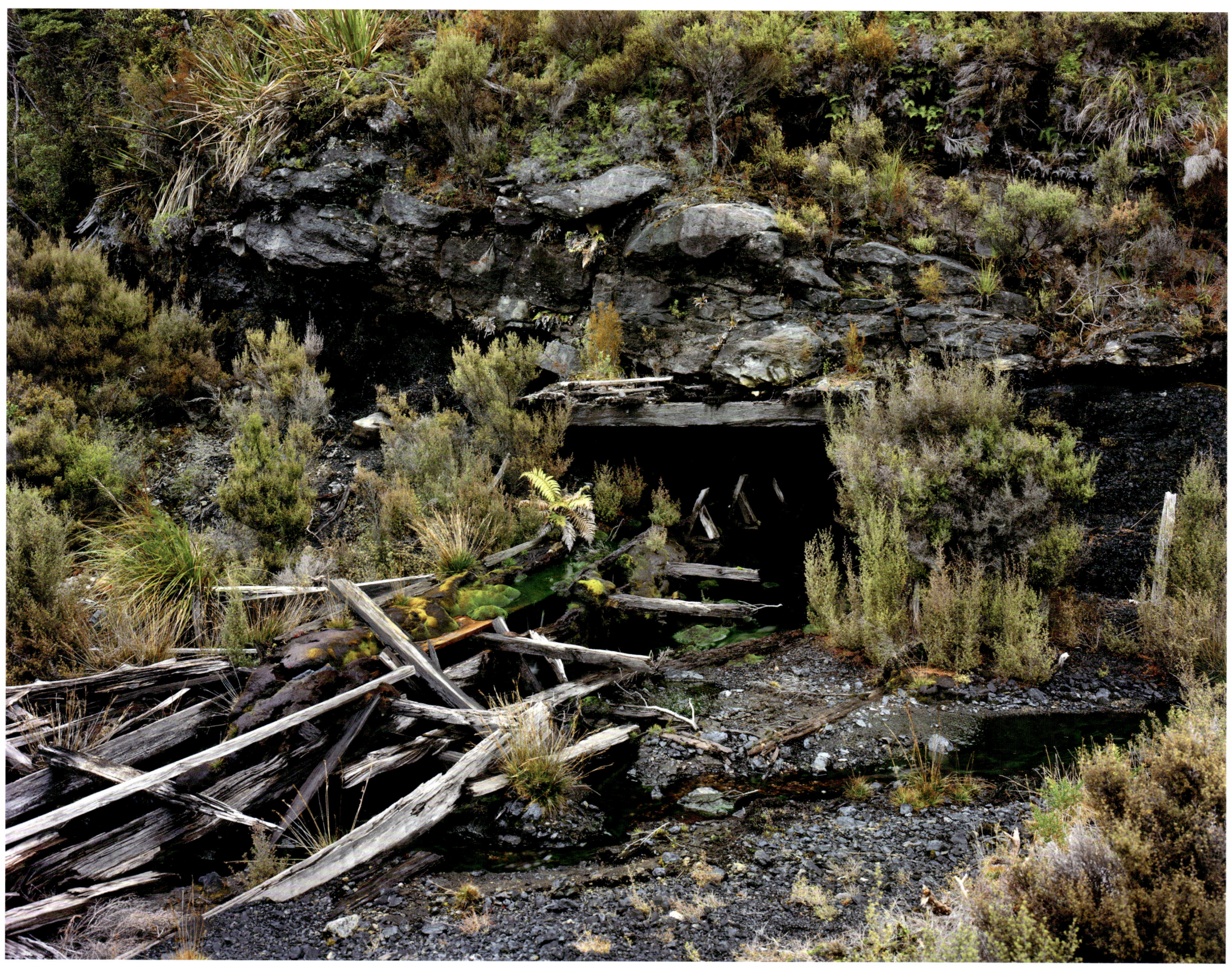

Woolshed and Oaks, Acheron Bank Station, Near Lake Coleridge, 2018

John Oakden arrived in Australia from England with his family in 1834, aged sixteen. Today, he is known as a pastoralist, and for his part in expeditions carried out between 1838 and 1852 that made him the first European to 'explore' parts of South Australia, such as the Murray River, Kadlunga, and what would become 'Oakden Hills'. Through these, he befriended a younger run holder, William Robinson, and became manager of his Hill River Station in Clare Valley. The young Robinson was known not only for his vast station but also for his involvement in the Rufus River Massacre of 1841, in which at least thirty Aboriginal people were killed by a large party of police dispatched by Governor George Grey and others in what they called 'justified retaliation' after warriors had tried to push back against settlers moving into their land.

Impressed with Oakden's farm experience and exploration abilities, and sensing that New Zealand was the next place in which money could be easily made, Robinson commissioned him to travel to the South Island to find pastoral land to purchase. In 1854, just two years later, Robinson sold his River Hill Station, apparently for a huge profit. Then, after what has been described as a wrangling of questionable legality, he purchased over 40,000 acres of the best flat land in the region around the Cheviot Hills on the Canterbury coast for almost nothing. Following Robinson's lead, Oakden, too, settled in New Zealand in 1855, purchasing the Acheron Bank Station. A considerably more remote and challenging section, it is located west of Christchurch, hundreds of metres above sea level, and near the source of the Rakaia River in the foothills of the Southern Alps.

Acheron Bank Station had been established in 1853, making it one of the earliest sheep runs in New Zealand. By 1857, Oakden is said to have had 2,500 merino sheep running across its 20,000 acres. He continued to operate the station until 1878, when he sold it to John Murchison, after whom a river and town would later be named. Murchison had begun as a junior farmhand at Acheron but had eventually risen through the farming ranks. By the time of his death in 1904, he had become the owner not only of Acheron but also of Lake Coleridge and Glenthorne Stations, which he combined to run as one enterprise.

Today, the farms again operate independently, but continue to produce merino wool. Well on its way to collapse, the two-story woolshed at Acheron Bank is perhaps the most evocative vestige of the farm's early history. Thought to have been constructed under Oakden in the late 1850s, if this is true, it is one of New Zealand's earliest surviving wooden industrial buildings. Geoffrey Thornton photographed it for his 1986 book *The New Zealand Heritage of Farm Buildings,* commenting: 'It is not customary to consider that ruins have any significance in the New Zealand scene—indeed some will assert that we do not possess any for we do not have the great heritage of masonry structures that older civilisations have bequeathed. … [But] there are some ruins of interest, including woolsheds. … The deeply weathered timbers [of the Acheron Bank woolshed] make it a picturesque ruin set among trees … [although] it is now in a ruinous state and its days are numbered.'

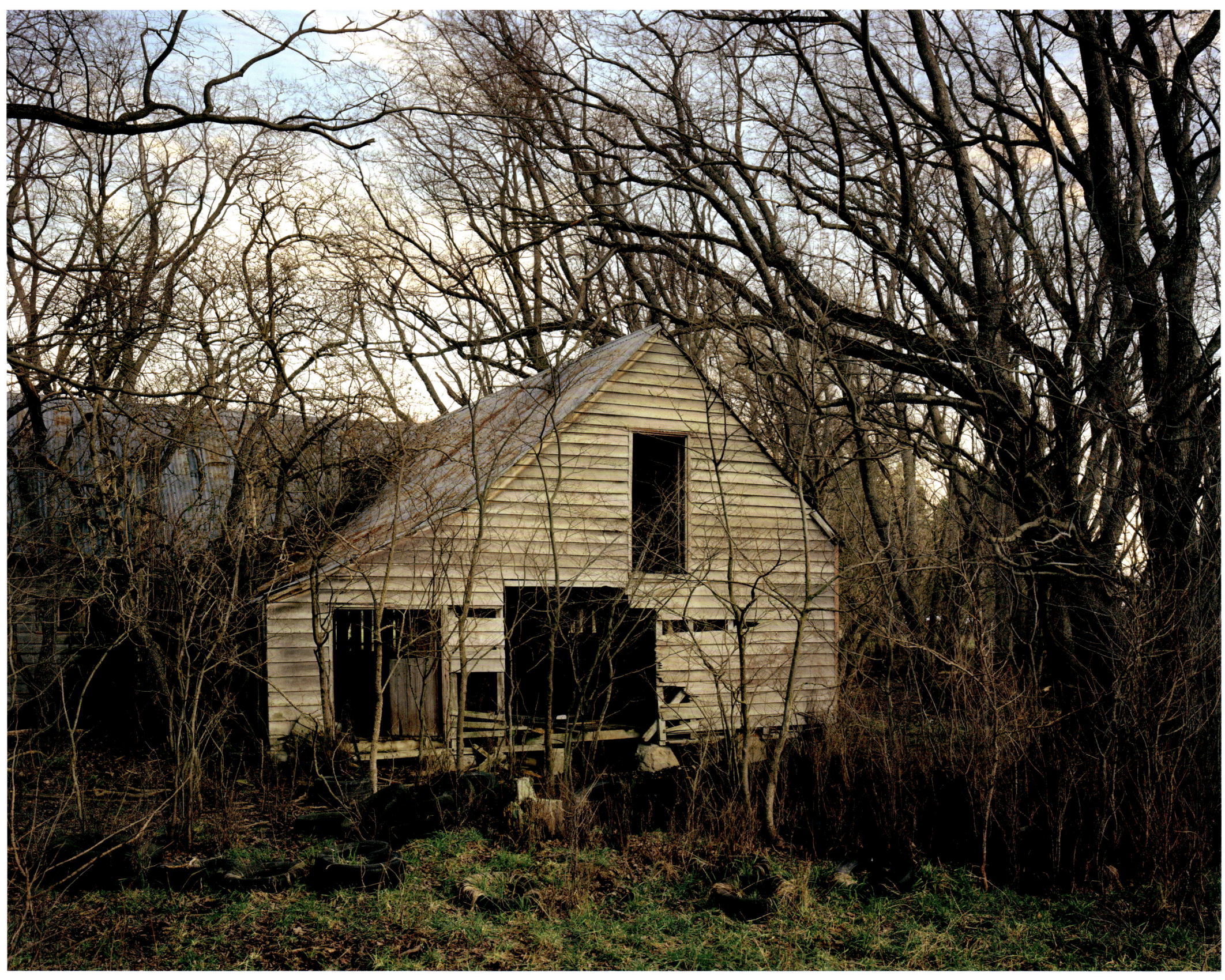

Generator Room, Former Fleming and Company Creamoata Mill, Gore, 2018

Thomas Fleming arrived in New Zealand from Scotland with his family in 1862, aged fourteen. In his youth, a string of jobs, ranging from cowboy to gardener, ultimately led him to wheat harvesting and flour milling near Ōamaru. After several years working in management, he and some partners bought their own mill and set about assimilating local competitors. In 1879, they opened a large new mill in Invercargill, and in 1883, they expanded further, purchasing Gore's first flour mill (built in 1877). By the end of the decade, they had expanded the facility with a four-story brick building in a Victorian style.

In 1909, Fleming and Company introduced what would become its most famous product, Creamoata. This oatmeal porridge was among the first 'fast oats' in the country, and over the next decade, its clever marketing saw it rise dramatically in popularity. Sold in an alluring yellow box, it was billed as 'Cream o' the Oat', and soon afterwards, 'The National Breakfast'. In the early 1920s, however, it permanently entered the national consciousness with the introduction of company mascot Sergeant Dan. Developed by a leading Auckland advertising agency, Dan was little drummer boy meets military cadet. Wearing an oversized army slouch hat and a green-buttoned shirt tucked into his shorts, and with a military pace stick over his shoulder, he made proclamations such as 'Every child needs a hot cereal breakfast all year round, say the doctors!' and 'Creamoata makes youngsters grow'. Dan appeared on everything from board games to spoons, and his popularity enabled Flemings to boast at one time that its factory in Gore was 'producing three-fifths of the oat foods used in the dominion'.

In 1889, Flemings Invercargill mill was razed by a fire, and in 1912, another fire struck the Gore factory. They rebuilt at Gore, but six years later, almost to the month, fire again levelled the mill, its cutting-edge machinery falling four stories into the basement. The mill was once again rebuilt. This time it was entirely constructed of fire-resistant ferro-concrete, and the latest fire safety measures were instituted. Widely described as the best and largest mill in Australasia, the art deco factory stood over twenty metres high and was fitted out with new machinery from the Pneumatic Scale Corporation of Boston.

The last member of the Fleming family who retained an interest in the company divested in 1953, and Flemings was purchased by Northern Roller Mills. In 1969, it merged with food producer Wattie's, which in turn merged with Australasian multinational Goodman Fielder in 1988. In 1993, Champion Flour Mills (then synonymous with flour in this country) also folded into the group, and Flemings came under the Champion umbrella. Around this time, Wattie's was purchased by multinational Heinz, and in 2000, the Creamoata factory in Gore was shuttered as production was shifted to Australia. Finally, in 2006, Nestlé acquired the Flemings brand as part of an acquisition of Uncle Toby's from Goodman Fielder. They discontinued Creamoata, and most of the Flemings line, two years later.

By the early 1990s, most of the wheat produced in New Zealand was used in the production of stock food, while the wheat consumed by people was imported from Australia or Japan. Since 2005, the former Flemings mill in Gore has been operated by Sergeant Dan's Stockfoods, which also acquired the intellectual property of Sergeant Dan.

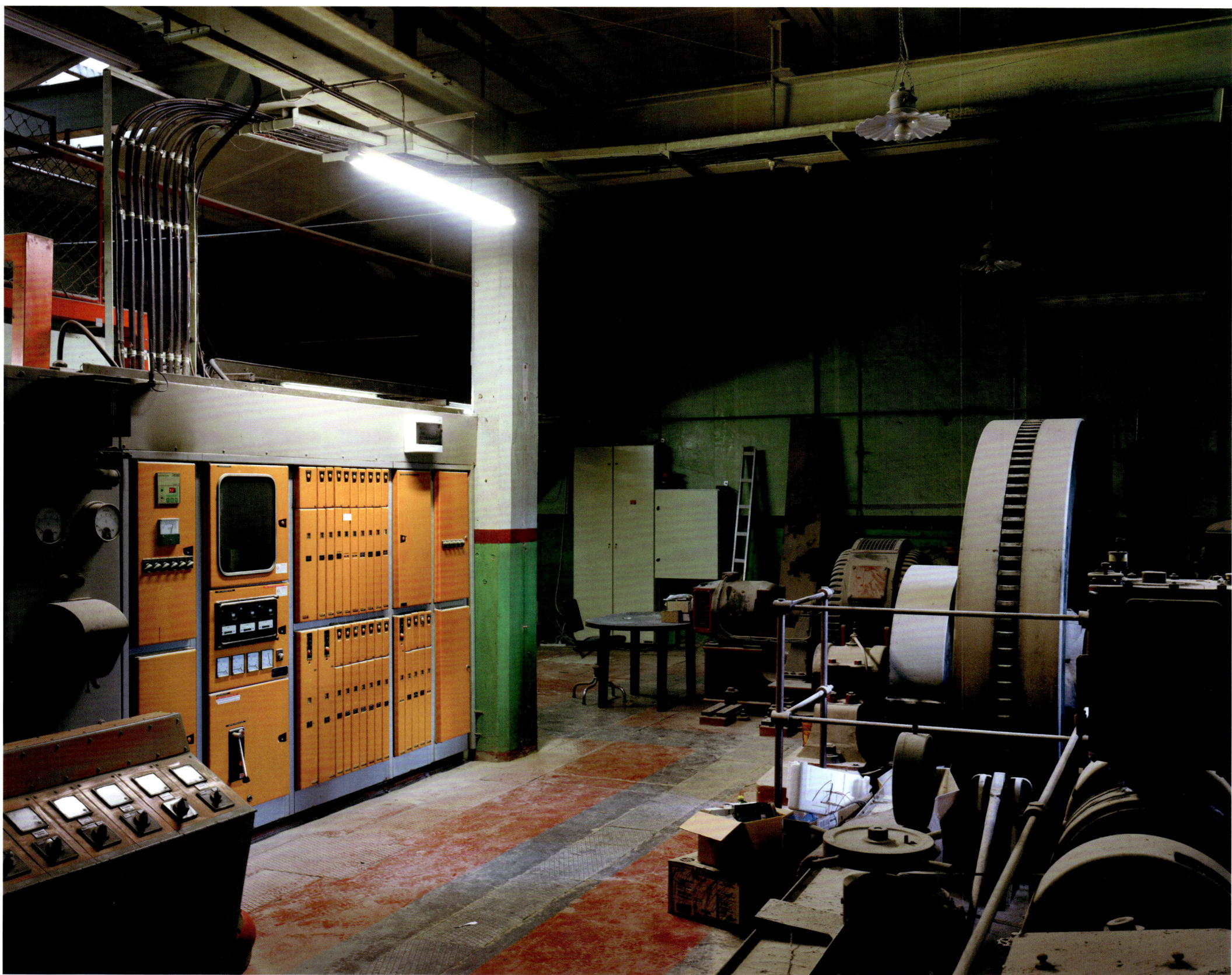

Spring Creek Mine and the Road to Rewanui, Dunollie, West Coast, 2016

The former mining settlement of Dunollie lies a couple of kilometres inland from the rugged coastline of the West Coast, beneath the kind of steep, rainforest-clad mountains for which the region is known. In 1903, a promotional flyer advertised 'a magnificent opportunity for speculation and investment' with 'The Creation of a new Town in connection with the State Coal Mines'. Dunollie was to consist of 160 freehold sections, to be sold by auction at the Greymouth Opera House. Located between the bend of Seven Mile Creek and the railway line that followed it up to the mines at Rewanui, the settlement sought to capitalise on the mines springing to life along the waterway by offering their workers housing closer than the existing settlement, Runanga, a kilometre away.

Near what was once the Dunollie train station is the Spring Creek Mine, the last underground coal mine to operate in New Zealand. Opened by state-owned Solid Energy in 2007, Spring Creek produced 'coking coal', for which there is presently no alternative when it comes to creating sufficient energy to produce steel and concrete. The mine formed a key part of the industrial ecosystem in the Greymouth region, together with the nearby Cape Foulwind Cement Works. It was also an important job provider, employing around 230 locals (most of whom had previously worked at other mines like Stockton), and a boon to the local economy.

In 2010, however, the Pike River disaster—the country's worst mining disaster since 1914—called the future of underground mining in New Zealand into question. The privately owned Pike River Mine lies less than thirty kilometres from Spring Creek, across a mountain range. On 19 December, at the beginning of summer, methane explosions ripped through the mine, killing twenty-nine men between the ages of seventeen and sixty-two. The tragedy dominated the New Zealand news cycle for years, with ongoing investigations into its cause and the miners' bodies remaining unrecovered due to the lingering risk of explosion.

In response to Pike River, new scrutiny was placed on the safety of underground mining. In 2012, the entire workforce at Spring Creek was made redundant, and later that same year, over 1,000 people marched in nearby Greymouth to protest the closure. Their message was that badly paid work in the tourism industry, to which the West Coast had been told to 'pivot', would not replace highly paid mining jobs in their communities. Spring Creek, however, remained closed. In 2015, risk-reduction amendments were made to the Health and Safety at Work Act. Designed to protect workers, the changes made it almost impossible to operate an underground mine legally and economically in New Zealand, and in 2017, after failing to find a buyer, the Spring Creek Mine was flooded and sealed.

As I drive through Dunollie's frost-dusted streets at dawn, smoke from coal burners rises against the dark hills. Most of the houses built by the first miners have gone, and those that survive are separated by now vacant lots. Nearly all the remaining homes have recently been painted, their lawns and gardens immaculately maintained. The pride of the town is still evident, as is the difficulty of going somewhere else, now that the local industry has vanished and property values have slumped.

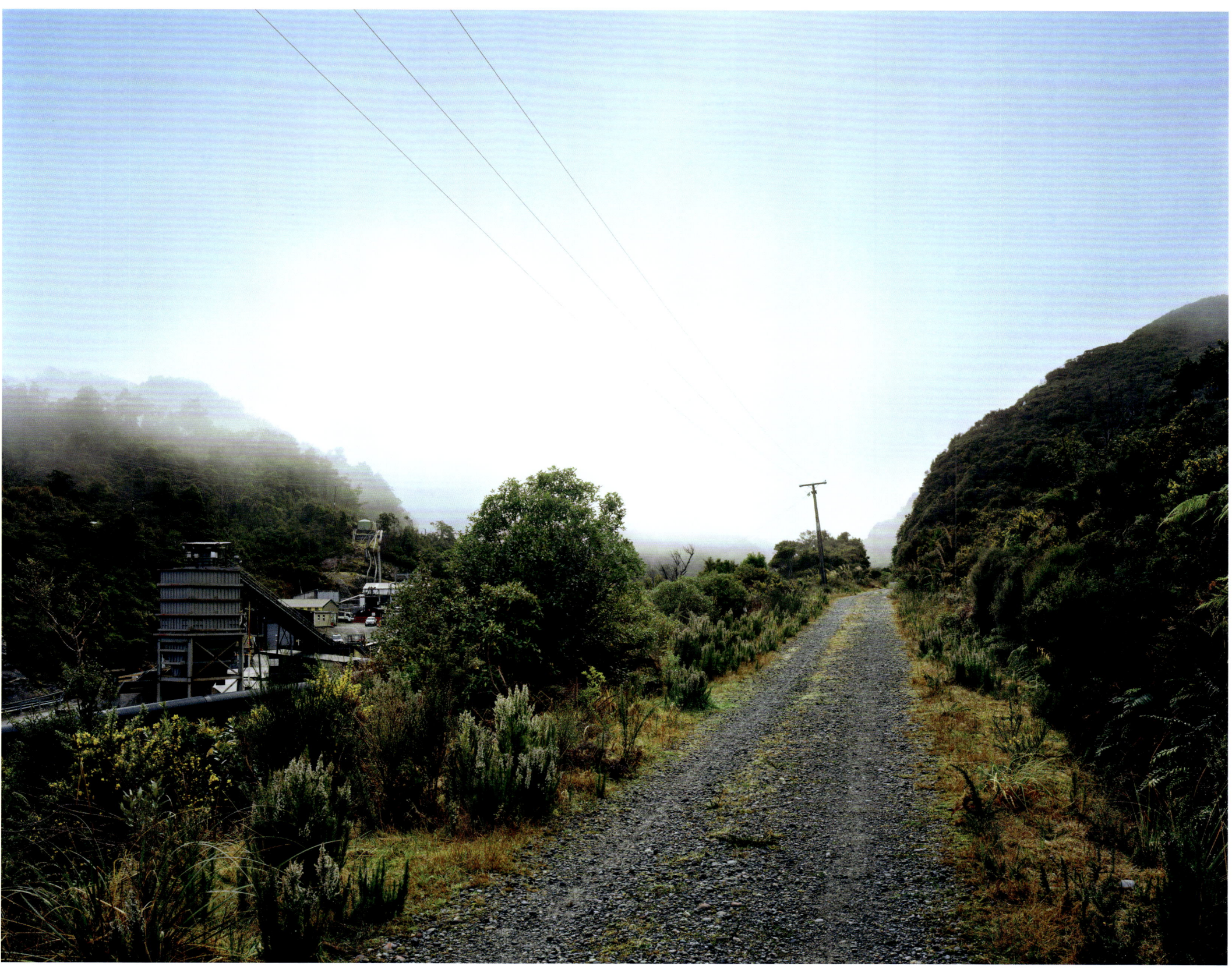

Engineers' Workshop, Rewanui, East of Dunollie, West Coast, 2018

Greymouth, the West Coast's largest town, lies at the mouth of the Grey River, on what was once a coastal wetland. Since 1872, at least seven major floods have brought the wide, swift, and steel-grey waters of the river into the town's streets, the flooding sometimes lasting for days. After one of the largest floods, in 1988, a seawall was built along the river, and this has protected the town since. But, set so close to sea level, the town has an uncertain future. On the seawall, two of the country's oldest and last pre-container ship port cranes stand like sentinels, frozen in place by rust, where not so long ago they moved coal from mines like Rewanui onto ships twenty-four hours a day.

Across the river from Greymouth and eight kilometres north, the small town of Runanga broods beneath the foothills of the Paparoa Range. Māori of the region once scaled its steep hills and river gorges, hunting birds upon the precipitous spurs above the rainforest. Although their settlement was gone before Europeans arrived, research suggests that an important whare rūnanga (meeting house) stood in the area giving the town its name. As Europeans ventured to this region, it was at Runanga that coal was first found in 1867. However, it was not until 1898, when a rail bridge was constructed across the perilous Grey River, that the coal industry truly began.

The Seddon Government demarcated the north side of the Grey River as a State Coal Reserve in 1902, and two years later, the Point Elizabeth No. 1 mine at Rewanui began producing coal. Following this, the settlements of Runanga and Dunollie sprang to life. The mining activity was also supported by the development of the Rewanui Branch train line, which ran ten kilometres uphill along the sheer gorge of Seven Mile Creek from Dunollie to its terminus, the mining area of Rewanui.

More than a dozen mines would operate over the next decades in and around Rewanui and the surrounding valley, the insatiable desire for coal—to propel New Zealand's shipping, railways, steel, and cement production— leading to operations in some of the most extreme conditions in the country. The famous Liverpool mine, which opened in 1913, sat near the top of the 700-metre Paparoa Range in the sheer upper gorge of Seven Mile Creek. So remote was the settlement that it required its own incline tramway, split into two parts, for access. It eventually came to be known as Siberia, for its penal-colony-like isolation as much as for its relentless wind, freezing rain, and winter snow.

As coal prices slumped globally during the 1980s, the mines at Rewanui finally closed in 1984, and the Rewanui Branch was removed the following year. Just three years later, heavy rain caused a severe landslide that destroyed most of Rewanui's buildings and killed its caretaker, Keith Butler, whose body and car were never found. Today a plaque in his memory is etched into a large rock where the settlement used to be.

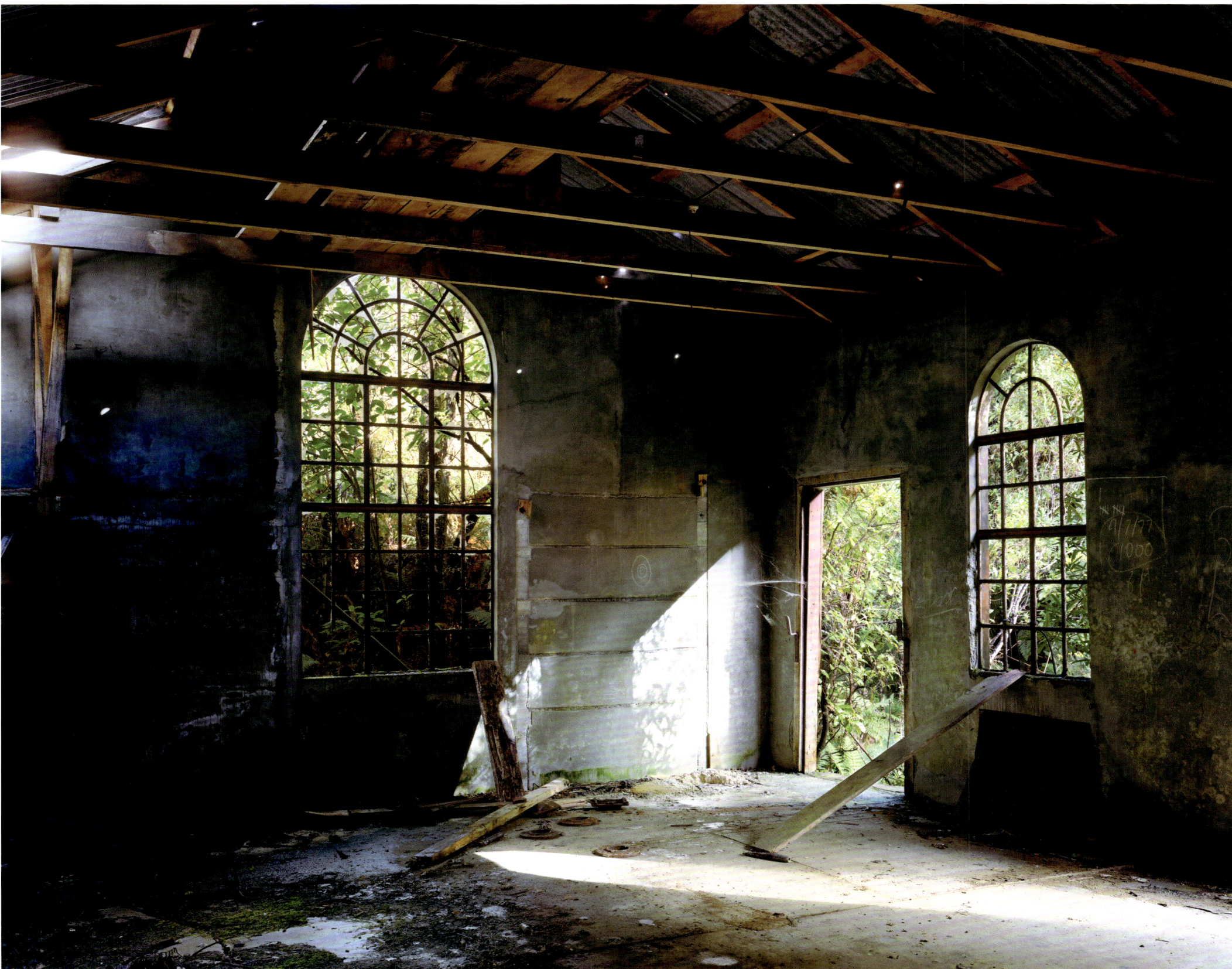

Rain over the Coal Bins at Kiwi Mine, Ten Mile Creek / Waianiwaniwa, West Coast, 2018

New Zealand's worst mining disaster took place at the Brunner Mine, near Greymouth, in 1896, when an explosion killed sixty-five miners, or half the underground workforce. The event triggered a national debate about mine safety, and in 1901, the Government responded with the State Coal Mines Act. The legislation allowed the Government to create mines that would have higher safety standards and provide a reliable national coal supply. They rapidly became the country's primary mining employer, and several of their operations on the West Coast, including Strongman, Denniston, Stockton, and Millerton, became famous. Unable to match the employment conditions at the state mines, private mines adapted by doing more with smaller teams and undertaking more risky work.

In the precipitous valley of Ten Mile Creek, north of Greymouth, a series of private mines worked for nearly six decades, until the price of coal declined in the 1980s. At nearby Government mines, teams of 100 to 200 men worked in shifts, with each person performing a specialised role. By contrast, at the private mines, groups would be limited to as few as four men, and several distinct mines would often operate in close proximity. This situation was in part facilitated by hydraulic mining, which eliminated much traditional labour. More importantly, however, miners for private mines were selected for their ability to fill numerous roles, such as prospecting, engineering, building, electrics, plumbing, and equipment maintenance. The collectives also employed a democratic ideology, with everybody—including the mine manager, who set the hours—sharing an equal portion of the gruelling and dangerous physical work.

The catch of these operations, though, was that the less-than-ideal nature of the coal seams and the use of gravity-based hydraulic mining often meant that mine shafts were located on extraordinarily steep terrain. In 1979, a short documentary produced by the Government's National Film Unit, *Coal Valley*, captured the combination of tenacity and foolhardiness required for the work. Focusing on the different operations at Ten Mile Creek, it shows work at the independent mines Harrisons, United, Snowline, Alpine, and Kiwi. In one scene, while carpooling to work, the miners discuss the freedom of independent mining and its strong connection to family tradition. Their pride and 'do it yourself' attitude are evident, as is their dogged determination; winter or summer, rain or shine, they work along precipitous cliffs and mountain tops, and even above a 200-metre waterfall. In another scene, miners from Kiwi Mine casually enjoy their morning tea in a tin hut built on a ledge cut into a sheer cliff, some 300 metres above their mine's coal bins. Their commute back to the mine shaft is a casual jaunt across planks from which a fall would mean certain death.

Over several years, I have spent weeks in the Ten Mile Valley trying to trace the mostly eroded cliff and mountain paths used by the miners. Setting aside the politics of coal, it's difficult not to admire their ingenuity and hardiness. Still private land, each time I visit the valley more of the operations have disappeared, claimed by the West Coast's wild weather and Government-mandated site remediation before the land can be sold. By 2018, the large steel coal bins at Kiwi Mine—which was the first to open in the valley in the 1920s—were the main remnant of their labour.

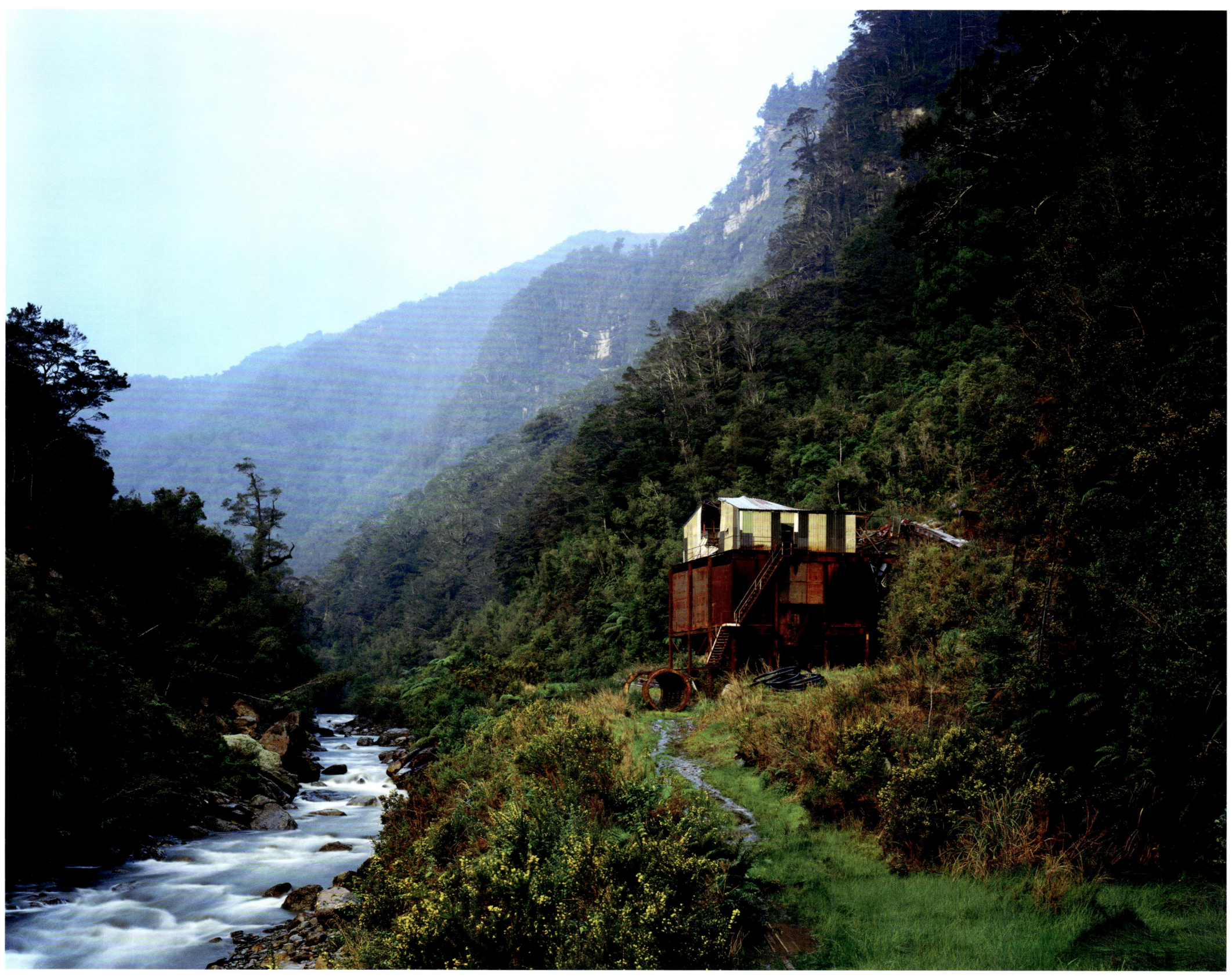

Miners' Hut, Near Alpine Battery, Lyell Creek, West Coast, 2018

In 1862, a group led by the Māori prospector Eparara was exploring around Lyell Creek, sixty kilometres east of Westport, when they discovered a gold nugget weighing nineteen and a half ounces (half a kilogram). Word of the sizable 'dumbbell shaped nugget' quickly spread, and the township of Lyell sprung to life almost overnight. One of the more picturesque of the West Coast gold rush locations, Lyell sat on a ridge above the confluence of the creek and the Buller River. The Lyell Ranges surrounding the site were then clad in lush old-growth forest. The geologist Julius von Haast had bestowed the name Lyell while exploring the West Coast in the 1850s in tribute to the 'father of geology', Charles Lyell, one of the first scientists to propose that the earth's geology was shaped by continual processes.

In the initial stage of the gold rush, nuggets and alluvial gold were readily found in the creek, but the easy pickings were soon exhausted. It was only when a party of Swiss prospectors discovered the gold's source, an auriferous quartz lode five kilometres upstream from the township, along the steep gorge, that the true wealth that lay beneath the Lyell Range was revealed. They established the Alpine Mining Company with a public share offering, and then set about constructing an elaborate wooden tramway to move the mined quartz down the almost sheer cliffs, below which an enormous twenty-head stamping battery (imported from England) was assembled beside the creek.

The quartz seam was unusually enduring, and the Alpine Company's stamping battery became Lyell's soundtrack, the noise of iron smashing rock echoing down the gorge at every hour of the day. The township underwent an explosion of growth, and in less than a decade after its founding, most of the surrounding rainforest had been logged or cleared. Meanwhile, its main street was now home to numerous businesses, including multiple hotels, a school, a bank, and two newspapers, and, at its peak in the 1880s, the population was over 2,000 people. The growth was largely driven by the success of the Alpine Mining Company, which employed over 200 men at the time and, despite competition, extracted over 80,000 ounces of gold, with over 150,000 pounds of quartz being removed and crushed in the process. Their winnings ultimately comprised nearly 90% of the gold found at Lyell.

Finally, though, the Alpine Company lost the bearing on their gold seam. Changes in ownership and amalgamations followed, but with no new seam forthcoming, the company laid off its workers and was out of business by 1900. Some of the miners carried on regardless, even appealing to the Minister of Mines for support, but no relief came, and by 1912, the operation was over for good. The loss also spelt the end for Lyell, and in 1963, the hotel, which was the last remnant of the town, burned down. Today, what was once a bustling hive of activity is an empty field maintained by the Department of Conservation as a campground. It comprises one end of the 'Old Ghost Road', an eighty-five-kilometre hiking and cycling route that follows old mining trails and is hoped to help the West Coast pivot from industry into tourism.

In the hills above the campground, amid regenerating beech forest, is Lyell's graveyard, its handful of headstones and wrought-iron grave borders almost lost beneath roots and fallen leaves. Further up the valley, deeper into the bush, a solitary miner's hut hangs on, just above the former Alpine Battery.

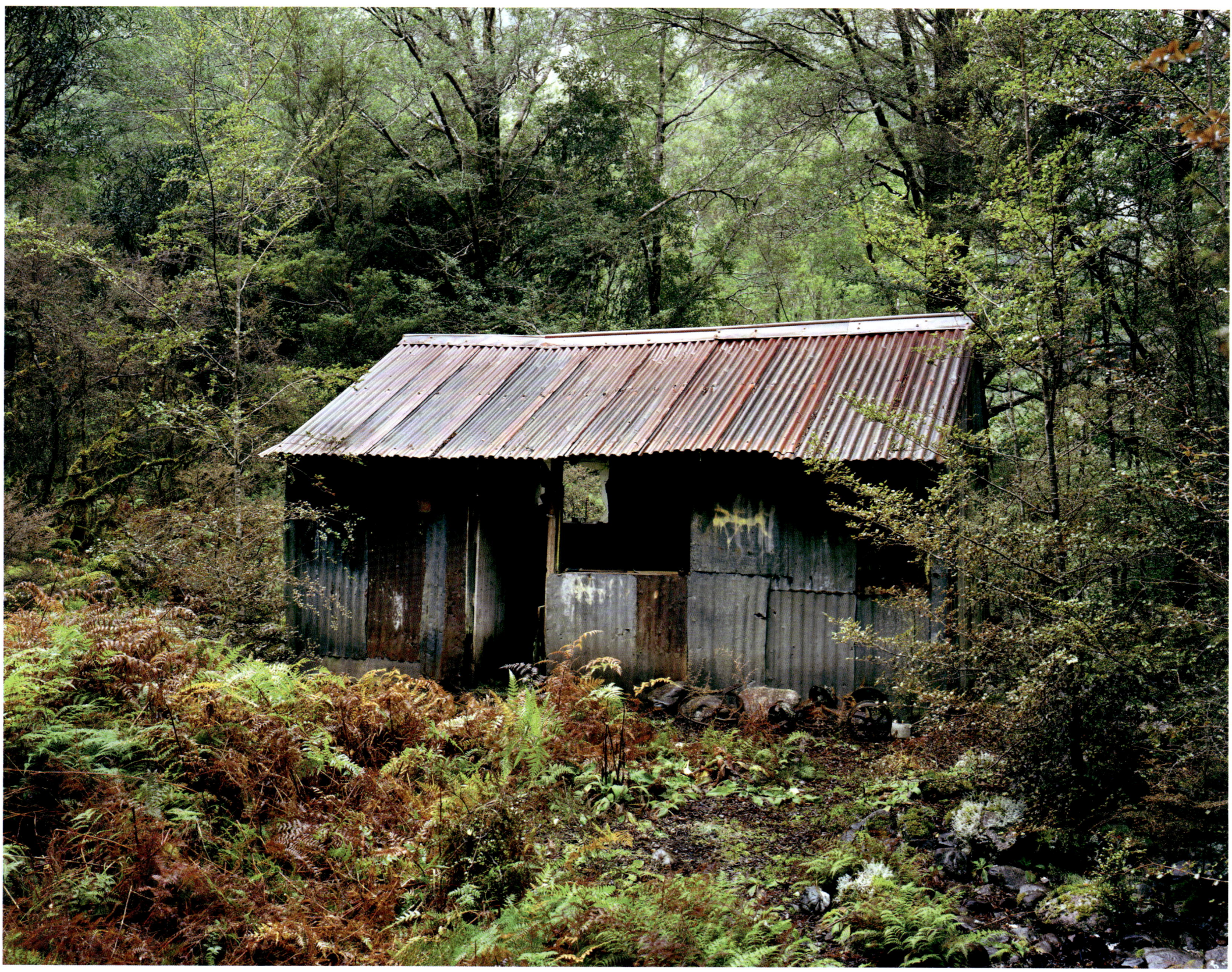

Homeward Bound Battery, Gold Burn or Rich Burn, North-West of Macetown, Otago, 2018

In the Arrow Gorge, a plaque on a stone monument reads, 'William Fox discovered gold near here in 1862.' However, it is now known that it was local farmhand Jack Tewa (known as 'Māori Jack') who first discovered gold in the Arrow River. He brought the news of his find back to Rees Station in Queenstown Bay, where he worked. Two men then departed for the river, and with just rudimentary panning, they were soon finding up to twenty ounces of gold per day. A week later William Fox showed up at the river, and, unfortunately for the local geology, he had been followed. Station owner William Rees reflected, 'Fox like a fool must need go to the Dunstan [for supplies] and as a consequence he was watched and followed.' The absurd sequence of events became known as 'the great foxhunt' and it sparked a rush at what would become Arrowtown.

By December, less than five months after Tewa's discovery, over 1,500 miners were camped at the base of the Arrow Gorge. As the miners explored the river, it wasn't long before a canvastown (tent settlement) began taking shape some fifteen kilometres further upstream from where the rush began. Named for the four Mace brothers, who first staked claims at the site, Macetown sat at the confluence of the Arrow River and the Gold Burn or Rich Burn, where the narrow gorge of the Arrow opens into a lush valley around a shallow and braided section of the river. Above the valley, the Harris Mountains and Mount Soho rise dramatically to heights of over 1,700 metres. Each year, as winter came, miners who decided to stay put would find themselves cut off for months at a time— first by ice and snowfall, then by the dangerous and unpassable volume of the Arrow River as the snow melted.

Despite the harshness of the alpine climate, the extent of the gold saw Macetown swell to a population of over 3,000 miners at the peak of the rush in the 1860s. But as the easily found alluvial gold ran out, the people left as quickly as they had arrived, most departing for the greener pastures of new gold claims on the West Coast. In the 1870s, the emergence of quartz mining saw large numbers return to Macetown; its main street acquired stone and wooden buildings, and a population of nearly 400—most of whom worked at the new mines. However, quartz mining made the work increasingly dangerous. Mostly found high and far into the mountains, accessing and extracting it required the creation of mines and support structures in extreme locations. But, with tenacity, ingenuity, and perhaps gold fever, huge mining operations came to life. Networks of sluicing and aerial cableways were built into the sheer rock so that with water and gravity, giant chunks of quartz could be moved downhill and crushed in the iron stamping batteries below, in preparation for the extraction of the gold.

Some distance up the Rich Burn from Macetown, the Homeward Bound Battery was one of the largest and last gold stamping batteries to operate in Otago. Its iron components were manufactured in Chester, England, and it was first assembled in New Zealand around 1884, at Waipori in Central Otago. The battery was moved to its current location around 1912—a monumental undertaking, with each of its ten iron 'stamps' alone weighing in excess of 625 kilograms. With the surrounding mountains being treeless, its timber had to be hauled, piece by piece, some twenty kilometres upriver from Arrowtown. Despite nearly forty years of mining at the site, the Homeward Bound claim went bust just four years after the battery was installed. Since the mine was the last in the area, its closure spelled the end of Macetown, which was soon abandoned.

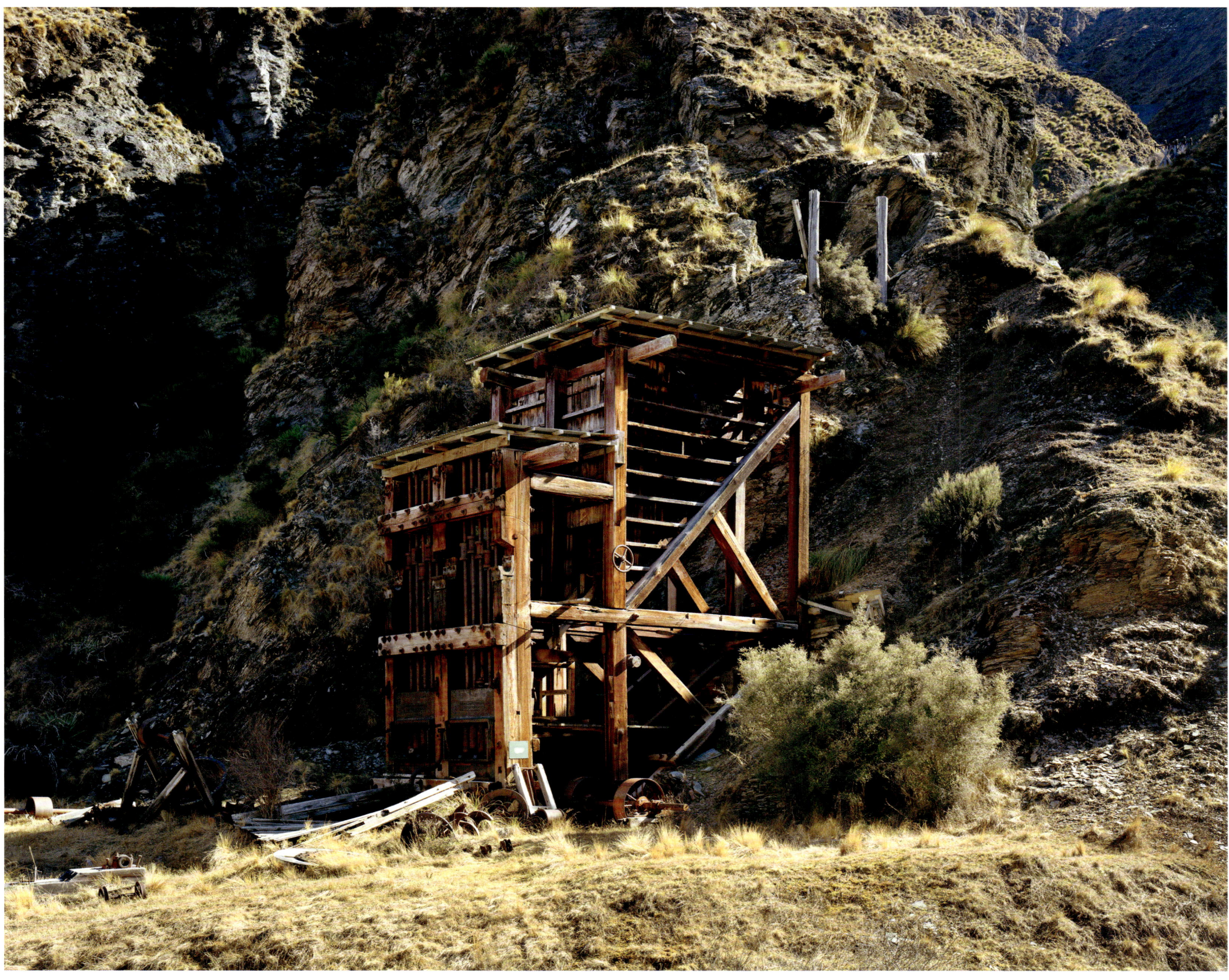

Cyanide Tanks with Ice, Premier Battery, Near Advance Peak, Otago, 2018

A few kilometres upstream from the Homeward Bound Battery, but higher in elevation, Premier Battery lies deep within the Harris Mountains. Among the most remote and forbidding gold mines ever to operate in New Zealand, even today it is challenging to reach the site. First, a fifteen-kilometre four-wheel-drive route traces the gorge and bed of the Arrow River. Cut by miners with nothing but pickaxes and packhorses in the nineteenth century, the trail crosses the river (which quickly becomes treacherous with rain) some thirty times, before finally reaching what was once Macetown. Here, the gorge shrinks, and not long after, the old mining trail becomes passable only on foot, climbing 600 metres higher and further kilometres into the mountains. The narrow pack track—which falls in and out of tributaries and river crossings—then disintegrates further, threatened by slips that continue to pull what remains of it into the valley below.

In the last decades of the nineteenth century, the mining complex around Premier Battery employed as many as 300 men. To be near the mine's workings, they lived in the remote valley from which it operated, housed in tents and makeshift stone huts that offered little protection from the elements. All the same, the isolation and extreme conditions remained better than walking the ten-kilometre track (which in winter could be covered with snow) each day from Macetown. Even living near Premier Battery, though, most of the miners still had to climb hundreds of metres up to the mine shafts where they worked each day. The most notorious was the Sunrise Mine, located just below the 1,749-metre summit of Advance Peak and known as the 'highest gold mine in the colony'.

Today, the remains of stamping batteries to crush quartz, and the cyanide tanks which extracted the gold from it, still stand in place. With the dangers of the cyanide process now known, though, it is disturbing to see the proximity of the tanks to the crumbled stone foundations of the miners' huts and Sawyers Creek, a major tributary of the Arrow River. The process of gold cyanidation was invented simultaneously in South Africa and New Zealand, and the world's first successful trial took place at Karangahake, near Coromandel, in 1889. In the system, crushed gold-bearing quartz rock was washed in a solution of potassium cyanide and water. Then, after agitation with air and filtration through zinc, the gold was cleanly separated. So successful was the invention that its patent was acquired by the New Zealand Government in 1897, and its widespread adoption saw the Government recoup its research outlay quickly, charging just a small royalty.

The Premier Company was said to be the most successful of all those that worked around Macetown during an intense half-century of activity. When they packed up shop in 1905, their operation had lasted an almost unheard-of thirty years. Over a century later, the primary legacy of their toil is now the toxicity of the site. Due to its remote location, the cyanide tanks are now almost the last remaining in the country. Decades after its closure, the Prohibition Mine, near Reefton on the West Coast, remained so contaminated with arsenic that just having lunch in its vicinity could cause poisoning. In 2016, the toxic remnants of that mine were cleaned up by the Government at a cost of $2.6 million. Premier Battery's cyanide plant still awaits remediation.

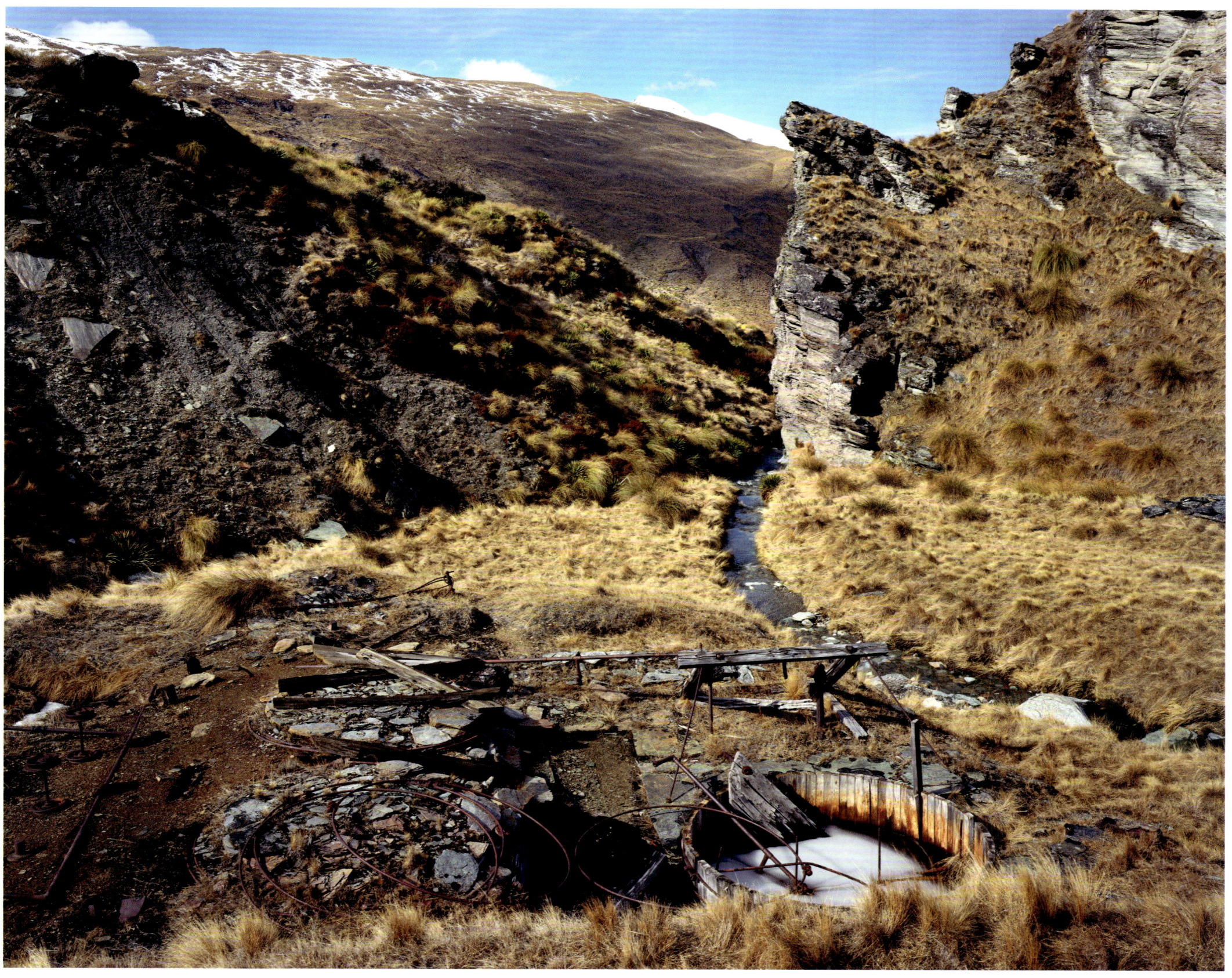

Acid Mine Drainage Remediation, Sullivan West Mine, Denniston Plateau, 2018

South of the Denniston Incline, and at a remove from the plateau's other works, the state-owned Sullivan Mine opened in 1952. It flourished for nearly three decades, closing in 1980 when the practically accessible parts of its coal seam had been exhausted. A new Sullivan West Mine was then established, west of the original workings on a still more remote site above Rapid Creek—its two new mine shafts offering a different angle of approach to the original coal seam and making it viable once again. Utilising hydraulic mining, Sullivan West became one of the safest and most efficient operations in the country. Workers at other hydraulic mines still had to perform some dangerous work at the coal face, but here, a machine known as the 'monitor' did the riskiest digging work, allowing miners to spend far less time in parts of the mine most at risk of ceiling collapse and explosion.

In 1994, the Sullivan Mine closed. With its gravel access road remaining intact, the site—which lies on Department of Conservation land—gradually became an illegal rubbish dump. Remains sufficiently well secured to survive scrap metal hunters were slowly buried by rubbish, which piled on to the former site like an archaeological dig in reverse. In 2004, the mine's owner, Solid Energy, finally cleaned up the rubbish and remediated both mine sites. With the once-giant coal bins and other structures removed, the only remnants present today are concrete foundations, shaft entrances, and a giant winch. Over the years, Denniston's wild weather has deteriorated the remote access road, which is now popular with mountain bikers and four-wheel-drive enthusiasts.

Like countless former mines all over the world, Sullivan West has produced toxic 'acid mine drainage'. This begins when mine diggings expose rocks containing sulphur-bearing minerals to oxygen, surface and subsurface water, or snow melt. The contact creates sulfuric acid, which in turn releases combinations of heavy metals, including iron, lead, arsenic, and mercury. The acidic water and metals then inevitably move into waterways, wreaking havoc on aquatic, bird, and plant life, as well as people downstream, unaware of its presence.

I could find no data for New Zealand, but a 2004 study in the *Encyclopedia of Energy* cited acid mine drainage as the primary cause of polluted water in the United States; in 1995, over 4,688 miles of waterways were affected, with an estimated USD $5 billion required to remediate them. At Sullivan West, a solution—versions of which have been tried successfully overseas—is being explored in a small-scale trial. Beneath one of the leaking mine shafts, a channel of limestone has been created. Containing the acid drainage, the rock bed will slowly reabsorb the heavy metals from the stagnant water, eventually restoring the balance of acidity.

Modern mining operations mostly contain and manage acid mine drainage before the problem begins. However, there is currently no system or budget in place to remediate the thousands of defunct mines that operated in New Zealand during the past century.

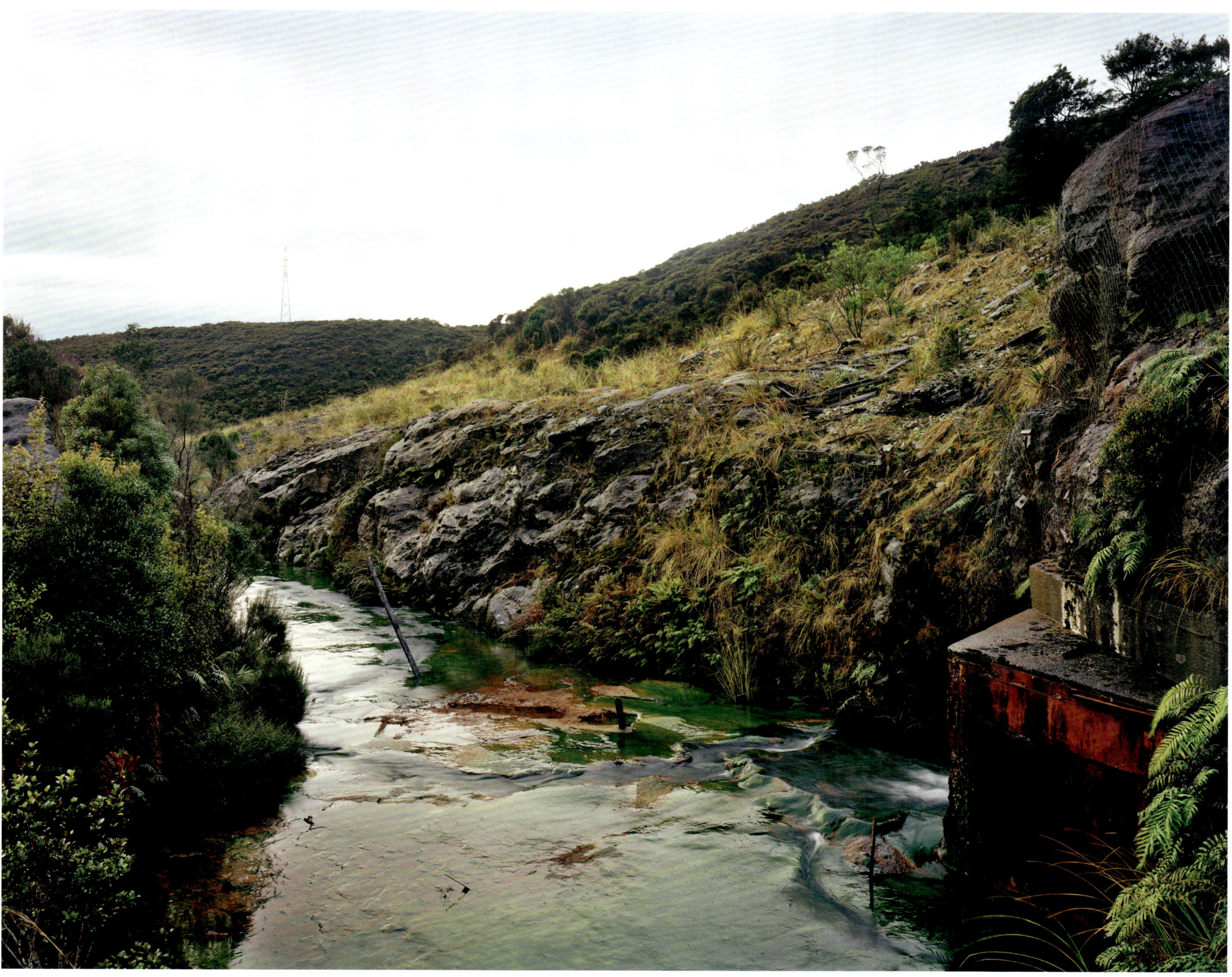

Remains of the Mine Bathhouse, Denniston Plateau, West Coast, 2019

Once a man was settled down with a wife and family of small children he was owned—every inch of him—by the mighty and powerful Westport coal company of the day. Mining was the only job offering and the only job he knew anything about. He was committed to earning a living for himself and family and couldn't afford to move from The Hill to any other place. He was owned by the regulations that bound him and every yard of the road he trudged to work. He was owned by the black and cavernous mine itself: without it, where was his living coming from? He was owned by his allegiance to his fellow-workers. He was owned by many outside influences which came with his daily work. He was owned, in certain ways, by The Hill itself.

So wrote Cecilia Adams in her book *The Hill*, published in 1971. A miner's daughter and miner's wife, she spent over twenty years living at Denniston, raising two children during the township's 'golden age' in the early twentieth century and serving as the plateau's first teacher. Despite the weight of her words, though, it is her love of the place that comes through most clearly in *The Hill*—along with her insistence on the strength of Denniston's community, in which miners made lives for themselves against the odds on inhospitable rocky terrain, where few plants would grow, and a cemetery couldn't be built for a lack of topsoil.

At Denniston's height, around the turn of the nineteenth century, the township had more than 800 residents and a multitude of businesses, including five hotels, a public pool, and even a hospital. In early years, reaching the plateau and township meant the choice between an arduous trek up the pack track, over 600 metres in elevation, or risking life and limb riding coal buckets up the Incline. By 1900, a gravel road had reached the township, but with Westport twenty-five kilometres away, and cars uncommon before the 1960s, miners still chose to live on the plateau. In 1911, over 1,400 people were based there, not only at Denniston but also at the smaller settlements Coalbrookdale and Burnett's Face.

In the 1970s, miners and their families began moving away from Denniston as the last mines closed, and soon, it became a ghost town, with just a handful of homes standing. Today, only one or two are still occupied, and of the rest all that remains are the scattered foundations of steps and chimneys, gradually being reclaimed by regenerating scrub. Of the many former shops and public structures, the only traces are the concrete of a swimming pool, two small dams, and the collapsed bath houses—the first, from 1939, and its replacement from 1984, which operated for just eleven years. On its floor, the ventilation system now lies in pieces amid broken asbestos cladding covered in a patina of mould.

The vast engineers' workshops, coal bins, and imported cableway and Incline, have long since been dismantled for scrap, or simply bulldozed off the cliff edge.

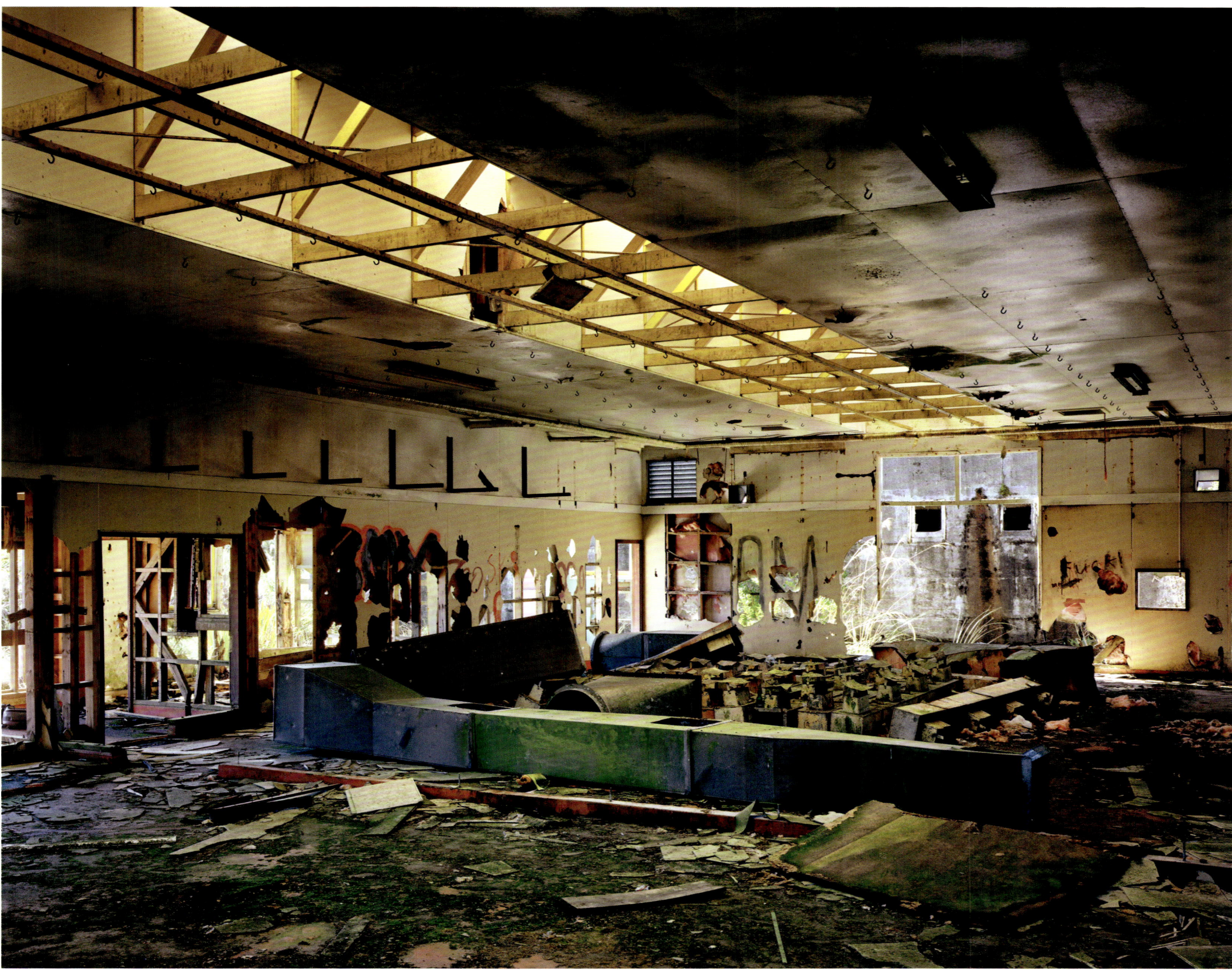

Remains of the Sefferston Schoolhouse, Moke Creek, Otago, 2019

West of Queenstown, a road winds around Lake Wakatipu before a turnoff ascends the foothills of Ben Lomond towards Moke Lake. The source of Moke Creek, the body of water moves through a sheer gorge before it joins Moonlight Creek, and the mighty Shotover River. Gold was discovered in the area by Australian prospector George Moonlight in 1862. Despite the harsh terrain and weather conditions, a canvastown of over 3,000 miners soon sprang up in the vicinity of Moke Creek and, in time, stone houses, a post office, a hotel, general stores, and even a school were added.

At many other sites, gold was found far below the surface or in hard quartz, but here it lay almost entirely among the gravel and stones of the riverbed, extractable through panning, sluicing, and, later on, dredging. What was easily found was also easily exhausted, though, and as went the gold, so went the canvastown. After this, only a small population remained, who worked dredging the rivers more deeply, and combing over the mountains of river stone tailings left piled along the creeks by previous miners. But although the rush was brief, it was one of the richest ever seen in New Zealand; in *Gold Trails of Otago* (1970), June A. Wood notes that by the end of the rush, 'over $8 million [$160 million today] of gold had been extracted and sold'.

Sefferston, as the Moke Creek settlement came to be known, is named for a Crimean, Vasilio Seffer, one of the first storekeepers there. Seemingly unfazed by the alpine conditions, he grew his own tobacco and made his own butter, cheese, and wine. As the settlement disbanded, his son, John Seffer, became the final inhabitant. The wooden hut in which he lived for decades is now the last building standing. For a time it was occupied by the writer Barry Crump, who wrote several novels there, and later, it is said to have been a 'public library' that housed over 500 leather-bound books up to the 1970s—although it is unclear who frequented the remote athenaeum.

Moke Creek is today private property, part of the vast Ben Lomond station. When I visited in 2019, it was the beginning of winter. The only access is a four-wheel-drive farm road that follows the creek hundreds of metres up into the hills, where patches of ice, mud, and slips threaten to drag the vehicle into the gorge below. As the trail winds further towards thousand-metre-high mountains, it ascends and descends, crossing in and out of swift and freezing creeks. Finally, it reaches the old Sefferston Schoolhouse and, nearby, Seffer's hut, my accommodation for the night. At 3am, though, my stay is cut short by the invasion of a disturbingly large possum that seems to have entered through a gap in the stone fireplace. Still half asleep, I retreat through the sub-zero night to the front seat of my truck.

Beyond the hut, and the mountains of river stone tailings, the walls of the schoolhouse—barely hanging on— are all that mark the former settlement.

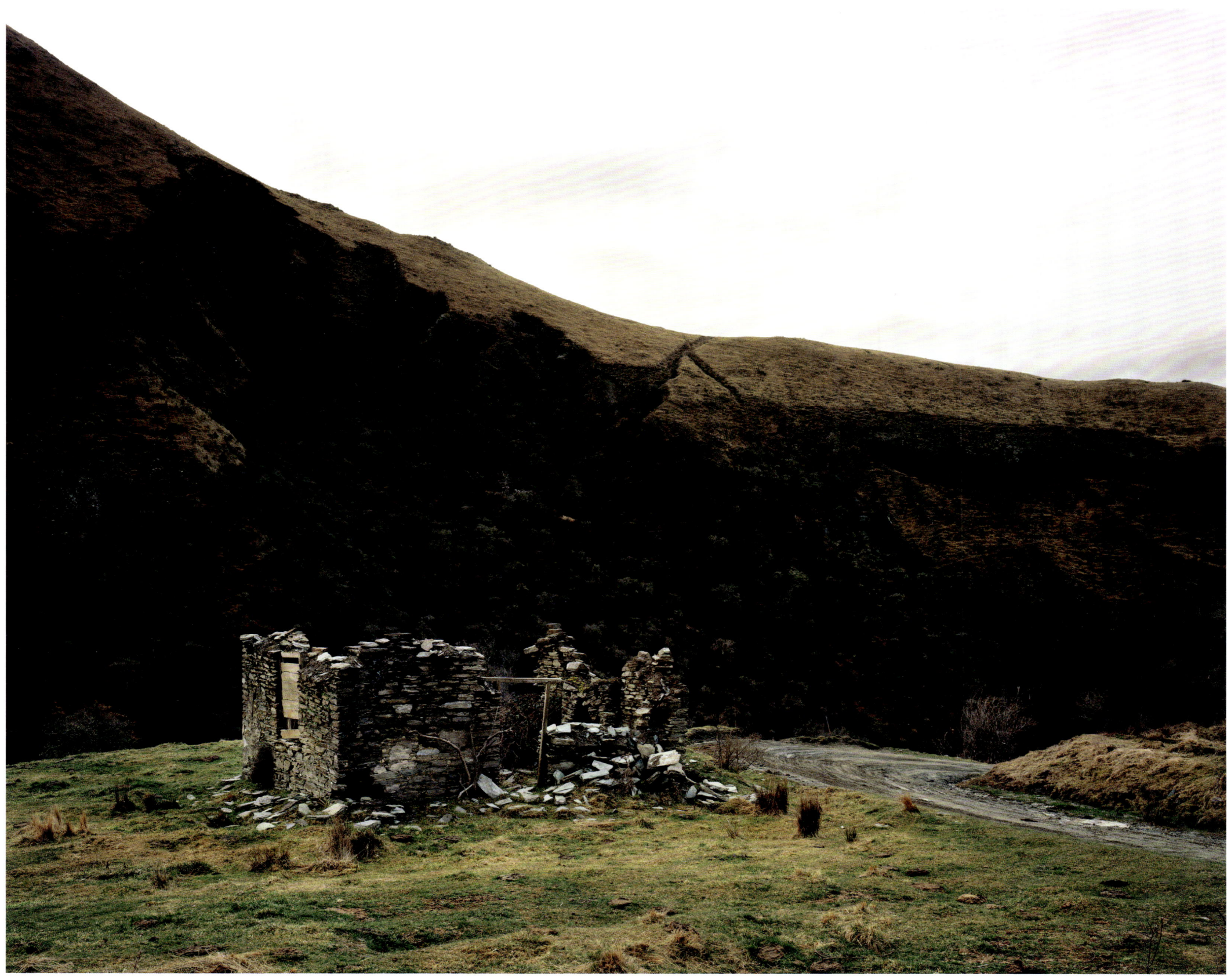

Chimneys and Tanks, Demolition of the Cement Works, Cape Foulwind, West Coast, 2019

Not far from the coastal town of Westport, the prominent headland Tauranga (meaning 'anchorage') juts into the Tasman Sea. For centuries, its sheltered cove was a resting place for voyaging waka (canoes). Captain James Cook visited the area in 1770, during his first journey to New Zealand aboard the *Endeavour*. Just off the coast, he encountered bad weather and a strong wind, which, he wrote, 'repelled his ship from the shore like an omen'. So, without ever stepping foot on land, he renamed Tauranga Cape Foulwind. In 1846, the artist and surveyor Charles Heaphy, then on an expedition from the top of the South Island to the West Coast, also reached the Cape, writing that as he gazed across Tauranga Bay it was the 'prettiest view in the world'. He was likely taking in the western side of the bay, which is one of the only fur seal colonies on New Zealand's mainland.

Industry, however, is not concerned with views, and by the late nineteenth century, multiple quarries were operating around Cape Foulwind, which became known for cement production. In the first decades after European arrival in New Zealand, little cement was used, since Portland Cement from Britain had to be imported by ship in wooden barrels. But as national railways were built from the 1870s, cement became necessary for tunnels and bridges. The material was increasingly used in other kinds of construction as well, and by the end of the 1880s, multiple cement plants were operating around New Zealand with plans in place for more.

The process of manufacturing cement is resource intensive, requiring—among other things—calcium-rich limestone, chalk, coral, or shell deposits; oxides from argillaceous (clay-like) materials, such as shale, slate, marl, and estuarine mud; silica sand; iron oxide; and bauxite. The raw materials then require crushing, cleaning, and filtering, and mixing to the correct proportions and purities. Finally, the blend is fired in giant steel cylindrical kilns to 1450°C, a heat beyond even stoneware ceramics. As with the production of iron and steel, almost the only way of achieving such a temperature at scale is using metallurgical (or coking) coal. This rare and valuable kind of coal is abundant on the West Coast. Thus Cape Foulwind was selected as the site of a major cement works by the New Zealand Cement Company—a consortium of four British cement, shipping, and finance companies—in 1958.

Over the next six decades, the Cape Foulwind Cement Works built much of New Zealand's infrastructure and cities. A report from 1998 records Cape Foulwind as accounting for 42% of cement production in the country that year. The closure of the works in 2016 dealt a devastating blow to the West Coast economy and resulted in the loss of hundreds of jobs. While many environmentalists cheered the change, it is a sad irony that cement now must be imported again, and the carbon footprint of this process vastly eclipses that of producing it locally. At Cape Foulwind, the industry was truly local; limestone and marl came from a quarry just two kilometres away, coal came from mines within twenty kilometres of the plant, and the final product was shipped from the nearby town of Westport.

Following the plant's demolition, the former site was sold to a group of property investors in 2020. It has since been subdivided for lifestyle blocks and dairy farming.

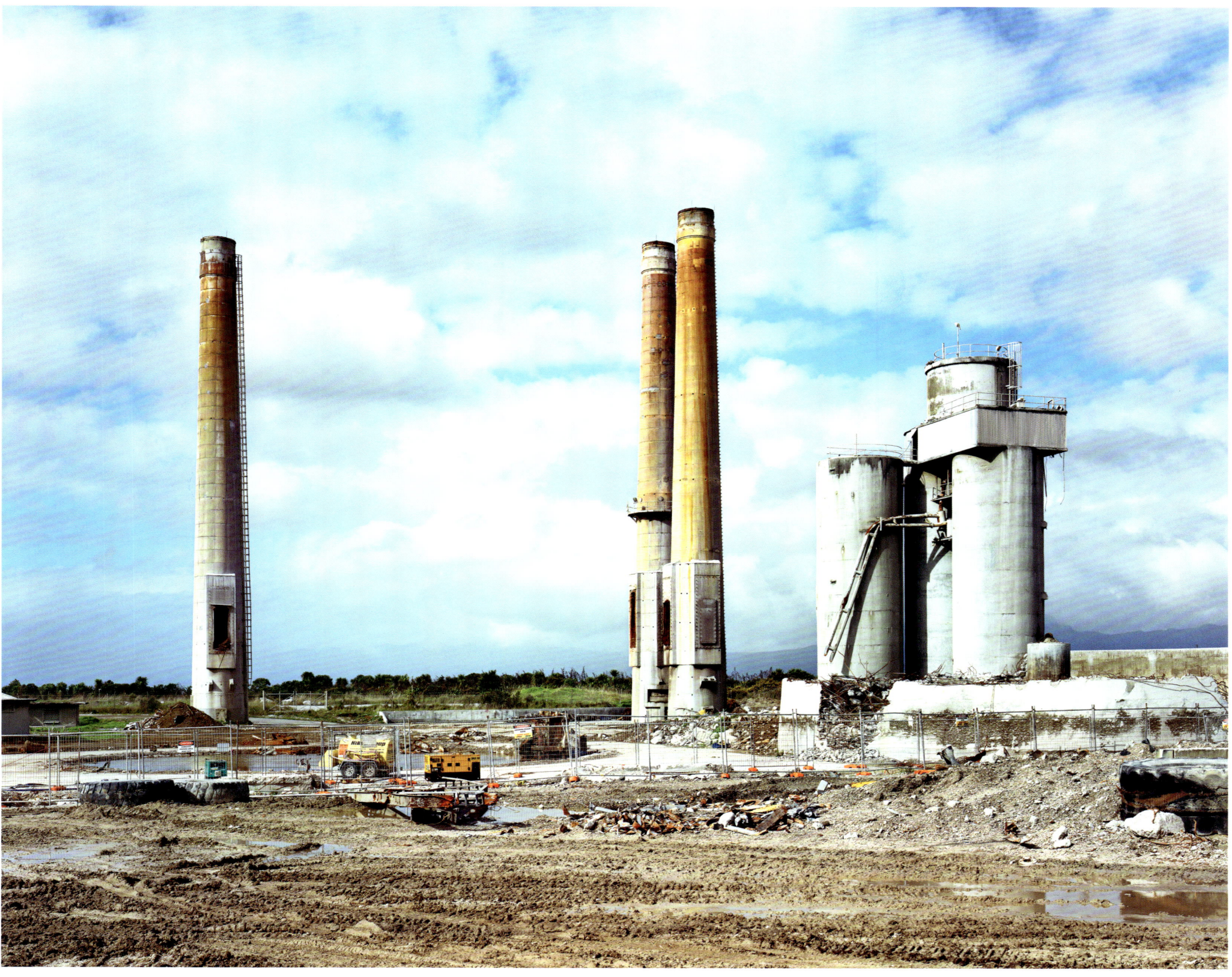

Dusk, Fishing Shack at Lake Onslow, Otago, 2019

Halfway along the Clutha River, and near the settlement of Roxburgh, a gravel road leaves the highway, winding up treeless hills interrupted only by scattered schist outcrops. Soon, the route becomes more clay than gravel, and for some forty kilometres it traces the ridgelines; on either side, the hills disappear into shadow as the road climbs nearly 1,000 metres towards Mount Teviot. There, an almost Martian landscape reveals itself, the hills rippling towards the horizon in every direction before melting into haze. The road then descends again, and before long the sheltered basin of Lake Onslow comes into view around a bend in the road, its water shimmering beneath the tussock-clad hills.

It took the fever of a gold rush in the 1860s to first lure Europeans into the depths of this remote, sub-alpine plateau. As they arrived, they encountered a breathtaking 'scroll plain', a rare alluvial formation in which a river, following a shallow gradient over millions of years, folds back upon itself to produce a pattern of complex oxbows and braids, among a network of tributaries that appear from above like calligraphy. To explorers in search of gold and a steady supply of water to aid its extraction, the wetlands were viewed as a mixture of opportunity and hindrance rather than as a wonder. Named Dismal Swamp, they were used to supply water to mines. In 1890, the waterway was then dammed to create Lake Onslow, which was named after the Governor of New Zealand from 1889 to 1892, William Onslow, Fourth Earl of Onslow. In creating the lake, though, more than half of the scroll plain was flooded.

In the early 1980s, during the 'Think Big' interventionist period of the right-wing Muldoon Government, large dams and hydroelectric power stations were built along Otago's Clutha River. Even the remote Lake Onslow received a new dam, which raised the water level a further five metres in a modest hydroelectric scheme. A television documentary on the construction of the Benmore Dam by the state-owned National Film Unit provides perhaps the most illuminating line about this period, the voiceover by media personality Selwyn Toogood proudly stating, 'The streams, now idly flowing through remote valleys, will be put to work, and compelled to perform their share of labour.'

A new 'think big' project of sorts emerged in 2020, when the Ministry of Business, Innovation and Employment established the NZ Battery Project to investigate a pumped hydro scheme at Lake Onslow as a solution to New Zealand's 'dry year' problem. The lake would become a 'battery', being filled with water pumped up from dams on the Clutha 500 metres below during times of high rainfall. In dry periods, water would be released back down, reducing dependence on fossil fuels as a backup for electricity generation. To store sufficient water, however, Lake Onslow would require damming once again to raise its level sixty metres. When the plan was announced, there was debate about feasibility and cost, as well as environmental impact of the project. Beyond destroying the last of the scroll plains, Onslow is a habitat of the rare Teviot flathead galaxias, a fish found only in a few areas of Otago, and nowhere else in the world.

An $11.5 million feasibility study released in early 2023 estimated a cost of $15.7 billion (up from earlier estimates of $4 billion) and indicated that the project would not be operational until the late 2030s. In December 2023, the plans were scrapped by New Zealand's new right-wing National Government as part of their 100-day plan.

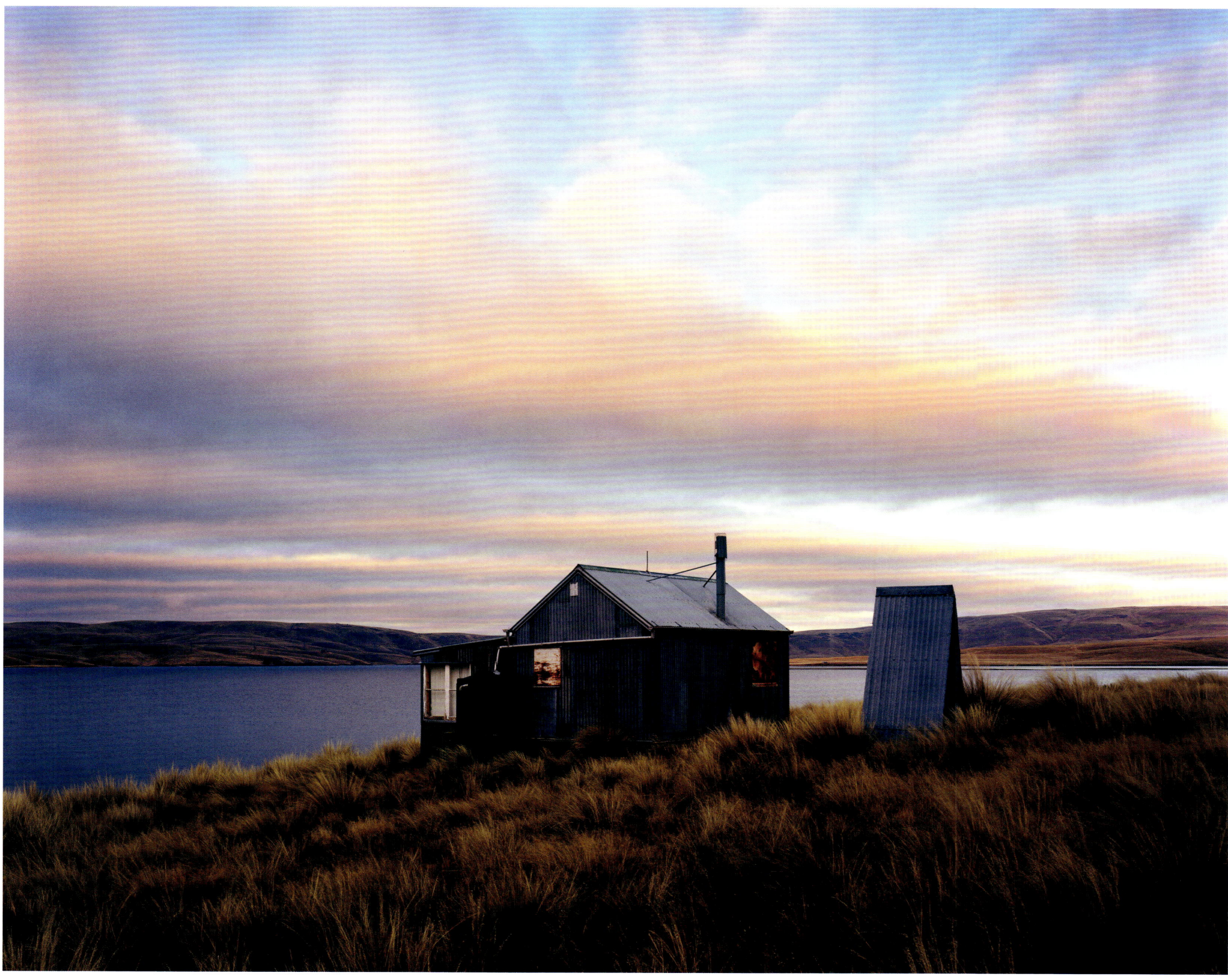

Poppet Head, Golden Progress Mine, Oturehua, Ida Valley, Central Otago, 2019

Following New Zealand's largest gold-strike at Gabriel's Gully near Lawrence in May 1861, miners ventured further into Otago's rugged plateaus. In 1862, another discovery was made in the gorge of the Clutha River near Dunstan (now Clyde) sparking a new rush. By happy coincidence, this roughly coincided with the opening of the first road access into the hinterland, the Dunstan Trail. For at least a decade, farmers had been dividing the tussock-covered hills of the region into sheep stations, but with no road into the remote landscape, growth had been limited. Stretching over 175 kilometres between Dunedin and Dunstan, the new route was almost a straight line on a map, but on the ground, it crossed numerous mountain ranges, four of which were up to 1,300 metres.

Treeless and unsheltered by its open topography, the route left miners exposed to cold nights, torrential wind and rain, and heavy snow. Nevertheless, they flocked to the area in their thousands, seeking to escape the drudgery of tenant farming in their home countries, make new lives, and find fortune. As the Dunstan rush cooled, the land surrounding the trail was explored further. Numerous miners began staking small claims around North Rough Ridge, a nearly thirty-kilometre mountain range on the eastern side of the Ida Valley. It seems that the most successful rush on Rough Ridge took place in 1864, and some time later attempts were made to extract quartz from the Golden Progress Mine. Mining continued for many years in the area; however, since most of the gold was bound up in quartz, North Rough Ridge became less appealing than other locations in the region like Saint Bathans, where gold lay in more easily workable alluvial gravel near the surface.

Already present when the miners arrived was Blackstone Hill Station, established in 1857 and one of the earliest runs in Otago. Māori had been present in the area much longer, calling it Oturehua (meaning 'place where the summer star stands still'). According to archaeological research, from as early as the fourteenth century, Māori would follow the Shag River over a hundred kilometres into Central Otago to collect food and stone in the lush Ida Valley in summer. Just east of what became the Golden Progress Mine is the best example of an early stone quarry in the area. Here, large amounts of silcrete were quarried from numerous pits to produce blades. Centuries later, Europeans renamed the area Rough Ridge and a settlement of the same name developed on the Ida to service the mines. The Māori name was returned in 1907 as the railway line reached the town.

In 1931, the *Alexandra Herald and Central Otago Gazette* wrote, 'Saturday last was a red-letter day for Oturehua, when the official opening of the Golden Progress Mine took place. It was what might be termed an ideal day. It was beautifully bright and warm. There was a particularly large gathering, including quite a number of the fair sex.' To work the site, a new company had formed a few years before, and now they injected massive capital into the operation. Above a forty-six-metre vertical shaft, from which horizontal drives (tunnels) were made in every direction, they constructed a fourteen-metre poppet head. In addition, they acquired a ten-stamp battery powered by two large steam boilers to crush the quartz. Just five years later, however, the mine was closed, as the project failed again. The stamping battery was dissembled and shifted to another site in Otago.

Today, the poppet head at the Golden Progress Mine is the last of its kind in Otago, and one of only two remaining in New Zealand. It has survived because of Otago's dry climate and its construction from a weather-resistant Australian hardwood.

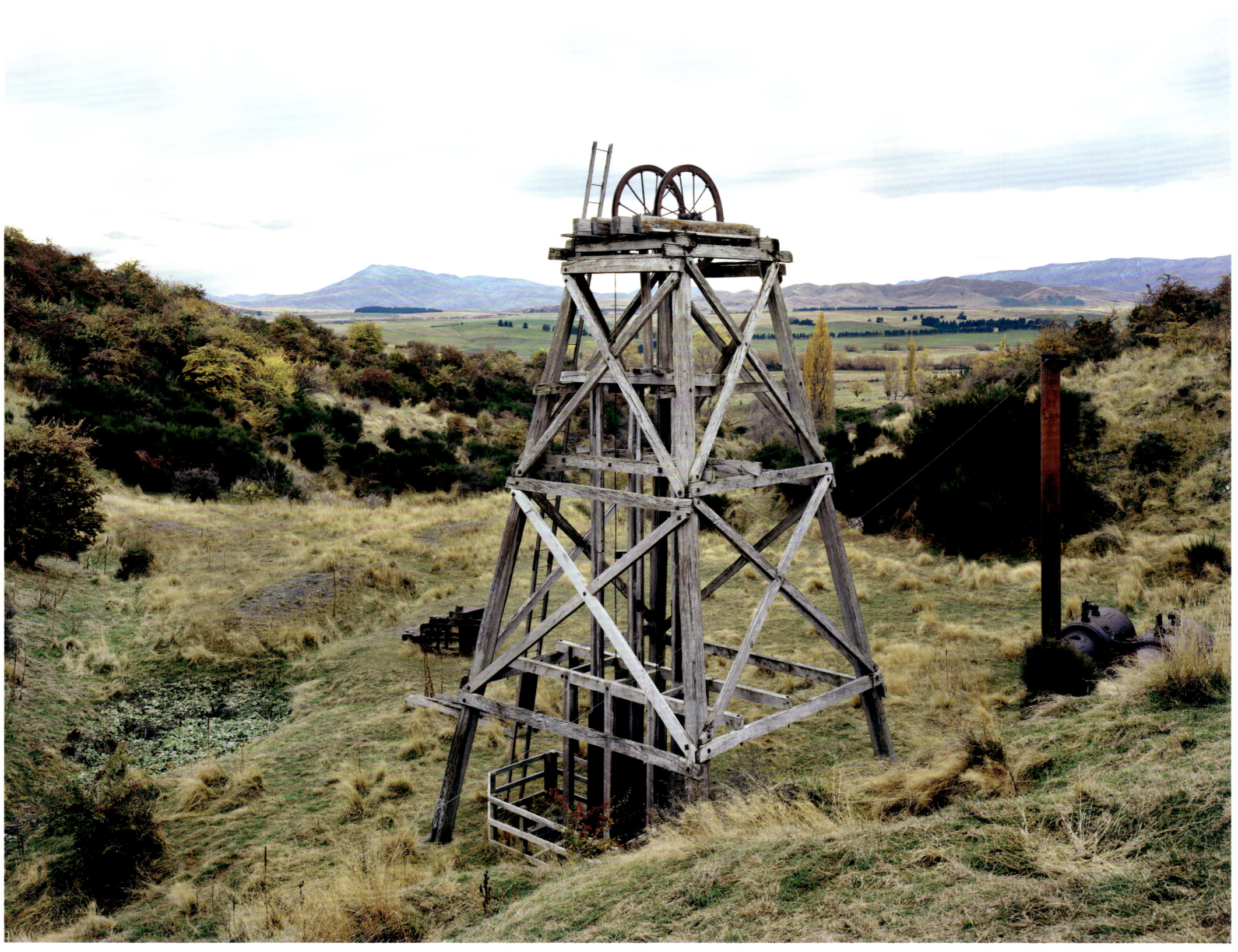

Morning Fog, Disused Stables at Earnscleugh Station, Near Alexandra, 2019

Over a two-year period beginning in 1856, British civil engineer and artist John Turnbull Thomson surveyed most of the lower half of the South Island, naming places and features. His intention was to use Māori names where they existed, but the national surveying authorities rejected the idea, so he used names from Northumbria on the Scottish Border, where he was born. Across the Clutha River from Alexandra and Clyde, the lush green valleys beneath a tussock-covered and rocky high-country reminded him of the landscape around the Earnscleugh Water, south-east of Edinburgh. Thus, a second Earnscleugh, 11,000 miles from Scotland, came to be.

Covering nearly 70,000 acres, Earnscleugh sheep station was founded in 1862, and its owners soon grew rich supplying the gold-rush-driven growth of the area. It was Earnscleugh's co-owner William Fraser who infamously first introduced rabbits into the Otago region. With no natural predators, they swiftly colonised the ecosystem, grazing away grass and vegetation on hillsides until rain and storms caused dramatic erosion. So rapid and drastic was the damage that sheep farming soon became unviable, and Earnscleugh Station was abandoned to the Crown in 1885. A similar fate would befall many other stations around Otago, as further rabbits were introduced or migrated from Earnscleugh.

As is often the case, with environmental disaster came capitalist opportunity. From 1902, the Earnscleugh Station's new owner, Steven Spain, set about turning the rabbit pestilence into profit. First, he sold rabbit pelts, then, during the First World War, he built a factory for the processing and canning of rabbit meat. The cans supplied soldiers and the international market in Europe, and it is alleged that in France labels on the cans said 'poulet' (chicken). Through this trade, Spain amassed a fortune, and in 1919, he was able to commission architect Edward Anscombe to design a two-story mansion, workers' quarters, and stables. Anscombe was known for his large public buildings in Wellington and Dunedin (including additions to the campus of the University of Otago, where he was resident architect for two decades), and he conceived the home on a grand scale. Blending outdated Jacobethan and Edwardian styles in an eccentric fashion, the building was ironically dubbed by locals 'The Castle'.

The mansion's endless expenditure, a post-war market collapse, and failed property speculations, conspired to be Spain's undoing. Although the home was habitable, it was never fully completed and became known as 'Spain's Folly'—a cautionary tale, if ever there were one, about the perils of vanity and conspicuous consumption. In the years that followed, several of Spain's seven children lived in the mansion, with family frictions eventually reaching such a pitch that a brick wall was constructed through the middle of the house to divide it. Later, the myth of the home grew further still, with the publication of *Castle on the Run* (1969), a wry memoir about growing up in the house by Spain's granddaughter Gay McInnes.

After passing through several hands, the Earnscleugh Station was purchased in 2022 by an Auckland couple who run a tourism company and work in building project management. The two men 'fell in love with the home and stables' and began a comprehensive restoration of the house and attendant buildings, with the stables being converted into an artist's residency.

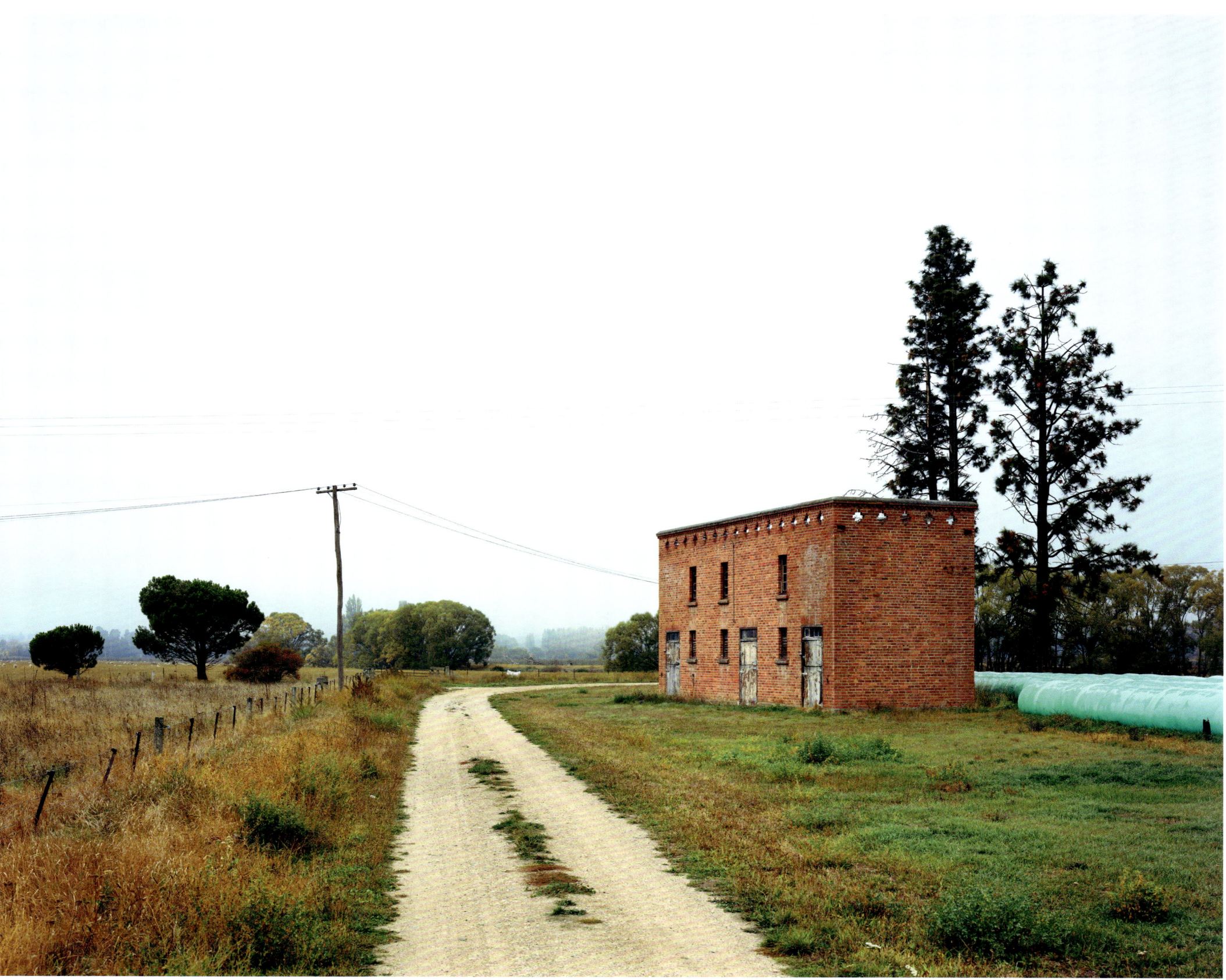

Musterers' Quarters and Kitchen, Home Hills Runs, Ida Valley, 2019

In the lower South Island, on the boundary between Canterbury and Otago, the Saint Bathans and Hawkdun Ranges rise to a height of nearly 2,000 metres. High on their slopes, alpine tributaries begin to form the Manuherikia River, which descends 1,000 metres across over 85-kilometres of high-country tussock and lush valleys before joining with the Clutha River. In the 1850s, this part of Otago's high country was subdivided into pastoral leases by the Government and became home to some of the region's earliest and largest farm stations. A decade later, in 1862, when gold was found in the Manuherikia Valley, the stations grew further, supplying meat and wool to the settlements that sprang to life.

In 1882, four of these stations—Blackstone Hill, Highfield, Home Hills, and Lauder—were leased by the Dunedin firm Ross and Glendining. Founded in 1862 by entrepreneurs John Ross and Robert Glendining, it grew to be one of New Zealand's largest manufacturing and warehousing companies, boasting of operations 'in all centres of the colony' and in London. In 1879, Ross and Glendining had opened the Roslyn Woollen Mill at Kaikorai Valley, near Dunedin; with the addition of the four Manuherikia Valley stations, which comprised more than 150,000 acres of land and 90,000 sheep, the company produced much of the wool required by the mill. And with a factory staff of over 500 people at the turn of the century, and a chain of retail stores, the company was one of the first, and most powerful, vertically integrated businesses in the country.

By the early 1900s, it had become cheaper to purchase wool than produce it, and Ross and Glendining let the leases on their runs lapse, the stations going on to be subdivided, to meet the demands of a growing settler population. The company held on to the Roslyn Mill until 1969, when synthetic wool and overseas imports began to take over, and it was sold to Mosgiel Woollens. That business went into receivership in 1980, and the mill subsequently became a business park. In the 1970s, following the closure of such industries in Otago, a number of artists began depicting old farm buildings like those at Home Hills, creating a genre of landscape painting and photography imbued with nostalgia for a vanished and masculine pioneer life. Now a minor New Zealand industry itself, this brand of regionalism, with its sentimental and pictorial clichés, ensures a steady production of coffee table books, prints, and postcards.

Similar attitudes are also pervasive in the advertising and film industries, both of which regularly decontextualise the landscape of Otago and Aotearoa as a whole, presenting it as uncontested when it is anything but. A rare exception to the rule is Jane Campion's *The Power of the Dog* (2021). Adapted from a novel by Thomas Savage, and filmed at and around Home Hills, it explores the tropes of pioneering masculinity and was nominated for eleven Academy Awards.

Further along the gravel road from Home Hills is Oteake Conservation Park. Gazetted in 2010, it is free to visit year-round. Together with adjoining public conservation land, it protects nearly 200,000 acres of tussock and mountain land.

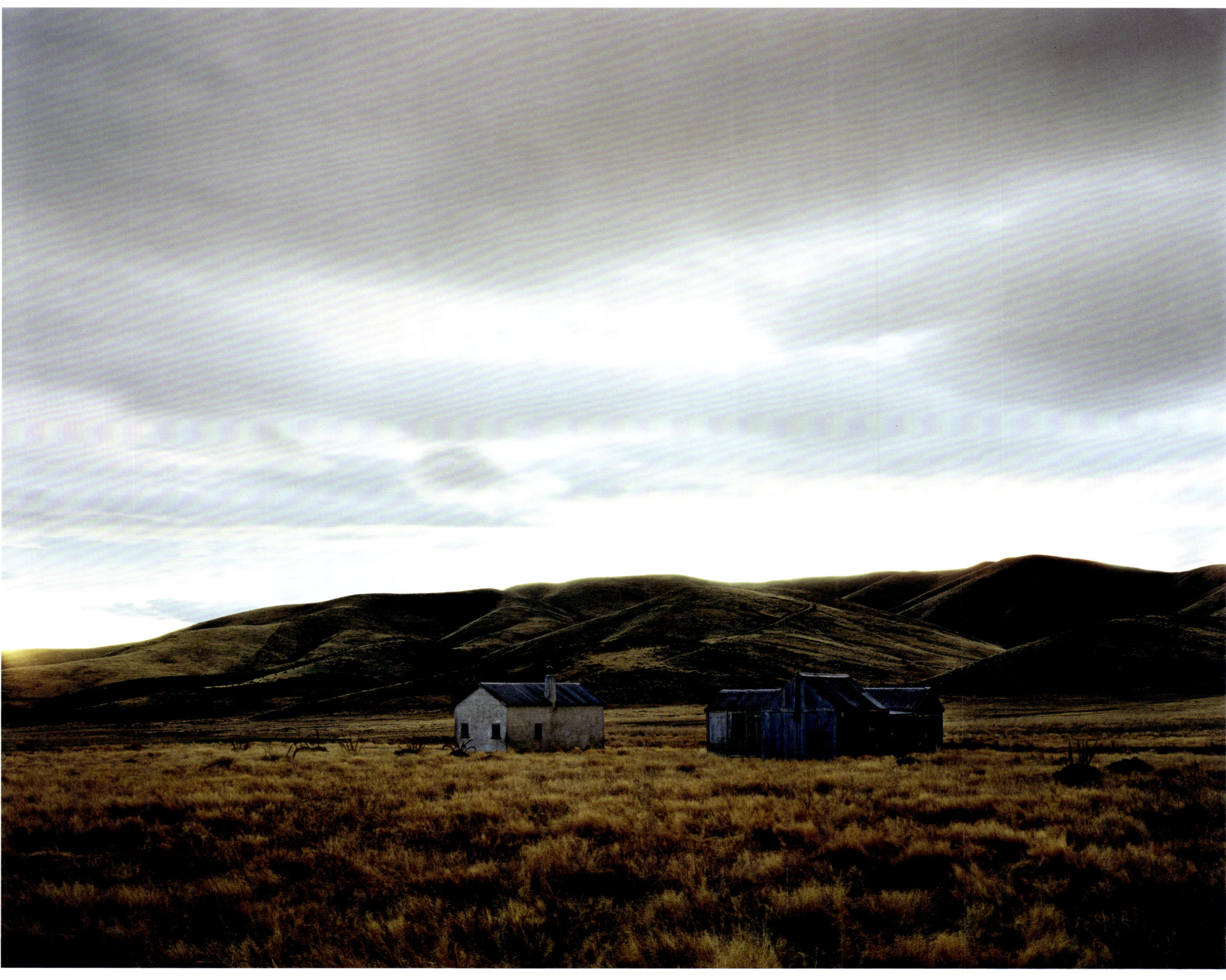

Fog over the Stamping Battery, Young Australian Mine, Carrick Range, 2019

A year into Otago's first gold rush in 1862, a new discovery made at the confluence of the Kawarau and Clutha Rivers saw the town of Cromwell quickly form as miners and wealth flooded into the area. Gold dredges trawled the rivers day and night, and, across the Kawarau at Bannockburn, miners made early use of hydraulic gold mining to scour the earth from the hills and separate rock from gold. Some found riches at Bannockburn, but it was the owners of the water rights and dams that powered the mining who profited the most. Just two years after the rush had begun, though, the number of miners around Bannockburn was already dwindling and the hopes of those who remained shifted to the Carrick Range.

In 1871, the *Dunstan Times* wrote, 'We are all indulged in great "expectation" ... building townships fast as we can, prospecting for fresh reefs and at the close of every day asking as Micawber [an optimistic character from Charles Dickens's *David Copperfield*] would do, whether anything fresh has turned up. We have one embryonic hotel nearly finished, another in the course of erection, one store, several respectable private houses, and a goodly number of residences of less ambitious character. We have claims taken up in every direction, and [have followed] several new lines of our reefs.' But as at Bannockburn, the optimism was in vain. After four years of effort, and only one remotely successful reef, the settlement referred to by the paper, Quartzville, had already been abandoned, and the miners had moved on again, following the reefs a further five kilometres up the Carrick Range and establishing Carricktown.

Despite the move uphill, the miners' fortunes failed to improve, and soon Carricktown was also abandoned. Today, wild blackberry, broken stone fenceposts, and schist remnants of walls and chimneys are all that mark the settlement. After Carricktown, the trail continues to climb the Carrick Range, and soon it is above the lowest clouds—the thick tussock giving way to sub-alpine grasses and lichen. Many kilometres further still, now following the old water race, the silhouette of the Young Australian Mine's waterwheel comes into view, far below in Adam's Gully. Constructed in 1875, the surreal eight-metre-high structure, now restored by the Department of Conservation, sits at an elevation of 1,067 metres. Above it, the ambitious, gravity-driven water race—built between 1872 and 1877 to drive the mining operation—still flows an incredible thirty-five kilometres around and across the range.

But the back-breaking labour involved in the construction projects was soon rendered pointless. After just a year of operation, rainfall caused 'a large influx of water' to flood the shafts of the Young Australian Mine, ending activity for two decades. In 1896, an investment in the latest cyanide-based gold-processing equipment was made at the still supposedly profitable reef, but due to the remote and steep location, this also proved unsuccessful. Now the waterwheel sits alone like a statue on the hillside. Kilometres away, in a neighbouring tributary, where the last attempt at mining was made, the stamping battery the wheel was built to drive barely hangs on, having weathered decades of winter snow.

Beneath the Carrick Range, at Bannockburn, fields of stone tailings and a spring bloom of wild thyme introduced by the miners upon its scarred landscape are the other most tangible traces of their toil.

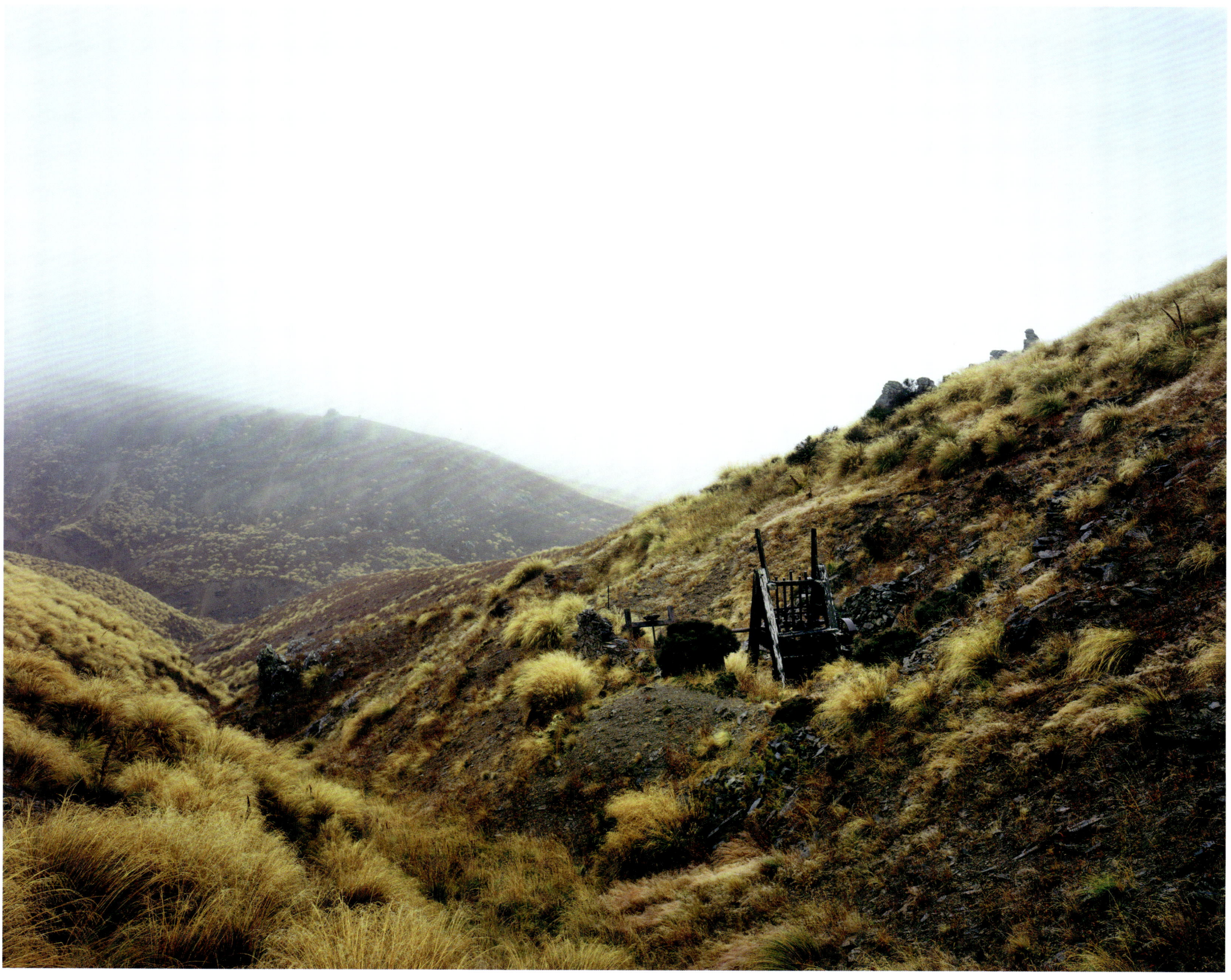

Approaching Snowstorm at Nightfall, Kopuwai (Old Man Range), Otago, 2019

High above the Clutha River and Nevis Valley, Kopuwai (Old Man Range) rises to 1,682 metres at the peak of its long ridgeline. Looking out from it to the east, thousand-metre-high plateaus stretch to the horizon, while to the west dramatic mountain peaks rise and fall towards Lake Wakatipu. Often sitting above the clouds, the summit of Kopuwai is surmounted by a twenty-six-metre schist outcrop also known as Kopuwai, which stands like a sentinel. In Ngāi Tahu telling, Kopuwai was a malicious giant. Attended by two-headed dogs, he preyed upon hunting parties who ventured into the remote ranges and the gorge of the Clutha River below. Kopuwai met his end after he enslaved a young woman named Kaiamio, the sole survivor from a group he had murdered. She eventually seized on his single weakness: that he would become drowsy in the warm nor-west wind. While his dogs were away hunting, she managed to flee, returning with a war party that killed Kopuwai and his dogs—leaving them frozen in their present, rocky form.

In December 1862, the Campbell brothers found gold at what became 'Campbell Creek', in the remote wetland plateaus behind Kopuwai. Though the miners likely didn't know the Māori story, they, too, saw Kopuwai as a human form, and named him the Old Man. With the Campbells' discovery, miners flooded into the area, and more than a thousand metres beneath Kopuwai a 'packers' village' named Chamonix (after a French mountain settlement) formed to service the mines. It was an arduous trek to reach the village from the nearest town, Alexandra, and then harder still to get to Campbell Creek, up and over the mountains. Nonetheless, by the time gold was found again, even deeper into the range at Potters, Chamonix had over twenty stores, including a blacksmith's shop, among a sea of shanties, tents, and stone houses. Despite its alpine exposure, the mountainous route between Chamonix and the mines was highly trafficked, and fearing an early snowfall in the coming winter, the local government marked the route with tall wooden snow poles in the autumn of 1863.

The first snow of the year fell in July 1863. For most of the miners, it meant the end of the season, and they retreated to Chamonix or Alexandra. But a large number elected to stay and endure the winter, in fear their claims would be 'jumped'. Soon, the snow had piled higher than anyone expected and, as the track along and over Kopuwai's ridgeline became almost impassable, the remaining miners began running out of fuel and food. By 11 August, as an abnormally heavy snowstorm descended on the range, they were on the brink of starvation and had no choice but to set out for Chamonix. A week later, exhausted and near-dead men began staggering into Chamonix bearing news that parties leaving from Campbells had been caught in a blizzard with below-zero temperatures and whiteout conditions on the barren range. As word of the disaster spread, newspapers feared and reported at least fifty dead—although more recent research suggests the number was likely closer to twenty.

In 1929, a monument was erected to the miners who perished in the great snow of 1863 beside Roxborough Road and George Creek, just a few hundred metres below the location of Chamonix, which had been thought lost to history since the incident.

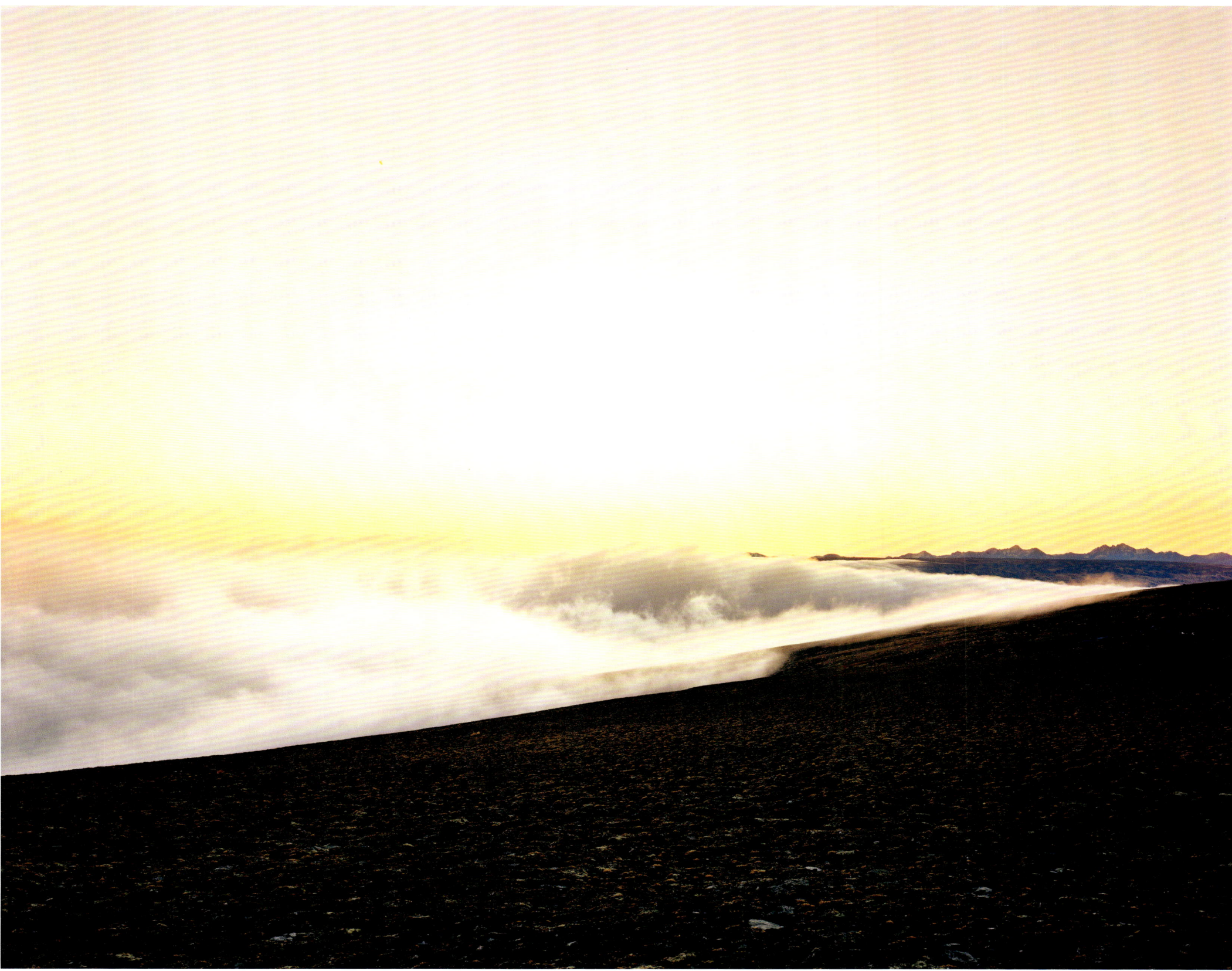

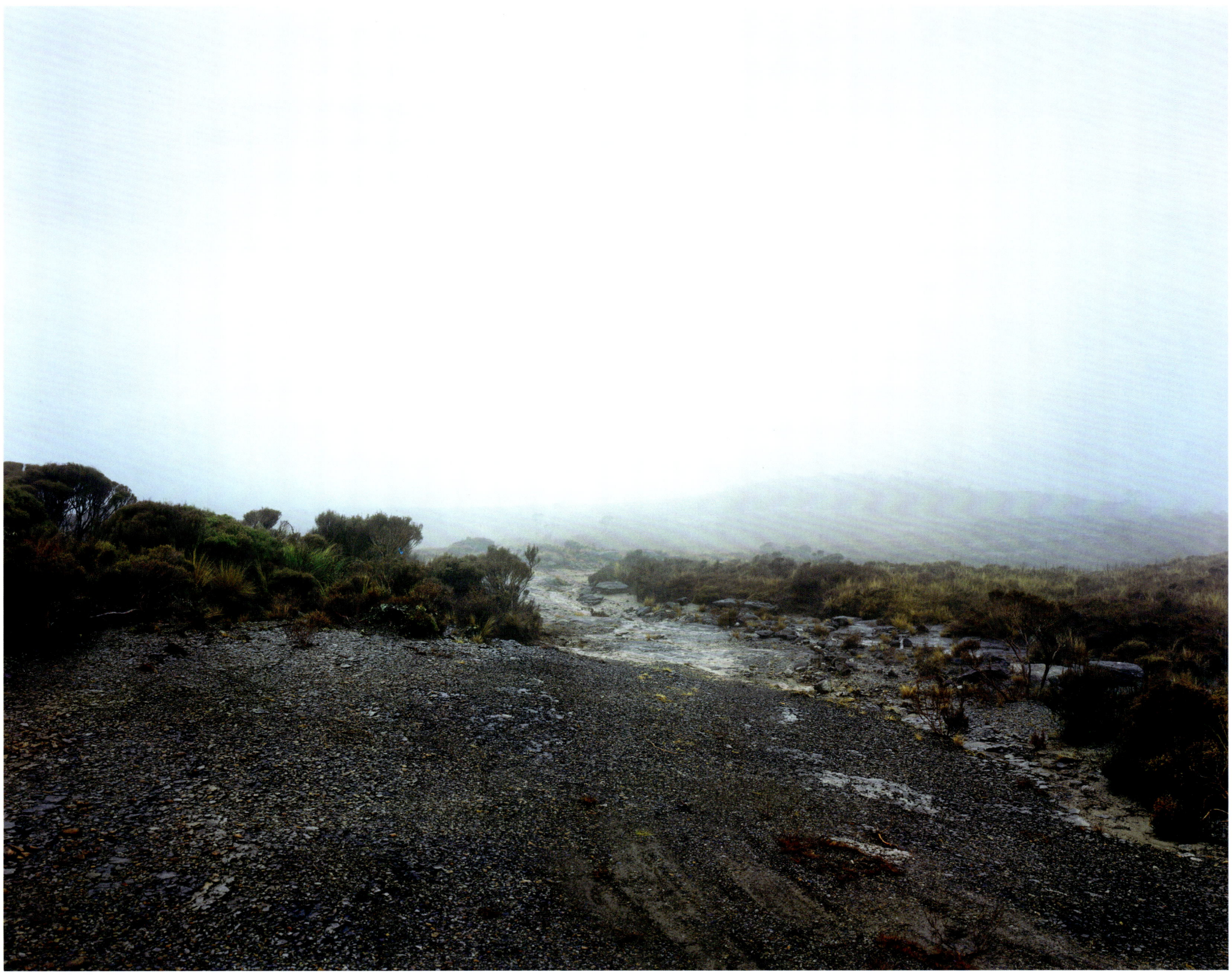

Afterword

LOST ON DENNISTON

Perhaps it was the sleep deprivation, but as we descended the thousand-metre plateau after being trapped overnight in a storm, I somehow felt as though the threads of the photography and research I had been doing over the last decade were finally coming together. Now almost dusk, the writer I was travelling with and I were in the SUV of an ex-miner turned local tour guide who had answered our call for a ride back to town.

The day before, we had set out following an old mining road on the rocky and treeless Denniston Plateau on the South Island's West Coast. The narrow trail was new to us, and after barely ten minutes of slow descent, it began deteriorating. Decades of rain had gouged its gradient into sandstone steps, so even in a modified four-wheel-drive, the gravel that still clung to the rutted surface barely stopped the car from skidding. I had spent weeks and months on roads like this: long abandoned mining trails in the backcountry of the West Coast, Otago, Southland, and elsewhere. So, with familiarity having led to comfort, we carried on.

It was a beautiful early-winter afternoon, calm and cloudless. Almost out of nowhere though, it began to rain. Too rough and slippery to reverse kilometres back up, we continued following what was supposed to be a loop out. At the bottom of the hill, with nowhere to turn, we drove across the rocky riverbed, launching into a narrow and almost forty-degree clay cutting. Now the track wound steeply upwards, climbing over one hundred metres, before flattening somewhat on a spine-like ridgeline. After what felt like an hour of driving, the escape of the plateau tops was in sight, but as the last bend in the road came into view, the trail disintegrated into rocky steps again. This time, though, a foot or more high, and rising until they disappeared into the fog. Suddenly, it felt darker too. The last sun of the day muted by the weight of an increasingly heavy grey sky.

Left: Dusk, Fog and Rain on the Denniston Plateau, 2016

Rain ran down the sandstone steps, making them so slippery it was hard to stand up. Even if driving this incline was possible, the risk of rolling was too high. The only way out was back, and we started a twenty-point turn on a singular patch of muddy ground which veered towards the cliff edge. Almost immediately we were stuck. One wheel spun in the mud, two more on the wet sandstone, while the last rotated off the ground. Our scramble to dig out or gain traction in the rain, playing out at an almost unreachable spot on the plateau, which was over thirty kilometres from the nearest town. But with the area almost void of sticks and even small rocks to help us, and the light nearly gone, we were forced to stay put for the night. Wedged between the truck and the cliff's edge, my one-person tent barely fit on the muddy patch; meanwhile, my friend tried to sleep upright in the passenger seat of the car, which was so full of equipment that the chair couldn't recline. Far from town lights, and above a layer of low cloud, the darkness was total. The rain became torrential, and vivid nightmares of being washed off the hill, or the car rolling and crushing me, woke me again and again.

By morning, the rain had abated into drizzle, and fog swept in along with a hint of snowfall in the air. The cold had also sapped our phone batteries, and with calls for help retrieving the car unfruitful, we left the vehicle and set out on foot across the scrub-covered plateau. The temperature was close to freezing, and the Denniston wind—notorious among coal miners—had picked up too. Exhausted, we tried to follow tracks that differed from the generalities of the Topo Map. The fog had now become thicker, and with visibility barely metres ahead of us, we circled back on ourselves, following dead ends to cliffs too sheer to descend. After at least an hour of wandering in icy scrub off trail, with almost no sense of direction, I wondered for the first time if we were lost. The countless tales I'd read of explorers meeting their ends in fog on mountains or in valleys forced themselves on my sleepless mind. Finally, though, we found an old mining trail that matched the GPS, and trusting it we walked through the whiteout, eventually reaching the relative civilisation of a gravel mining haul road. Making a last call with our phone batteries almost gone, the tour guide answered and agreed to pick us up for the price of his petrol. Forty minutes further along the haul road, we were greeted by a modern SUV, and we slowly returned to room temperature.

SELLING NEW ZEALAND

This experience, and others like it, have over time given me a new level of empathy—and complicated respect—for the hardships faced by the people who built New Zealand's early industries. One was my great-great-grandfather, who moved to Milton in 1861 with the gold rush and became a farmer, horse breeder, and, later, hotel operator. Facing eviction and seizure of farmland in Scotland, he first travelled to Australia during the gold rushes, before immigrating here, where being able to acquire Māori land in the South Island almost for free, he found 'success'. His story is similar to those of tens of thousands of other Europeans who immigrated to New Zealand in the nineteenth century, many also tenant farmers, or likewise attempting to flee poverty, servitude, or the dangerous and sometimes deadly conditions of factories and mines.

In present decolonial discourse, it is often common to view colonisation as binaries of positive and negative, because in many cases this is a more accurate version of history than that concocted—and then taught for a century—by colonial authority that sought to manufacture consent for their seizure of land and power. In visiting hundreds of industrial sites around the country, and meeting those who worked in them (or their descendants), I increasingly saw that binary truth can elide the fact that colonial powers were equally happy to exploit their own people and other non-Western immigrants if it meant they would benefit. In short: the simplification removes class conflict from the discussion. As Catherine Comyn writes in *The Financial Colonisation of Aotearoa* (2023), 'Finance was and remains pivotal to the colonial acquisition and exploitation of Māori lands and resources.' Enterprises like the New Zealand Company—one of the main retailers of immigration, as well as land speculation—keenly took advantage of Māori and Pākehā alike. Towards Māori, they undertook exploitive land deals, abused cultural differences in understanding of land 'ownership', made false promises of sharing and cooperation, and actively profited from stolen land. Towards Pākehā, they targeted Europeans desperate to emigrate as a way out of class oppression, selling what mostly turned out to be a false dream of class mobility—or independence and success through hard work—but omitting that most immigrants would enter a country that was still actively in the process of being stolen through manipulation, threat, or force.

Of the European immigrants, many paid their life savings to move to 'New Zealand'. Upon arriving, time and time again they discovered that the housing and green pastures they had been sold did not await them. Instead, they often found barren, swampy, or forested pieces of land not suitable for occupation—a desperate situation which made many of the settlers once again a permanent underclass, much as they had been before they arrived. The grift is more explicit still with women from lower classes, and Chinese miners—for just two examples. Promised freedom and opportunity, in most cases they found themselves servants, often in worse situations than they had previously been in, and ultimately never earned enough to return home. Even for men—for whom this period offered greater independence—the need to survive often meant taking any work that was going—much of it in dangerous and isolating industries, such as mining and logging. Across the length of the country, nearly every industrial site I visited marks tragic incidents in which workers died or were seriously injured: in falls from cliffs, explosions, factory accidents, mine shaft collapses, floods from swollen rivers, and a hundred other grisly fates, far from home. An often ignored element of this, too, is that many of these industrial workers were Māori, who suddenly needed money to survive in what had become a capitalist wage economy overnight, as land that had provided sustenance for centuries had now been taken.

ENVIRONMENTALISTS FROM THE CITY

When I first started visiting industrial sites, and one of their early epicentres, the West Coast of Aotearoa, I had what I'd describe as a relatively typical environmentalist viewpoint. I'd always been told mining was bad, something we should fight against, and I believed it almost exclusively was. The more time I spent researching, talking to workers and locals of industrial settlements, though, the more the binaries of these views were challenged.

In 2017, as we talked to the guide while driving down the hill from Denniston to safety, he asked, 'If you are environmentalists from the city, why don't you support coal mining? The kind of coal produced on the West Coast isn't for fireplaces. It's coking coal, which is the only way to create enough energy to produce steel, concrete, and aluminium.' His comments made plain the reality that if we want a sustainable future—green buildings, cities, public transport, and the rest—then for now we still need coal to produce those materials. And although he didn't say it, we also need a litany of rare metals, only acquirable through mining, for technology—at least, if technology is to be part of any of our solutions as nearly everyone believes it will be.

As I spoke with miners and those in their communities around the country, again and again, in a resigned tone, they explained something along these lines to me. Hurt as much as perplexed by their portrayal as environmental villains, they described how they, their friends, and their families—often over generations—broke their backs and in some cases gave their lives to extract the resources upon which our cities and modern existence is built. I think of their words, too, when later I read about the unbelievable amount of steel and concrete we use in nearly every structure—from skyscrapers to public bike racks—from their foundations and up. A 2019 article in the *Guardian* titled 'Concrete: the most destructive material on Earth' opens with the observation, 'After water, concrete is the most widely used substance on Earth. If the cement industry were a country, it would be the third largest carbon dioxide emitter in the world with up to 2.8 billion tonnes, surpassed only by China and the US.'

Yet in decades of reading on environmentalism and sustainability, I don't recall the essential role steel, concrete—and by proxy coal—will play ever being part of the discussion, because the conclusion is upsetting: true sustainability can only come from consuming less, and building things that last; changes that would require fundamentally moving away from a marketplace and ideology of infinite growth and a belief in profit above all.

To most of us, though, the battle lines have already been drawn. We are either environmentalists who distrust industry or we are anti-regulation and anti-environmental protection, and believe business should have free rein. The contradictions and complexity are buried by passion or propaganda, driven and engineered by media, corporate, and political interests. A story springs to mind about a friend arriving at a prestigious college campus in the Midwestern United States, where some of his classmates were celebrating the closure of a nearby Rust Belt coal mine. The students had crossed the country to study at the expensive school, many using trust funds filled by parents who had become rich through companies that extracted resources and polluted the environment. They did not see, let alone feel, the hypocrisy, because socio-political tribalism is so sadly effective at whipping people into frenzies about things they barely understand. Nuance and complexity fall to the wayside while media outlets—serving corporate messaging as much as politicians—fan the flames, so we keep clicking and consuming advertising like a snake eating itself.

Back home, and sitting in apartments built with West Coast coal, concrete, and steel, many New Zealanders also celebrate the closure of mines, claiming an environmental victory. But such closures are actually a new manifestation of an old colonial and capitalist ideology. We still need and use the same resources, but now outsource their production to the so-called Global South, so we can put the reality of our environmental footprint out of mind, and can continue to trade on the perception of New Zealand as a tourist destination that is marketed as being 'clean and green', '100% pure', and 'Middle-earth'. In reality, we have only shifted the production of industry that goes against the brand to places where working conditions, worker safety, labour rights, and environmental standards are worse, and have worse outcomes. Instead of coal taking a boat to a cement works a few kilometres away from where it was once mined on the West Coast, now the coal, the cement, or both, come to us from the other side of the world. Resources criss-crossing the oceans, travelling back and forth to circumvent labour laws, climate regulations, and taxes, before crashing into New Zealand with a vastly greater carbon footprint.

TECHNOLOGICAL DREAMS

At home in Auckland, I end up sitting beside a progressive politician at a friend of a friend's house. When I bring up issues people on the West Coast have raised with me, their attitude is dismissive; they remind me of American politicians who suggest that labourers from the country's countless dead or dying post-industrial towns should simply move to Silicon Valley and retrain. But is ever smarter tech really the only correct future? In barely a decade, artificial intelligence has gone from something we knew would eventually displace countless jobs, to something that is here at the fast food drive-thru, as much as in every creative field. Suddenly it seems completely sane to wonder if, in the not-too-distant future, art, writing, and creativity will still be driven by people. Even if human creativity manages to survive the coming wave of technological advance, will its integrity and power remain? In the time since I first wrote this afterword in June of 2024, A.I. has progressed from caricature-ish image generation where people never have the right number of fingers, to apps that can generate video so realistic that people are now regularly convinced by their use in fake news on social media. Meanwhile, another new app can turn any still image into a realistic video that rewrites history however it is prompted to.

As ideas of truth and history are increasingly destabilised, a large part of this project is about remembering. About trying to understand the industries by which—and partially for which—an entire country was colonised, and most of its natural resources consumed in barely a century. What do the crumbling or now vanished ruins of industry, once so influential that settlements came to life to support it, now mean? What did the lives of those who built them, handmade plank by plank, and handmade brick by brick, amount to? Today, in the afterglow of industry, capitalism touches everything, so much so that even our desire is inextricably bound within its machinations. Whether fifty or one hundred and fifty years after the structures photographed were built, what do these industrial monuments symbolise now that the wealth extracted is long behind us, and even the towns that rose around them have often vanished back to wild grass and creeping weeds?

Are today's technological dreams just an analogue for the colonial and industrial dreams this project depicts? In its day-to-day use, technology seems clean, streamlined, and slick. But from the factories with poor working conditions and the precious metals required for technology's creation to—for just one example—the millions of hard drives discarded annually by the vast data centres that invisibly support our commerce and communication, this modern industry is obviously every bit as destructive as industry of the past, and probably more so. But as technology grows ever more inseparable from our existence, the demand for electricity to power it and for rare—also rapidly depleting, and destructively mined—precious metals only increases. Hand in hand with modern mass production, another afterglow of industry is plastic, nearly a century of which is now quietly transforming into microplastics, which, moving through the oceans and every fish and being on earth, are suspected to slowly give us all cancer. Meanwhile back on the ground, the increase in production that industry also brought left most soils worldwide so overworked by agricultural lime (and more modern monocrops) that they are now failing, or beginning to fail. All are part of industry's now greatest legacy, climate change—which despite the somewhat successful efforts of propaganda campaigns dreamed up by people who once worked for Big Tobacco, and now work for Big Oil, remains a scientific fact. In the shadow cast by these issues, the subjects of this book also serve as sad markers of the progress of climate change from its small beginnings in the nineteenth century during the industrial revolution to its snowballing at roughly the end of the Second World War, as industry proliferated in the era known now as the Great Acceleration and the Anthropocene. A period in which measures like carbon emissions, loss of rainforest, water consumption, species extinction, surface temperature, and finally population all increased at vastly unprecedented rates.

Faced with this reality, the continued survival of our species is seriously challenged by the idea, popularised by Slavoj Žižek, that 'it is now easier to imagine the end of the world, than the end of capitalism'. Capitalism, by necessity, requires constant growth, despite our only home being a planet with finite resources. The mess we are in is a painfully simple paradox. Our desire for 'endless growth' is fundamentally at odds with what has now become clear is our only potential salvation: to want less. How do we even begin to rethink the all too human desire for growth and acquisition that drives almost every person on this planet?

THINKING BIG

In late 2019, I bought my first home, one of four small two-bedroom units that were built in the 1960s. Slowly, I renovated the unit to make it more sustainable, insulating the walls, floor, and ceiling with recycled materials and replacing old joinery with double glazing. But when I decided to sell in 2024—spurred by a need to move to the edge of the city in the Waitākere Ranges rainforest—it quickly became clear that despite ethical renovation, property value was a numbers game based almost entirely on metrics like rooms and floor area. Having also extensively replanted native trees around the units, this realisation, which accommodates neither sustainability nor nature, was depressing to accept. As was how few people in this country were willing to accept a smaller but well-designed space. After all, how much space do we really need to sleep between going to work and coming home to watch a streaming series while we doom scroll on our phones?

While I was renovating, a Silicon Valley venture capitalist purchased the old house in front of the units. Once owned by one of Auckland's first professors of native flora, and just months after his widow's death, a century-old kauri and pōhutukawa were cut down, along with every other trace of nature on the land. Next went the bungalow itself. Built in 1910, it was one of the first homes in the area, made entirely of old-growth native timbers from the Waitākere Ranges rainforest. In their place came a mansion designed by an architect from Los Angeles. Although built for just two semi-retired people, the 'home' rises to a height of three stories, across over 650 square metres on a street where 200 to 300 is typical. As a society, despite everything, we still seem to view homes like this as aspirational. But is this level of resource usage and consumption really so, or is it more truly an illustration of the boredom and emptiness at the heart of our capitalist belief system?

The mansion's floor plan is large enough that it could fit ten of my two-bedroom units—housing twenty to thirty people—while the mansion's design houses just two. As long as we as a society still revere this kind of consumption rather than scorn it, we will struggle to face the challenges before us.

LOST ON KŌPŪWAI

In travelling the length of Aotearoa, and visiting nearly every settlement across it, the vast majority of people I met were kind and supportive. Wanting the stories of their land, industry, and businesses told, they helped where they could, then left me to work—whether in factories, at mines, homes, stores, or driving and wandering the distant parts of their farms or lifestyle blocks. All the same, as the decade in which this work was made unfolded, the growing inequality of this country, especially in many formerly industrial districts, became more and more evident.

Several times, the wrong back road led to ominous encounters. After exploring defunct mines on a privately owned West Coast hillside with permission, we had to make a quick exit from a house with PVC plastic for walls, after the owners wondered out loud if we'd been given the tea laced with hallucinogens. In central Otago, I was told about an old mine deep in a private forestry block. Kilometres into the forest, as I trudged through the cold drizzle, I wandered into what was—or had recently been—an outdoor meth lab. At another mostly abandoned West Coast mining town, we followed bush trails that were deliberately obscured, and felt we were being watched. Later on, a local told us that people moved there for the seclusion, using it to produce marijuana or meth in the hills.

Many times, in these remote settlements where people had moved to be out of sight, people were hostile until convinced we weren't the police, the tax department, or some other kind of authority. Sometimes, my interest in their old buildings set them off, and they unloaded on health and safety regulations, historic building protections, council bylaws, environmental groups, Māori land stewardship, and so on.

The more stories I heard, and the more I learned, the more depressed I felt about politics and the environment. As politics increasingly fractured in new ways during this period, too, I visited places where society's division along lines of labour vs. tech and rural vs. urban made the new degree of economic inequality brutally evident. Increasingly, I took more risks, venturing further into more dangerous and remote parts of the South Island, trying to understand the early industrialists and workers I was following in the footsteps of so I could better understand the present.

In 2019—just before the world shut down due to the COVID-19 pandemic—I made the last trip of this project around Te Waipounamu / South Island. Near the end of months of working, and at the beginning of winter, I was on the 1,673-metre (5,489-foot) summit of the Kōpūwai Range, which towers above the Clutha River / Mata-Au in Otago, and is the highest elevation 'public road' in the country. Over what had been an unusually warm and cloudless day, I had hiked downhill through the tall tussock grass to photograph abandoned mines, and in the late afternoon I made it back to my car near the summit. A 360-degree vantage point, in nearly every direction the plateaus below stretched to the cloudless horizon, while to the west, heavy clouds massed above the valley, so that it felt as if the summit were floating above them. Setting up my old large-format camera, I began waiting for the sun to drop below the mountains. It was then that the wind picked up and changed direction; the clouds, which had been static for hours, now rushing towards the summit. In a panic, I took the last image in the book, packed up the camera, and ran towards the car. Over that couple of hundred metres, the rain- and snow-filled clouds reached me, and suddenly it was almost entirely dark.

As I arrived at the car, snow and rain buffeted the peak. Even with fog lights, visibility through the windscreen was less than a few metres ahead, and barely able to make out the edge of the gravel road, the only way to follow it was with one wheel bumping along the edge of the drainage ditch. One hundred fifty-six years before, after being trapped in heavy snowfall on another plateau behind Kōpūwai, more than a dozen miners had perished trying to escape across this ridgeline in a blizzard, and inside the raging storm their story went through my mind. Almost in a trance, I finally reached the farm gate that led downhill and off the mountain. Stepping outside to open it, the wind and freezing weather hit me, the chill pummelling me again and again, as I opened each gate, drove through it, then got out and closed it, over the thousand-metre descent.

Descending through two layers of clouds, as the steep and winding gravel road's unfenced edge threatened to pull the truck down into the darkness, at last I was out of the storm. Back on the sealed road below and able to breathe, I realised this project had reached its natural end. As I drove through the rain and night back to my cold cinderblock room at the campground, I thought about those miners again. Like the English coal barge wrecked on Mōkihinui's sand bar on this book's cover, the miners' deaths on this remote mountain range in Otago could also be read as a warning of nature's indifferent response to expansion and ambition which continues unchecked.

Chris Corson-Scott, November 2024
Tāmaki Makaurau Auckland

Bibliography

Adams, Cecilia. *The Hill*. J. W. Baty Ltd, 1971.

Adams, Mark, and Harry Evison. *Land of Memories: A Contemporary View of Places of Historical Significance in the South Island of New Zealand*. Tandem Press, 1993.

Adams, Mark, and Nicholas Thomas. *Cook's Sites: Revisiting History*. Otago University Press, 1999.

Binney, Judith. *Encircled Lands: Te Urewera, 1820–1921*. Bridget Williams Books, 2009.

Binney, Judith, Atholl Anderson, and Aroha Harris. *Tangata Whenua: An Illustrated History*. Bridget Williams Books, 2017.

Blackley, Roger. *Two Centuries of New Zealand Landscape Art*. Auckland Art Gallery, 1990.

Blackley, Roger. *The Art of Alfred Sharpe*. Auckland Art Gallery, 1992.

Brownson, Ron. *John Kinder's New Zealand*. Random House, 2004.

Busch, Glen. *Working Men*. National Art Gallery, 1984.

Cleveland, Les. *The Silent Land: A Pictorial Record of the West Coast of the South Island of New Zealand*. Caxton Press, 1966.

Diamond, J.T., and B.W. Hayward. *Kauri Timber Dams*. Lodestar Press, 1975.

Diamond, J.T., and B.W. Hayward. *The Maori History and Legends of the Waitakere Ranges*. Lodestar Press, 1979.

Ell, Gordon. *New Zealand Ghost Towns and Glimpses of the Past*. Bush Press, 1988.

Ell, Gordon, and Sarah Ell. *Adventurous Times in Old New Zealand: First Hand Accounts of the Lawless Days*. Bush Press, 1994.

Fox, William. *The Six Colonies of New Zealand*. University of Otago, 1971.

Gundry, Sheridan. *Making a Killing: A History of the Gisborne-East Coast Freezing Works Industry*. Tairawhiti Museum, 2004.

Hall-Jones, John. *Goldfields of the South*. Craigs, 1982.

Hall-Jones, John. *Goldfields of Otago: An Illustrated History*. Craigs, 2005.

Harris, Aroha. *Hikoi: Forty Years of Māori Protest*. Huia Publishers, 2004.

Heaphy, Charles. *Narrative of a Residence in Various Parts of New Zealand*. Capper Press, 1972.

King, Michael. *Māori: A Photographic and Social History*. Heinemann Publishers, 1983.

King, Michael, and Robin Morrison. *The Coromandel*. Tandem Press, 1993.

King, Michael. *The Penguin History of New Zealand*. Penguin, 2003.

Lippard, Lucy R. *Undermining: A Wild Ride Through Land Use, Politics, and Art in the Changing West*. The New Press, 2014.

McGill, David. *Ghost Towns of New Zealand*. A.H. & A.W. Reed, 1980.

McLean, G.J. *Spinning Yarns: A Centennial History of Alliance Textiles Limited and Its Predecessors*. Alliance Textiles Limited, 1981.

Muir, D.C.W. *Mataura: City of the Falls*. Mataura Historical Society, 1991.

Monbiot, George. *How Did We Get Into This Mess?: Politics, Equality, Nature*. Verso Books, 2016.

Morton, Timothy. *Ecology Without Nature*. Harvard, 2007.

Nolan, Tony. *Gold Trails of the West Coast*. Reed, 1975.

Palmer, A. Laurie. *In the Aura of a Hole: Exploring Sites of Material Extraction*. Black Dog Publishing, 2014.

Park, Geoff. *Ngā Uruora: The Groves of Life: Ecology & History in a New Zealand Landscape*. Victoria University Press, 1995.

Park, Geoff. *Theatre Country: Essays on Landscape & Whenua*. Victoria University Press, 2006.

Pascoe, John. *Explorers & Travellers: Early Expeditions in New Zealand*. Reed, 1983.

Panoho, Rangihiroa. *Māori Art: History, Architecture, Landscape and Theory*. Bateman, 2015.

Phillips, Leigh. *Austerity Ecology & the Collapse Porn Addicts*. Zero Books, 2014.

Pound, Francis. *Frames on the Land: Early Landscape Painting in New Zealand*. Collins, 1983.

Quilley, Geoff, and John Bonehill. *William Hodges, 1744–1779: The Art of Exploration*. Yale University Press, 1994.

Reed, A.H. *The Story of the Kauri*. A.H. & A.W. Reed, 1953.

Reed, A.H. *The Gumdiggers: The Story of Kauri Gum*. A.H. Reed, 1972.

Reid, R.C. *Rambles on the Golden Coast of the South Island of New Zealand*. The Colonial Printing and Publishing Company, 1886.

Roth, Bert, and Janny Hammond. *Toil and Trouble: The Struggle for a Better Life in New Zealand*. Methuen Publications, 1981.

Sameshima, Haruhiko. *Bold Centuries: A Photographic History Album*. Rim Books, 2009.

Scott, Dick. *Fire on the Clay: The Pakeha Comes to West Auckland*. Southern Cross Books, 1979.

Scott, Dick. *In Old Mt Albert*. Southern Cross Books, 1983.

Scranton, Roy. *Learning to Die in the Anthropocene*. City Lights Books, 2015.

Temple, Phillip. *Presenting New Zealand: An Illustrated History*. New Holland Publishers, 2001.

Thornton, Geoffrey G. *New Zealand's Industrial Heritage*. A.H. & A.W. Reed, 1982.

Thornton, Geoffrey G. *The New Zealand Heritage of Farm Buildings*. Reed Methuen, 1986.

Thornton, Geoffrey G. *Cast in Concrete: Concrete Construction in New Zealand 1850–1939*. Reed, 1996.

Wood, June A. *Gold Trails of Otago*. Reed, 1974.

List of Works

St Heliers Beach (New Year's Day), Auckland, 2013
1400 x 1750 mm

The Neighbour's Garden, Mt Eden, Auckland, 2012
1100 x 1350 mm

Remains of the Controlled Mine Base, Rangitoto Island, 2013
1400 x 1750 mm

Fuel Pump in a Clearing, Rangitoto Island, Auckland, 2013
1000 x 1250 mm

Reservoir Pipeline at Dusk, Big King / Te Tātua-a-Riukiuta, Auckland, 2013
1100 x 1350 mm

Gorse in a Development, Pinehill, Auckland, 2012
1200 x 1500 mm

A Pōhutukawa Saved from Development, Rosebank Road, Auckland, 2013
1100 x 1350 mm

A Boathouse Among Pōhutukawa (After Winkelmann), Hobson Bay, Auckland, 2015
1100 x 1350 mm

Kotanui Island and Rangitoto (After Kinder), Whangaparāoa, 2013
1200 x 1500 mm

My Father (Ian Scott) Painting Beneath a Pōhutukawa, Okoromai Bay, Whangaparāoa, 2013
1100 x 1350 mm

Land Development Beside Waikumete Cemetery, Glen Eden, Auckland, 2014
1300 x 1600 mm

Nihotupu Auxiliary Reservoir, Waitākere Ranges, Auckland, 2014
1100 x 1350 mm

Remains of Black Rock Kauri Dam, Piha Gorge, Auckland, 2014
1100 x 1300 mm

Rain over a Development, Whangaparāoa Peninsula, 2014
1300 x 1650 mm

Mark Adams Retouching Photographs at Studio La Gonda, Karangahape Road, Auckland, 2013
1500 x 1890 mm

My Father's Studio, Three Months After His Death from Cancer, Mt Eden, 2013
1500 x 1890 mm

Bulldozed Farmland in Albany, North Shore, Auckland, 2014
1350 x 1660 mm

George's Tunnel, Waitākere Dam Tramline, Auckland, 2015
1100 x 1350 mm

Evening, The Frank Sargeson House, Esmonde Road, Auckland, 2015
1100 x 1350 mm

John Perry in His Workshop, Former Regent Cinema, Helensville, 2015
1100 x 1350 mm

Mark Adams at a Former Garden and Settlement Site, Āwhitu Peninsula, 2015
1400 x 1750 mm

Kauri Dam Remains, Coromandel Ranges, Near Tairua, 2015
1400 x 1750 mm

Pūriri Tree in Waterfall Gully, Shakespear Regional Park, Whangaparāoa Peninsula, 2022
1400 x 1750 mm

Undersea Cables, Former Degaussing Station, Pink Beach, Whangaparāoa, 2015
1400 x 1750 mm

Poutu Dam and River Diversion, Rangipo, Tongariro, 2015
1100 x 1350 mm

Former New Zealand Shipping Company Offices and Wool Store, Tokomaru Bay, 2016
1100 x 1350 mm

Last Light, Tokomaru Bay Wharf, Waimā, East Cape, 2016
1400 x 1750 mm

Collapsing Roof, Gisborne Sheep Shearers Wool Store, Tokomaru Bay, 2016
1400 x 1750 mm

Waikaretāheke River Diversion (After Lusk), Lake Waikaremoana, 2016
1100 x 1350 mm

Manager's Office, Waipaoa Freezing Works, Outside Gisborne, 2016
1000 x 1200 mm

Sawmill at the Lane and Brown Shipyard, Whangaroa Harbour, Tōtara North, 2016
1100 x 1350 mm

Wildflowers in a Development, Katikati, Near Tauranga, 2015
1000 x 1250 mm

Limeworks, Frenchman's Gully, Near Te Manunui Rock Art Site, Canterbury, 2016
1100 x 1350 mm

A West Coast Sawmill Relocated to the East Coast, Temuka, 2016
1100 x 1350 mm

Henry Simon Purifier, Former Aero Flour Mill, Temuka, 2016
1400 x 1750 mm

Loading Fertilizer, Former Empress Flour Mill, Waimate, 2016
1300 x 1650 mm

Collapsing Kiln, Mākareao Limeworks, Blue Mountains, Otago, 2016
1250 x 1600 mm

Boiler Room, Former McGill's Flour and Oat Mill, Milton, 2017
1300 x 1650 mm

Boilers Behind the Bruce Woollen Mill, Milton, 2017
1100 x 1350 mm

Spinning Machines, The Bruce Woollen Mill During Receivership, Milton, 2016
1200 x 1500 mm

Gregg and Company Chicory Kiln, Clutha River / Mata-Au, Inch Clutha, 2016
1100 x 1350 mm

Winter Morning, Marawera Flour Mill, Near Tapawera, 2016
1100 x 1350 mm

San Pedro Drying in the Upper Level of the Hoffman Kiln, Former McSkimming Brickworks, Benhar, 2016, 1100 x 1350 mm

Remains of McCallums Mill, Ōpārara, Karamea, West Coast, 2016
1000 x 1200 mm

A Poet Writing Before the Falls and Freezing Works, Mataura, 2016
1400 x 1750 mm

Winter, Powerhouse at the Old Escarpment Mine, Denniston Plateau, 2016
1000 x 1250 mm

Collapsing Coal Bin, Escarpment Mine, Denniston Plateau, 2016
1400 x 1750 mm

Saplings Growing Among the Sawmill (After Cleveland), Kopara Village, West Coast, 2016
1100 x 1350 mm

Late Evening, Looking North Towards the Limeworks, Clifden, 2017
1100 x 1350 mm

Bridge at Middle Break, Denniston Incline (After Lock), West Coast, 2016
1000 x 1250 mm

Winter Morning, Remains of the Coal Barge S.S. Lawrence, Mōkihinui, 2016
1250 x 1600 mm

Ngarua Limeworks (Looking Towards Abel Tasman), Tākaka Hill, 2017
900 x 1100 mm

Hop and Tobacco Kilns, Beneath Tākaka Hill, Near Riwaka, 2017
1000 x 1250 mm

Hop Kiln and Barn, Stanley Brook, Motueka Valley, 2017
1000 x 1200 mm

Chinese Miners' Hut, Illustrious Energy Mine, Central Otago, 2017
1300 x 1650 mm

Scientists Performing Autopsies on Some of the 350 Pilot Whales that Beached and Died, Farewell Spit, Golden Bay, 2017
1250 x 1600 mm

Musterers Quarters (After Barker), Lake Coleridge Station, Canterbury, 2018
1100 x 1350 mm

Overgrown Workshop, Elliotvale Coal Mine, Otago Coast Forest, 2018
1000 x 1200 mm

Winter, Sullivan Mine, Denniston Plateau, 2018
1100 x 1350 mm

Fluming and Adit, Mt William North Mine, Near Stockton, West Coast, 2016
1100 x 1350 mm

Woolshed and Oaks, Acheron Bank Station, Near Lake Coleridge, 2018
1000 x 1250 mm

Generator Room, Former Fleming and Company Creamoata Mill, Gore, 2018
1300 x 1650 mm

Spring Creek Mine and the Road to Rewanui, Dunollie, West Coast, 2016
1100 x 1350 mm

Engineers' Workshop, Rewanui, East of Dunollie, West Coast, 2018
1300 x 1650 mm

Rain over the Coal Bins at Kiwi Mine, Ten Mile Creek / Waianiwaniwa, West Coast, 2018
1400 x 1750 mm

Miners' Hut, Near Alpine Battery, Lyell Creek, West Coast, 2018
1000 x 1250 mm

Homeward Bound Battery, Gold Burn or Rich Burn, North-West of Macetown, Otago, 2018
1100 x 1350 mm

Cyanide Tanks with Ice, Premier Battery, Near Advance Peak, Otago, 2018
1100 x 1350 mm

Acid Mine Drainage Remediation, Sullivan West Mine, Denniston Plateau, 2018
1100 x 1350 mm

Remains of the Mine Bathhouse, Denniston Plateau, West Coast, 2019
1100 x 1350 mm

Remains of the Sefferston Schoolhouse, Moke Creek, Otago, 2019
1000 x 1200 mm

Chimneys and Tanks, Demolition of the Cement Works, Cape Foulwind, West Coast, 2019
1200 x 1500 mm

Dusk, Fishing Shack at Lake Onslow, Otago, 2019
1000 x 1250 mm

Poppet Head, Golden Progress Mine, Oturehua, Ida Valley, Central Otago, 2019
1100 x 1350 mm

Morning Fog, Disused Stables at Earnscleugh Station, Near Alexandra, 2019
1000 x 1250 mm

Musterers Quarters and Kitchen, Home Hills Runs, Ida Valley, 2019
1100 x 1350 mm

Fog over the Stamping Battery, Young Australian Mine, Carrick Range, 2019
1100 x 1350 mm

Approaching Snowstorm at Nightfall, Kopuwai (Old Man Range), Otago, 2019
1400 x 1750 mm

Dusk, Fog and Rain on the Denniston Plateau, 2016
1100 x 1350 mm

Acknowledgments

Several people in Aotearoa were instrumental in this project at an early stage. Ron Brownson (1952–2023), for his friendship, encouragement, many conversations, and later, institutional support at Auckland Art Gallery Toi o Tāmaki. He is greatly missed. I thank Mark Adams for the standard his work has set in this country. Along with sharing a studio and a printer, we shared many conversations, and several photography trips throughout this project. Countless conversations, and long trips around the South Island in 2016 and 2018, were also shared with Chris Holdaway. Following these trips, this project was developed further through publications of his words with my images by his imprint Compound Press. Harvey Benge, (1944–2019), was another person I also made regular photography trips (around Tāmaki Makaurau Auckland) with. Our conversations, and his extensive photobook library are part of this work, and he is also greatly missed. Since 2015, Trish Clark has regularly exhibited work from this project at Trish Clark Gallery, and I am grateful for her ongoing support.

Several people in the United States gave much needed support too. Michael Fried offered encouragement and dialogue at an early stage, and later made time to visit museums to look at art in Washington and New York. Darby Bannard (1934–2016) also provided early discussion and encouragement, though sadly we never got to meet in person. Kylie Wright's generosity with her knowledge of colour correction and printing was instrumental in developing the way my images look, and her spare room in Philadelphia let me spend time with the work in its museums. In New York, David Leventi made the drum-scans of most of the 8 x 10 film negatives in this body of work, which are elevated by the care and skill of his craft.

At Daylight Books, Ursula Damm's guidance and support as creative director brought this publication together. Simultaneously, copy editor Gabi Fastman carefully tightened and improved the text. Since we met in 2018, Daylight co-founder Michael Itkoff patiently encouraged this work becoming a book. Thanks to his work ethic and fortitude, at last it is.

Back in Aotearoa, Lara Strongman's encouragement and institutional support at Christchurch Art Gallery Te Puna o Waiwhetū was a great help. Likewise, Christina Barton, who exhibited part of this work at Te Pātaka Toi Adam Art Gallery in Wellington. Her research from that project became the foreword here, and her preliminary editing discussions and work as a reader much helped the development of the text. As an editor, Francis McWhannell also greatly improved these texts, which in many ways are a product of years of conversation. Designer Elliot Ferguson patiently honed a perfectly suited style and typography for this book, and we have also shared years of conversation about the ideas within. Hana Pera Aoake also provided a sharp preliminary edit of the text, and our conversations, too, have also influenced the work. I also thank Nigel Borell for his encouragement, and work as a reader.

James Gilberd has also supported this work though several exhibitions at Photospace Gallery in Wellington, and has regularly offered a spare room in that city on my way south to make work for this project. Photography trips in the North Island, and many conversations, were also shared with Solomon Mortimer. Additionally, Sarosh Mulla and Pac Studio (the architecture practice he co-directs), provided important support of this work, as did Chris Culverwell at PCL Imaging (who processed all the film), and Phillip Glamuzina at Progear Photographic, who among other support, helped our studio get a large-format printer, which improved our proofing and print process.

For their friendship, support, or conversation: Stephen Bambury, Chad Bevan, Kevin Church, Vannessa Cook, Julia de Cooker, Julia Durkin, Dan Eagle, Emma Eagle, Alberto Garcia-Alvarez, Ed Hanfling, Derek Henderson, Stephen Higginson, Georgie Hill, Rui Inaba, Simone Kaho, Michael Lett, Emil McAvoy, Hamish McKay, Stuart McKenzie, Warren Mendonsa, Shannon Novak, John Perry (1943–2021), Brydee Rood, Geoff Short, Zara Sigglekow, Lawrence Simmons, Caitlin Smith, Andrew Thomas, Julia Waite, Emma Walter, Areta Wilkinson, and peers in the Aotearoa photography community Edith Amituanai, Conor Clarke, Ngahuia Harrison, Jae Hoon Lee, Caroline McQuarrie, John Miller, Haru Sameshima, and Tim Veling.

Finally, my partner, Amanda Gruenwald, mother, Nan Corson, and my father, Ian Scott (1945–2013).

I also thank the countless people who shared their knowledge of local history and places. Without their openness, generosity, and access to these places, this work would not be possible.

Cofounder: Michael Itkoff
Creative Director: Ursula Damm
Copy Editor: Gabrielle Fastman

Editor: Francis McWhannell
Book Design: Elliot Ferguson
8 x 10 Film Scans: David Leventi
Colour Corrections: Chris Corson-Scott
Readers: Hana Pera Aoake, Nigel Borell, Christina Barton

The author has made every attempt to provide
information that is accurate and complete.

ISBN: 978-1-954119-45-1

Printed by Ofset Yapimevi, Turkey

Daylight Books
info@daylightbooks.org
www.daylightbooks.org